Stalking the Ice Dragon

Stalking the Ice Dragon

An Alaskan Journey

/ *Susan Zwinger*

The University of Arizona Press   Tucson

The University of Arizona Press
Copyright © 1991
The Arizona Board of Regents
All Rights Reserved
⊗ This book is printed on acid-free, archival-quality paper.
Manufactured in the United States of America.

96 95 94 93 92 91   6 5 4 3 2 1

Library of Congress Cataloging-in-Publication Data
Zwinger, Susan, 1947–
    Stalking the ice dragon : an Alaskan journey / by Susan Zwinger.
        p.   cm.
    Includes bibliographical references (p.   ).
    ISBN 0-8165-1202-7 (cloth)
    1. Alaska—Description and travel—1981- —2. Northwest Coast of North
America—Description and travel. 3. Natural history—Alaska. 4. Natural history—
Northwest Coast of North America. 5. Zwinger, Susan, 1947-   —Journeys—Alaska.
I. Title.
F910.5.Z85   1991
917.9804'5--dc20   91-11627
                                                              CIP

British Library Cataloguing in Publication data are available

This book is dedicated to
my three favorite nature writers:

Rachel Carson, who started us thinking;
Ann Zwinger, who raised me to think,
and Ed Abbey, out there in his desert.

Contents

Introduction: Getting Used to Going Home ix

Maps xii–xiv

Book One The Man Who Was All Covered with Mouths

  1 Earth-Sprung Tongues 3

  2 Asleep on the Tundra 11

  3 Crossing into Alaska 18

  4 Breathing for the Planet 32

  5 Frozen Desert/Burning Seas 59

  6 Return to Civilization 97

Book Two Fleeing to the Wilderness on Silk Threads

  7 The Art of Conducting Oneself 111

  8 East/West Convergence 123

  9 In Which Winter Strikes and
      I Am Entirely Surprised 141

Book Three Dream, Ritual, and Conversation for Return

  10 Easy Dream, Easy Money, Deep Water 159

  11 Darth Vader's Hometown 171

  12 Rough Beast's Progress Report 193

  13 An Oceanic Ending/Beginning 200

Select Bibliography 217

Introduction:
Getting Used to Going Home

Times-in-between-time are gifts. In 1987 I was in several such in-between-times—in career, in living place, in loss of a significant love, and in a value system flux. I left a self-satiated art scene in New Mexico for a vaguely thought-out, environmentally focused career in Seattle, Washington, trading the subtle earth colors of the Southwest for the deep green forests of the Northwest.

Times-in-between are gifts of opening: they thrust us stringless and nebulous into what at first appears to be the void because it is unknown. Because pain made me poignantly receptive, and nobody was there to define it, the void soon became furnished with vivid, fresh, raw experiences. I knew nothing of glaciers, of what to wear in tundra or how to walk on tundra, except what I had learned from brief flirtations on the tops of thirteen-thousand-foot peaks in the forty-eight connecting states. Somewhere in the labyrinthine attic of my dream-storage area there was an urge to go to Alaska. In the Southwest it had been out of the question: too far away, too expensive, too big, too cold, too this and that. Just a wisp of an idea.

Now events converged so it might just be possible: the death of my old pickup, which forced me to buy a slightly more reliable one; the proximity of Seattle to Alaska (Anchorites claim it is a suburb and warehouse for Alaska); the realization that there are roads and ferries and trains, other transport than extremely costly airborne adventures. I came to a slow realization, too, that the Northwest corner of the planet is neither covered with ice nor dreadfully cold in summer and fall.

But what was it I wanted out of following this dream? Just traveling was not enough. I needed profound change. I wrote in a black notebook:

> To live close to elemental power. Close to what is essential. To feel the noise of black water cascading down precipitous black stone. The avalanche and earthquake providing momentum; the ice worm and glacier lily providing solace; the gleaming green/purple mallard head from the Chiricahua on the Mexican border north to the Chena River near Fairbanks providing rhythm. Not external rhythm, as of traffic lights or Beethoven, but one felt within when all else is silent. The ululations of loon on a red lake at dawn deep within the middle ear.

I wanted to enter a new land not just by seeing it, but by allowing it to permeate six senses at once. Yet our sense receptors are imperfect. As in the pinhole cameras I made with school children from Quaker Oats boxes, into which every aspect of light comes dancing through a pinhole and gets reversed and flip-flopped, the image warps in odd lenticular bends on the negative. The journal becomes the darkroom in which sweat, fact and memory ferment in the dark and develop into images that, at their best, are a sort of psychic perfume to be shared for years to come.

I wanted to record a fresh reaction to the planet from the perspective of one steeped in the Desert Southwest. I chose unfamiliar earth hoping that, as one tectonic plate slamming into another causes faulting, vulcanism, uplift and earthquake, an intense change of place would catalyze my vision.

Travel journals to such places are abundant, but many of them carry on agendas quite different, and often at odds with, their outward intentions. A political mission turns scientific. A religious mission turns political, conquering. A scientific journey waxes rhapsodic. There are many mythologies put forth as self-evident truth, such as the Absoluteness of Science, or the myth that Techno-Supremacy Means Cultural-Supremacy (from my own country), or the hubris of pinning the biota from one of the last great wildernesses left on earth to a box of user-focused expectations. Surely this must ratchet over to a vision based on complex unseen relationships, an inspirited sense of the symbiosis of all, an ethical and passionate love of diverse beings for their existence alone, an awe of adaptive strategies and celebration of biodiversity for its own sake.

To me everything is a fabric, a whole, a world in which all (from microorganism to president) are entangled irrevocably in each other's oxygen tubes. One big Gordian knot.

Earth as medicine bundle is a concept as ancient as it is immediately appropriate. In pretechnological tribes, it was the worldview of everyone because people could *see* that it was true. The way one behaved toward the elk or the salmon or the trees did come back in a closely knit cause-and-effect bundle. Then we got big. The earlier worldview was cast off as primitive junk. Now we are back to it. The biosphere cannot bear us. The planet is so small that we devour the world. I wanted to go outward to places where human beings are small, to feel my place in it.

ARCTIC OCEAN

Barrow
Prudhoe Bay
Beaufort Sea

Point Hope
NORTH SLOPE
Christmas Tree Wells
ARCTIC NATIONAL WILDLIFE REFUGE

ARCTIC CIRCLE
BROOKS RANGE
Porcupine Caribou Herd
Inuv

GATES OF THE ARCTIC N.P. & P.
Atigun Pass
Porcupine River
Fort McPher

Coldfoot
Fort Yukon
UNITED STATES
CANADA
Fort McPher

BERING LAND BRIDGE N.P. & P.
Nome
Yukon River
HAUL ROAD
Circle

St. Michael
Fairbanks
YUKON CHARLIE N.P. & P.
Eagle

Ophir
DENALI N.P. & P.
Chicken
Dawson City

ALASKA
DENALI HIGHWAY

Bethel
Anchorage
Hope
Valdez
WRANGELL-ST. ELIAS N.P. & P.
Carmacks

NUNIVAK ISLAND
LAKE CLARK N.P. & P.
Seward
Cordova
Whit

Homer
KENAI FJORDS N.P.
GLACIER BAY N.P. & P.

KATMAI N.P. & P.
Bristol Bay

KODIAK ISLAND

ALEUTIAN RANGE

DEMPSTER RIVER HIGHWAY
ALCAN HIGHWAY

PACIFIC OCEAN

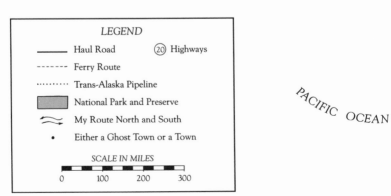

LEGEND

——— Haul Road   ⟨20⟩ Highways

------- Ferry Route

·········· Trans-Alaska Pipeline

▨ National Park and Preserve

〜 My Route North and South

• Either a Ghost Town or a Town

SCALE IN MILES

0   100   200   300

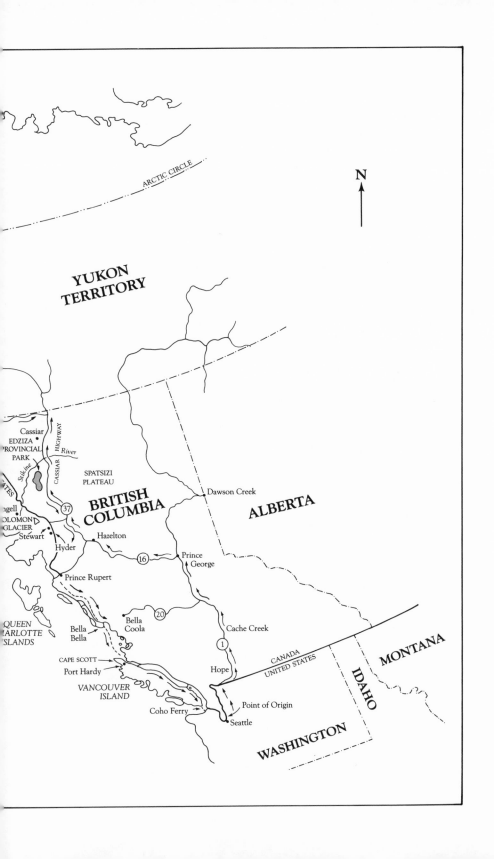

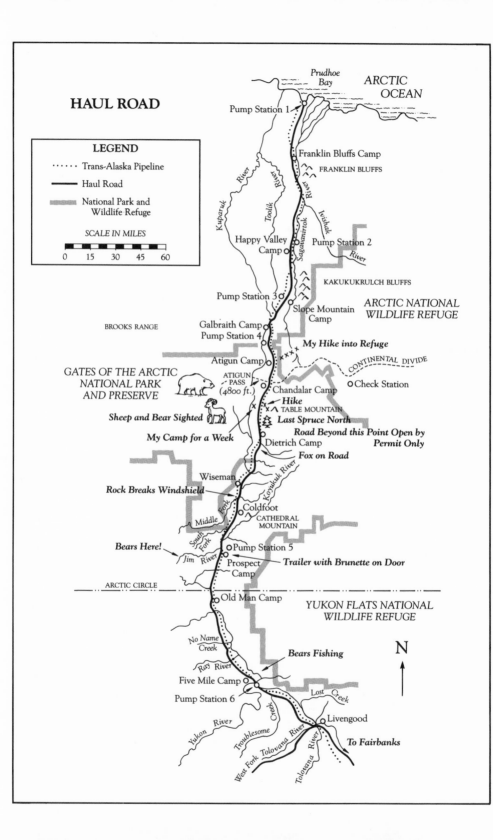

Stalking the Ice Dragon

BOOK ONE

The Man Who
Was All Covered with Mouths

1

Earth-Sprung Tongues

/ August 6:   West of Prince George, B.C.

The morning I leave, Seattle is absolutely clear: a stunning, unceasing
blue contrasted against white boats and steel buildings. The glint of
the many bodies of water and the crisp edge to a gold air seem to be
saying I should not leave.

The first night there is a sense of abandonment and loneliness I
had not expected, perhaps based on some gender expectations I have
of myself. Historically, it is the man who has left behind wife, children, the court, his kingdom, his queen, his lover to venture forth to
the unknown. His essence has always been to expand knowledge, to
conquer, to claim new lands, to grow spiritually, to haul back earthly
goods—mostly to haul back earthly goods.

At first there is no sleeping. On a bed built up to window level
on three months' supply of food and motor oil, there is no headroom,
and bright lights slither along windows all night. The aluminum canopy sits lightweight on the steel bed of the pickup like a set of beetle
wings, iridescent and functional. I cannot park on the level yet. Logis-
tical packing problems. Burning brake fluid smell. Screws coming

loose. The right tool, the wrong extension.

I work on the technical aspect of the small living space in back of the pickup and learn how to set grommets with a new kit. Off the back flap and tailgate I have designed a porch of mosquito netting, with two extending aluminum poles set off about four feet to the back. The bottom is weighted with a band of heavy material, which can, in turn, be weighted down with stones. An elaborate Velcro system for attaching it underneath the tailgate must be worked out. A poncho can be slung over the top of this for an extended living area.

HAZELTON VILLAGE

I drive due west, back toward the jumbled Pacific coast, then begin north again. It is impossible to drive simply north from Seattle and Vancouver up the coast: a jangled geology prevents that, so far. Just as one turns irrevocably northward toward the Arctic, there is an initial encounter with the first people to enter this continent: the Athapascans. Guess-estimates are as long ago as 25,000 years, although anthropology and the technology of dating are experiencing growing pains, and the numbers expand backwards every few years.

A thin bridge flinches over a deep river canyon, a deer's hide plagued by black flies. The weight of two trucks passing: the undulation nauseates and exhilarates me. Once, long ago, Athapascans lashed a thinner bridge out of cedar logs a quarter-mile long. The deep channel gives a dizzying glimpse of the Skeena River 500 feet below. I am relieved that it is forbidden to get out, to stare, swinging, a small flightless speck on the twitching span. This is the passage to Hazelton.

Hazelton is adjacent to the prehistoric village of Gitemaks, or Kitan-Maksh, "the place where people fished by torch." When whites came all the way up the Skeena River to its confluence with the Kisplox River in their sternwheelers, they discovered an artistically rich and sophisticated Athapascan culture. They simplified Athapascan names with regularity. For instance, the churning river below was called "iksh" (=out of) and "shian" (=clouds), meaning water out of clouds. Iksh-shian became Skeena. This same Skeena River, in a deep glacial valley, will spit me out on the Straits of Georgia as I head home three months later.

Through the naming of geography one encounters a people and their beliefs rooted in the land. Athapascans lived through harsh winters and used this downtime to develop complex ceremonies, art forms, and mythologies. Naming came not in abstraction of compass, pole, and global grid, nor after their superiors, but in topographical directions: up-river/down-river/place-where-the-rapids-are-difficult. Mountains are honored by naming them by prominent features, rather than after an individual who might never visit the place. Our own distance from the land shows in our not naming certain places "inlet of thunder water" or "place where earth's core heat comes to the surface and makes power."

Aboriginal languages of the British Columbian Athapascan make up one of the richest and most complex language groups in the world. They belong to six language groups as remote from one another as English is from Chinese. They are neither simple nor primitive, but are as logical, intricate, and precise as any language on earth (Levine 1983).

In some languages, such as Haida, verbs require special forms to be added to the front; these match the shape of an object in action. The pine branch, the comb, the feather—as opposed to a paddle or a spoon—would have within the verb a suffix meaning "of a pinnate nature."

Athapascans named things according to mythical beings, sea monsters, or danger points. They animated their world with supernatural beings, ghosts, and spirit guides. Springs or bends in the river would be connected with spirit guides or the place-where-so-and-so-found-a-woman. Mythologies are not limited in imagination either, as in the Zuñi myth in which people were still covered with slime and had their genitals placed on their foreheads, or in the Athapascan myth of the Man Who Was All Covered with Mouths.

Athapascan story-telling made the ordinary mysterious, impregnating each mountain and stream with meaningfulness. Each family had unique myths to explain its own ancestry, its relationship to animals, its strengths, totems, ceremonies, initiations, and privileges, imbuing each member with great dignity. A young Athapascan must have felt powerful in a landscape punctuated by sacred points of his or her origin.

Slowly, many of the places in Alaska and Canada are being returned to their original names by the people as part of an effort to save the Athapascan languages from extinction. A most famous example: Mount McKinley (McKinley never set foot inside Alaska) is once again Denali, which translates as "the Great One."

An adolescent Athapascan leads me through the totem lodges in his village, proud of his cultural heritage, longing for the nightlife of mine. I love the highly codified hummingbirds and orca whales, animals craftily retooled to the level of a secret language. As intriguing as iconography of Catholic saints, each object is interlocked with the ancient pantheon of animals; I long to become the hagiographer of Kitan-Maksh. A renegade from the twentieth-century art world, where I was an artist in Santa Fe, New Mexico, I would gladly swap celebrated but vacuous originality-for-originality's-sake for the long journey toward meaning.

My past in the Southwest arises again: Navajo and the Apache languages are so similar to the Athapascan that these culturally diverse people can understand one another. An estimated 2,000 years ago, according to the British Columbia Provincial Museum, ancestors of the Athapascan left southeast Alaska and traveled south along the California coast, into the interior of Arizona and New Mexico, to become the Navajo and the Apache! Others came to the interior of British Columbia, then moved eastward into subarctic regions of the Northwest Territory.

So slow was the evolution of their language that the Athapascan of Alberta could understand the Chiricahua on the Mexican border of Arizona. Slow change, in contrast to English, lies in the strength of tradition. In the Keresan language of the Acoma, Zia, Santa Domingo, San Felipe and Cochiti pueblos, the ability to compound syllables in naming enables the language to form multisyllabic, onomatopoetic sounds, which also are quite graphic in story-telling.

/ August 7:   Cassiar Highway

Woman-Travels-Alone up here is a nonsequitur. When I enter a
restaurant early in the morning, men gawk at me like deformed game.
As in Mexico, I do not look into eyes. They are speaking passionately
about something when I walk in, but forks pause in midstroke,
mouths remain open, and only slowly is the silence again broken. I
walk through their cat's cradle of stares, a cat through a sprinkler system, and sit down to face the immense Klastine Plateau rising up at
the door. I listen. They talk number of prongs, sizes and inches, and I
slowly learn that it is a large stone sheep they speak of, now fettered,
still warm, to a truck rack. It is only the first of many whole animals
that will stare blankly at me, twitching in an auto-neuro movement.
I wonder why they have not dressed it out as an investment in meat.
It is warm, and the heavy wool will soon putrefy the flesh in its own
furry oven bag. They go a long ways home.

A greasy breakfast. White bread soggy with bright yellow axle
grease, one slimy yellow-eyed beast surrounded by a metallic field of
machine-regurgitated potatoes.

It is inexpensive, and after his annoyance that I eat so little comes
the owner-cook's extensive pride at the speed with which he serves
this pie-shaped viscosity; but then, I've seen steers serve it up faster.

The inn owner speaks of the rumbles of volcanoes and earthquakes
nearby. Clashing continental plate tectonics: the subduction of the
Pacific Plate, a final fray to hit the jigsaw-puzzle continent. I passed
Edziza Mountain yesterday, a recently active flow, lava-strewn upheaval of blistered earth. No roads and few trails.

From Hazelton I have turned north on the infamous Cassiar
"highway." It may be technically shorter than the paved route that
swings way north and eastward out of St. George, but in wear and tear
and time it is longer. Still, it follows a chain of magnificent upheavals
where two continental plates crushed together, spilling out precious
minerals from the earth's core. The cost endured in car-mangling is
well compensated in beauty.

COLORADO 1971

What earth belched was hope, was chance
To tiny men scrawling on its surface.
A golden vein would take a wrist,
An arm, repeated easy dream
In difficult progression down.

Elements constantly renamed men
Or scoured them out. With hands
Which refused slow prairie plows, dug
Stubborn half-digested stone.
Jagged as their weather, these men
Have gone: descended into mines
And closed the door. Now, no more
Room for them to go.

Or so I thought from my perspective seventeen years ago, as I searched through the fragments left of Colorado gold mines. Not true: they came up to Alaska with Caterpillars instead of shovels, huge earth scrapers, not mules. Back in my childhood I would roam the Pikes Peak National Forest unfettered by roads, collecting old colored whiskey bottles, metal rifle parts, pack fragments, sardine tins, which created a mystique of rugged individualism and tremendous adversity. Penetrating the high Northwest is stepping back a century in civilization, when men left safety in droves for ephemeral chimera of instant wealth.

The distinction now lies in their trash. What was once picturesque is now grotesque.

Cassiar, the district in the extreme northwest of British Columbia, was named for two tribes, the Kaska and the Kaskamet, "dried beaver meat." The Cassiar Highway takes its name after the main profit-source of the district. Asbestos.

The highest asbestos mines in the world punctuate a vertiginous ridge of mountains with lime-green slag heaps. Nine miles up a dirt highway, in the summer ghost town of Cassiar, sits a four-story-high cone, a cynosural vision. It emanates a lighter-than-sky phosphorescent green. Ravens punctuate it with black iridescence. Up the stabilized side grows a constellation of moss. Deserted as if after a catastrophic event, Cassiar gives off an eerie pulchritude—the guts of earth spilling heavy metals down vertical mountains.

Asbestos is not the black, sinister-looking material I had imagined; it is quite lovely. Chrysotile-asbestos, discovered here in the mid-nineteenth century, consists of clear vegetablelike fibers found in conjunction with jade and serpentine. Under the microscope it becomes a jungle of translucent fringe lying at right angles to the surface of origin. Made up of lime, magnesia, and aluminum, this stone comes up from the molten interior of the earth.

Asbestos was used by the early Greeks to wick the oil lamps of vestal virgins. I always wondered exactly what vestal virgins did with most of their time, but apparently it was not spent in changing wicks: this stone is hardy. In the 1940s, a time of war and self-confidence in industry, we used its crude fiber for spinning, packing, tape, brake lining, shingles, paper, insulation, to protect metal surfaces, cloth, rope, yarn, cement felting, mattresses, mill board, cement slate, paint, tiles, and electrical machinery. A cheerful book from the Canadian Department of Mines (Cirkle 1910) shows photographs of early processing: asbestos lying in open wooly heaps about the machinery that cards and spins the glassy fibers.

Up here on the Cassiar Highway, scale towers beyond human proportion. Volcanic mountains shoot overhead: 3,000-foot layers pointing straight to the sky. How can existent space hold so much greater a distance than Kansas? The sanctity of Colorado is threatened. The vulnerability of humankind comes through for the first time! What this *immensity* means and why we seek it. This sense of hugeness creates an understanding of our historic urge to tame: wanting to control, to impose one's own proportions throughout such tumult. A human being is insignificant here. How did men feel out here for years at a time, many to die slow deaths in each other's brotherhood, until the last man was alone?

Last night, I fell asleep like a submerged log. This morning I find myself on a segment of gravel pit that doubles as emergency runway;

signs at either end advise one to take heed in case a plane comes at one down the road. There is no shoulder, no ditch, so that etiquette requires one to nosedive off the steep mountain into the trees, as far as I can figure.

To the east, the magnificent expanse of Spatsizi Plateau Wilderness, one of Canada's largest protected tracts of pure wilderness. Spatsizi translates as "red goat" in the Tahltan language; mountain goats here are fond of rolling in iron-oxide dust. Formerly visited only by Tahltan Indians, it was not penetrated by whites until 1926. Still roadless, it is, for me, impenetrable; trying it on foot would be limited and dangerous. I must be content to know that uncounted caribou, moose, grizzly and black bear, wolves, wolverine, beavers, and hoary marmots live unbothered here, entirely wild.

2

Asleep on the Tundra

*Sleeping on the tundra is like sleeping
with many tongues mumbling. A sharper wind.
Like a bear snorts, stops and starts in spurts.*

*Sleeping on the tundra is sleeping on the river
in a river kayak, where all night long
one must read river currents as many fingers
moving. Wind eddies sound like the loon sounds.*

/ August 7, Evening: Continental Divide on the Yukon
Territory/B.C. Border

Traveling west to Alaska, I have crossed into that otherworldly land
called "Yukon." Miles before Whitehorse on the Alcan, I discover the
Continental Divide looking particularly low for a Coloradan's eye. But
when I get out, there is a shock. Something, except for briefly on the
isolation of Pike's Peak, I thought I knew so well and find I do not.
    Tundra!
    Within a few square feet in the smelter of rain and rock, I find a
form of drugless hallucination. I thought I knew tundra from backpacking in the Lower Forty-eight, but nothing prepares me for this
delirium of sponge. Mounds of moss and lichen swallow my feet up
to the knees. Rosettes of rose, lavender, and rust bloom over lily
frost-greens. Miniature orange fungi spawn up through unions of
plant and algae.

The world is inventing itself anew!

How peculiar is the eye: at first it sees nothing, then a little, and then a proliferation of forms. At first I notice the mushrooms, the known forms: bright lavender *Cortinarius* slimy in the rain. Gilded giant *Leccinum aurantiacum* glow delicious and firm, like steak. Umbrellas of cinnamon red tubes, the *Boletus* curl upward in the wet.

Elysian colors beyond the known spectrum. Tomorrow the pleasure of cracking the cabalistic code.

But for now, the night anchors bruised cumulus to the mountain tops, casts the lakes in bluish silver. I am at peace, at last, with my own company. I have crawled through a labyrinth of worm tunnels and come out in an immense place to be free.

/ August 8:   Continental Divide, Yukon Territory

The ground is so lush with moss and mushroom, such diversity of species, that I cannot put my foot down. Rolling bedgear toward the front of the pickup uncovers a six-foot-long Masonite platform. On this I spread out artwares, notebook, maps, rulers, containers, reference library, stove, hot chocolate, and soups. It is best to work in a fine, wet mist, so as not to be tempted to explore. The weather is very obliging.

It is with the joy of a long-caged animal that I find myself in land so surreal that the mind cannot surround it. Tube mushrooms crowd out of earth like the fingers of a thousand dead men. They wave when I turn my back.

Strong-glowing *Suillus tomentosus*, bright yellow mushrooms in fairy rings, spin out across the slope like a lariat thrown in slow motion. A fairy ring forms as the whole plant grows and dies out from its center, sending out many individuals in a larger ring each year: one organism attached by miles and miles of mycelia. From pithy caps up to seven inches in diameter down to nubbins of toes, so many that they fill the scruffy forest like an explosion in a foam rubber factory.

Mushrooms are notoriously difficult to identify. These diverse critters adapt so specifically to each and every temperature and altitude change, host organism, soil base, that what it takes a plant generations to do, fungi do in just a matter of years. I am seeing cold-adapted species that, owing to lack of competition, may exist nowhere else in the world. I may be poking a saprophyte that prefers dead leaves of only the black cottonwood or dines exclusively on Sitka cones. Ten mushroom guidebooks and four hours later, I look up, woozy.

Why am I doing this?

What is it about fungi that so purely grabs at the imagination? What is it about those little spongy wenches, which refuse normal legged forms of fauna and the pretty symmetries of flora? In human terms, it is that peculiar juxtaposition of usefulness and mortal danger: most humans gasp when I tell them my passion, assuming that everything one finds is shoved into the mouth like a two-year-old. Others, such as myself, are endlessly entranced by the expansive colors, forms and textures, smells and tastes that fungi take on. Unlike gravity's beasts, which must have legs or slithering bellies, fungi are unperturbed by such practicalities as grasping extremities, heads and tails, opposing thumbs, or sense organs, as we know them. Instead, they ooze, loop, pulse, cover, reticulate, sprout, crenelate, drape, hang, and generally make themselves omniprevalent any way they please.

Laws of physics be damned.

BREAKFAST GARBAGE SCRAMBLE

    1 wet cheese soaked in icemelt and plastic bag
    2 soggy ends of onion and yellow bell pepper
    1 cooler-crushed egg
    3 *Suillus lakei* mushrooms, large
    1 anchovy for protein

To prepare: light small propane stove, rub on pan small amount of what might be olive oil from old plastic jar, simmer vegetables in their own juice, adding mushrooms. Once water has simmered off, scoot stuff to pan sides and dump in cooler-crushed egg. Sprinkle with spices from unmarked plastic screw/stack spice rack and chopped anchovy.

Healthy, but peculiar.

Finally it is morning, and I am allowed out to examine this strange new world:

All is spongy, soft, unknown. Even under the pastel fireworks are their inversions: implosions of color. No matter how many layers I mine for the tundra's wealth of life, more are revealed. The Little People are alive and well, as evidenced by suggestion of moss form and function.

Imagination is far outclassed by the audacity of evolution.

Tundra is one way to begin life. Lichens are the first to inhabit raw stone after the glacier: they can tolerate temperature extremes and dehydration, and can suck minerals out of hard rock. Dehydration allows them to plunge many degrees below freezing by becoming dormant. In laboratories, lichens "dead" for many years have sprung back into full bloom with the addition of water and warmth. Although lichens do not leave fossil records, it is assumed that these were the first beings to form before Earth had stabilized its atmosphere to oxygen. Some lichens are capable of creating their own atmosphere about them, and thus their low, ruffled shape to contain it. Under snow, they grow year-round. Some prosper in perpetual dark, and some prosper submerged. They are the first to colonize a completely burned area. Those growing in holes may develop luminescence (Bland 1971:44–9).

The mosses find infinite ways to be odd. Bryophyta can be amphibious; they can live submerged in water, so that a human foot placed upon them may sink in up to the calf. Most ancient beings, they were among the first to crawl hungrily out of the sea. Reproductive efforts create magnificent and odd forms: unicelled spores hang off the tips of bracts with brightly colored sex organs. In their sexual phase they may appear in completely different form than in the asexual stage. Tall bracts suggest space-age technology, towers, medieval spires, spears, gyres, radar discs, or prophylactics. Pear-shaped, egg-shaped, columnar with angles, elliptical, and covered with a cap called the calyptra, they may put on humanoid airs. Liverworts, not true mosses, also take bizarre forms in flat papery patterns or thin ribbons with peculiar pods and forks, umbrella shapes springing up from a flat plane.

Tundra plants are delicate and tough; their function is vital. They collect and hold rainfall, create bodies of water, feed reindeer, caribou, even people in the northern countries. They have tremendous capacity to hold water; in their first trickles begin entire rivers, entire drainage systems. Lichens create the original thin slips of soil on sheer rock. Sphagnum moss piles up deep loams in bogs, a rich soil with a fine memory.

Peat bogs have the excellent habit of swallowing humans, other animals, weapons, and history whole, preserving them. In the interior of Alaska, complete mammoths and bison genuflect in their viscous crypts, waiting for paleontologists to free them.

All forests begin in the lichen and moss, yet certain foresters believe in denuding even steep hills of all growth, in clear cutting followed by slash burning; they believe they reduce "competition" in this way, in order to rapidly grow a new crop of trees. There is a tragic flaw in this short-term logic. If mosses and lichens have been the basis of growth since the beginning of earth, and the trees live in a leafy, intricate symbiosis with lichens and moss, with fungus, squirrel, and winged seed-carrying shitting machine, then to destroy one is eventually to destroy the biological strength and diversity of the other.

/ August 9:   Continental Divide, Yukon Territory

With my shirt off and black muck up past my armpit, I squat here on the tundra. This soil of impeded drainage covers most of interior Alaska and northern Canada. From one foot to ten feet deep, the moisture lasts throughout the summer, regardless of rainfall, the result of melting permafrost.

I have dug down here and not yet hit ice, uncovering four distinct layers. First, under the moss, is organic peat, a rich black goop that

15

emerges from its slimy sockets with great sucking noises. I check: no one is around to mistake them for my bodily functions. The second layer down is mineral, more distinct in grain and more various in color than our old soils in the Lower Forty-eight. The next is a buried organic soil, and finally, too deep for my arm, the frozen substrata. After this dig I carefully replace the layers and pat the moss back into place; tundra takes years to recover.

The bog is penetrated by mysterious ice forms: wedges, pillars, and lenses, which leave weird graves on the surface when they melt. This accounts for the multitudinous lakes cast across the tundra plain, perfectly round lakes with flat, silt-covered bottoms. No fish, just oddly scattered sky coins.

Although philosophy thrusts itself onto tundra through the microcosm/macrocosm flip-flop of scale, tiny mosses to vast expanses, I try to avoid too much philosophizing. It's dangerous to the health, capable of suddenly sopping up one's mind with a smelly doctrinal sponge. The way a microscopic seed pod parallels a swirling galaxy, each following similar laws of physics, or the way parallel evolution creates similar life in diverse regions, tempts one to the teleological garbage bin. Not that it's not true on some larger scale we cannot comprehend, or some planetary-intentionality à la James Lovelace and Gaia. It's just dangerous as hell: a Big Daddy making it all work with perfect solutions too easily absolves us of our ultimate responsibility to our planet.

Ah, good. One more cup of cowboy coffee with the grounds in it and I will have offended half the universe. Always feel much better after that. "Let us make man in our image, after our likeness; and let them have dominion over the fish of the sea, and over the birds of the air, and over the cattle, and over all the earth, and over every creeping thing that creeps upon the earth." Dangerous.

To understand the precedence and attitudes of the Lower Forty-eight, it helps me to see Alaska as a frontier in progress. To comprehend an original law, such as the 1872 Mining Act, and its contemporary impact, it helps to understand the need from which it sprang: a wide-open frontier has to be conquered and claimed as quickly as possible. A "cruel" desert, complete with religious persecutors, sets

16

in motion defensive attitudes that set into motion actions toward the land that are perpetual and self-justifying forever, even to our planet's demise.

3

Crossing into Alaska

/ August 10

Before seven in the morning, the customs official disappears with
my license for an eternity. I feel vulnerable. Computers used in this
capacity frighten me: I remember my father's justifiable fears from
pre-war Germany, how a government can use information on people
as effectively as bullets. A family friend, Eni Jaspersen, smuggled out
social-work case records from her office under her clothes to protect
her client records from the Nazis, risking her life. Old Stern Face
comes back with my license. I have cleaned out garbage from the
truck cab in his absence, not realizing that this is a suspicious activity.

The crazy jumble of catastrophic upheaval, loosely and collectively
called Alaska, can be explained somewhat by very recent theories of
geology, plate tectonics. Yet it helps to remember that Alaska does not
follow the same physical laws as do the Lower Forty-eight. It seems to
have come from a different solar system.

When Earth was born of hot swirling gases, it began organizing
itself into a liquid sphere with a cooling surface, later to become rock.

At first, science viewed the planet as a solid, unchanging mass of hard rock; sometime in the 1950s, viable theories of continental drift began to develop based on unexplained ocean trenches and high ridges. The ridges were discovered to be the source of the molten earth core that spread over the sea floor. The continents were then understood to move on the same conveyor belt as did the ocean floor. The lithosphere, Earth's outer layer, turned out not to be solid. Only parts were solid.

These parts, the continents, float like patchy skins on top of a boiling cream-based soup. Immediately under the lithosphere is the asthenosphere, a partly solid layer through which molten interior rock rises and into which crumbles the lithosphere when plates are subducted. "Astheno-," from Greek *asthenes*, means without strength and refers to plasticity. According to a recent theory (Nance et al. 1988), all the continents drift together and then apart throughout Earth's history with fair regularity. Heat creates convection like a pudding boiling. The heat, resulting from the decay of radioactive material, has been declining since Earth's birth. Heat builds up under the continents, which, in turn, causes a bulge (a boil) to build up under them, and thus a "sudden" (in geological time) breaking apart.

In fifth grade I was fascinated with the plastic globe in our classroom, by the fact that Africa fit so neatly into the curvature of South and North America, and that Greenland came down like a broken china chip to fit the hole between Canada and northern Europe. As a budding visual artist, I drew this for a science project, but a fifth grade teacher pooh-poohed it as fantasy. It is only dully pleasing to be vindicated thirty years later by the Supercontinent Cycle theory.

Continents drift apart, leaving between them oceans, which dissipate heat more quickly. Up through central rifts of the oceans, which are cooling and sinking, come high ridges of molten crust, which create heavier and heavier ocean floors. The trenches are thought to be formed by the tearing apart of continents. As the ocean plates increase in size and weight, they begin to sink, moving as skateboards at centimeters per year, which slam back into the continents. Several things then may take place. One, the continent and ocean floor collide like two blocks, such as is happening in the Atlantic

19

Ocean, and are glued to the land mass. Or the plate may slide under the continent, as the Pacific and all its subsidiary plates do on the Pacific Rim, sinking back down into the asthenosphere until they reach a realm dense enough to stop them.

Under immense pressure, the plates are heating up, crumbling, tearing, folding, wrenching, torquing the edge of the land. Vulcanism begins again to create land, sometimes rising in huge batholithic punches as mountain ranges or entire cordilleras, sometimes blowing out in actual volcanic flows. Mountain uplift in the Pacific-type oceans is sudden in geological time. In the North Cascades, folded and faulted sea floors point jaggedly to the sky. Alaskan coastal ranges are not yet softened by the erosion of rivers, so they rise up straight out of the ocean with disconcerting abruptness.

An idea: here lies the reason that Alaska and B.C. are as yet still wilderness. The Pacific Rim was a jumbled carnage of rock; the youngest expansions and contractions of the earth were not conducive to easy travel. I find myself, like the rest of humankind, inevitably drawn to this last jagged frontier.

The Supercontinent Cycle theory accounts for the rhythmical ice ages, the periods of intense mountain-building, glaciation, and even the very nature of life, as evolution changes with mysterious pulses. These cycles are rhythmic and happen all over Earth. Distinct periods of mountain-building, together with subduction of ocean and continental plates, took place 2,600 million, 2,100 million, 1,800 million to 1,600 million, 1,100 million, 650 million, and 250 million years ago. Paleontological records show whole life types suddenly disappearing, such as at the end of the Cretaceous Period, when the dinosaurs and 80 percent of their cohorts disappeared, along with sudden emergences of new dominant forms (such as mammals) at the same time. A pretty theory, indeed.

What this model does not explain, however, is the Alaskan continent itself: its pieces appear to have come from all over the sphere, according to geologists. Its stone is hopelessly complex. In all its joining, rending, building up, wearing down, cracking with molten rock through the cracks, faulting and rejoining, some rocks seem to be from as far away as Australia. The Alaskan Coastal Range once swept past Los Angeles and is coming still. The Brooks Range leaves scientists in a scrap heap of speculation. Some say that it came across from northern Canada; others claim it is from quite far off; still others state that the sediment of the Brooks Range formed exactly where it is and has been there for some time. I, myself, prefer the Uranus theory.

TAIGA

My first experience with Alaska comes at Deadman's Lake. I am engulfed in taiga ("land of little sticks," in Russian), a low, tilting, circumpolar, boreal forest. The understory is thick with willows, dwarf birches, blueberries, lowbush cranberry, fireweed in bloom, labrador tea, rushes, sedges, and grass. This one is predominantly white spruce and paper birch in muskeg, while the dark scribbles of black spruce are assigned to higher tundra. The elegant balsam poplar and huge-leafed black cottonwood follow the rivers.

Throughout is the liquid song of the red-winged blackbird, a versatile species that spreads its individuals effectively through sparse vegetation by means of territorial song, thus saving itself from disease, predation, or starvation. A drumming of ruffed grouse wings begins: Could it be fall so soon? I sense that I am being watched by the hawk or the coyote, by the wolf or the eagle, with the intent curiosity of a higher predator. Or perhaps just by a mink down at the lake hunting stickleback. Or by a great white owl, awkwardly awakened, twisting its head around to watch me. Whoever it is, I am hushed, as if at the feet of a master. I am on their territory now, not humankind's.

These dark stick trees against snow must become ink lines etched on the clean copper plate, printed over and over again, sometimes with the track of the snowshoe, sometimes with the red swatch of moose blood, sometimes with the dance of magpie and raven, birds who winter here.

I stop for a cheap breakfast at the 1260 Inn. There is no menu: you just yell over the counter what exactly you want, which is a great relief after compound breakfasts with eighteen-wheeler titles.

In the 1260 Inn's dark, low-ceilinged bar is a museum-level collection of Northwest natural history paraphernalia, amazing unexplained objects. Such as the oosik, the penis bone, twenty-five inches

long, of *Obodenus rosmarus divergens* of the North Pacific. This most
fortunate creature haunts the pack ice and ice edges, and is at its
largest in the Bering and Chukchi seas. This largest of pinnipeds
(having finlike feet or flippers) weighs up to 1,600 kilograms and
sports canine teeth a meter in length. It also is blessed with huge and
powerful lips, which it uses to separate mollusks and arctic clams
from their shells, and mystacial (resembling a mustache) pads covered
with long, sensitive vibrasse, which it uses to feel out food on the
floor of the sea.

Although quite a desirable creature, not much is known about the
Pacific walrus's mating ritual. The ritual of its smaller Atlantic relation
was almost extinguished by whale hunters, who turned to this large
mammal for oil when they had extinguished the whale. It once was a
central source of oil, blubber, meat, and ivory for the Eskimo, but the
Inuit today are limited to taking only four a year and ivory cannot be
exported. So, after a near-extinction, the lovable walrus is in the process of recovering. The largest cause of death—hunting—has been reduced by the virtual disappearance of the dogsled and the attendant
need for meat: one ironic benefit of gasoline.

A trucker enters the cafe: "Thirty hours of snow, I've seen. You
couldn't hardly see that trailer over there [he gestures with his hand-
rolled cigarette to a van fifty yards away], comin' straight down." A
man across the room, a total stranger: "One hundred eighty inches of
rain a year. I once saw three inches fall in five minutes." The matronly
cook adds that "some of the old-timers say that in 1955 it was . . . ,"
and another weather extremity is listed. A major pastime in places of
great extremes, weather one-upmanship; if it is really awful, at least
you can file away a statistic.

Outside, a trucker is playfully torturing the cafe dog. Several
boozed-up Native Alaskans are putting more booze in the back of
their pickup. Someone in the gas station next door welds a trailer
hitch broken from hauling too big a load over the high pass. It jack-
knifed forward. The driver now screams into the telephone at his boss
in Valdez, who has given him the inadequate rig: "Risking my life to
save a couple bucks. Asshole!"

This seems to be a handy, cheap metaphor for Alaskan-style hubris: carrying too big a load for the hitch. Or stealing the company blind, as I heard a man boast he did with Alyeska.

/ August 11: To Tok

Consider the fireweed in the fields!

The fireweed singes Alaska a brilliant red, symbol of forest fire, death and rebirth. Characteristic of the central low tundra, entire fields are aflame with *Epilobium angustifolium*. It grows in disturbed soils and cool climes, from sea level high into the mountains, along the highways in intensely dense and extensive patches, persistent through underground roots. As with many other natural phenomena, what is soft, sweet, and pink in the Lower Forty-eight becomes a flaming intense red in vast swatches. It feeds caribou and mountain sheep and decorates tables. In fall, when the long white feathers of seed open and fly, again there is a glow when backlit by the sun. Fireweed along with alder and willow quickly begin reforestation after the glacier's tooth, a natural burn or, more recently, the Caterpillar's scrape.

Scientist James Larsen watched a fireweed in full bloom as the temperature plummeted to minus 26 degrees. The waxy flowers, which were covered with ice crystals, later thawed without damage and continued to bloom. Plants up here develop buds in the fall and are able to stop dormancy instantly at the first sign of spring warmth. Their remarkable ability to resist freezing is hidden in fundamental differences in protoplasmic composition. Most of the water is not in the cells, which causes damage to the cell walls, but rather in a free state outside. The growing period here is only a month or two, so that plants must have a good storage capacity for carbohydrates to allow growth to happen instantly (Larsen 1964).

Against the field of red, an old, old man walks along the highway with a heavy pack and a rifle. A long white beard. How grand a scale of time one must have to *walk* Alaska.

/ August 12: Chena Hot Springs Road

Thirty miles east-northeast of Fairbanks, 9:30 at night. I have driven off a side road in what looked like swamp, good for wildlife observation. Instead it is a dirt bike arena, land chewed up with targets for target practice. Alaskans shoot at immobile objects a lot; throughout state parks there are signs admonishing against such practice. Some of the outhouses have bullet holes in them. I would hate to be inside when the two-holer becomes a twelve-holer.

I have driven up a sharp rise. At the top I meet, nose-to-nose, a moose. She is a tall bag of bones with loose gray skin draped over a Tinker Toy frame. She appears four times as large as the truck. She looks up calmly, only slightly perturbed at the noise, so I cut the engine and watch her cumbersome magnificence, largest of deer, osterizing dripping ooze from the bottom of the swamp. The moose cow is dangerous with a young calf, so I look around. By this time of year the youngun would have gained 400 pounds in preparation for the hard winter. If it was a bull I was facing, he would be crowned with fifty or sixty pounds of antlers with a mantle of velvet lined with blood vessels. With this, he could spar with either a member of his own kind for herd dominance, or with my small truck, Die Fledermazda.

I feel honored to take a close range, elongated look at this greatest of deer, the holarctic *Alces alces*. She seems ancient, having emigrated across the Bering Land Bridge during the Illinoian Period of the Pleistocene. Her ancestry in Eurasia stayed down in coniferous forest, but here she has been steadily extending her feeding range northward toward the coast. Once the enormous Brooks Range stymied the moose, but in the 1950s she started toward the North Slope, encouraged by warmer climes and by the abundant willow browse along the river bottoms, which appeared as the glaciers retreated.

Her legs are extremely long; they have a long way to go before they reach the ground through forty-five to sixty centimeters of loose snow. She does not migrate, as do caribou, but travels locally between willow patches and seasonally between winter and summer feeding ranges.

Her eyes are dark and gentle, her whole countenance that of a lugubrious wisdom left over from an ice age. She is well built for the harshest of winters, her massive body conserving heat and storing huge amounts of energy. Capable of eating forty to sixty pounds of bog bottom a day (rich in sodium), she is capable of great power. I remember photographs of one of her kind, hackles raised, head down, charging a full-grown male grizzly. Twenty years ago she stood in greater numbers: in the 20,000 square miles of Nelchina Basin, there were 80,000 caribou and 30,000 moose in 1964. Eight years later, a 90 percent decline of caribou and a 50 percent decline of moose.

Her major predators are man, grizzly and, occasionally, wolves. Grizzlies take 85 to 90 percent of the calves by autumn, and wolves a few of the weaker individuals. Although hunting has become much more managed, the hunters have increased faster than has the moose population, and there is tremendous lobby pressure on Fish and Wildlife to ease up on hunting restrictions. In addition to thousands of visitors from all over the states, 1 in 80 of 500,000 Alaskans hunt moose, taking 3.5 million pounds of meat home for the freezer (Van Ballenberghe 1987).

My back wheels are also partaking of a primordial swamp ooze feast. Becoming worried that I may be disturbing her, I fire up and spin my wheels deeper. Now I have to rock back and forth to free myself. I do not choose to get out with the shovel in front of a 1,200-pound moose. The wheels free with a vulgar noise, and the truck springs forward toward the moose; I jerk the steering wheel to the left and back quickly down the rise. The next morning there are two sets of tracks up from the swamp, one of them mooselet.

An expired salmon floats stiffly near shore in the Chena River, and every once in a while I catch a death-sniff.

Chum salmon migrate up this river, and it is now closed to fishing during these spawning months. This fellow is part of the summer run of chum, beginning his long return before mid-July, all the way up the Yukon to the Tanana, and then into the Chena, through downtown Fairbanks, and up to the state park, where he is protected. He has spawned in some narrow channel, a back slough, in a warm Chena hot spring, or even at the very origin of the river, anyplace where the coarse river gravel and water are kept from freezing by movement.

These northern salmon bear many more eggs (up to 4,300) than do their southern fellows (as few as 900), making the increased fishing pressure in highly populated areas, such as Seattle, even more ironic. Here, from the fourth week of October through the first week in November, chum will overlap with the returning coho, which results in the digging up of each others' redds. These redds are larger than one would surmise from the size of eggs, ranging from three to nine meters squared, about. Even with this tremendous productivity, not many make it to fry (only 2.5 percent for this chum). Hatched in February through the Ides of March, the fry still has a heavy future in front of him: he leaves for the Bering Sea as early as April with stomach full of partial yolk sacks and invertebrates, hangs around the continental shelf a bit in the summer with the guys, and then the gang disperses to places far and as yet unknown.

The dance of diminishing returns: in 1961, only 71 fishermen took $15,000 worth of chum flesh; only 41,000 fish yearly on the Yukon from 1961 through 1968. Then in 1969 there was rapid growth in terms of both fish taken and fishermen catching them: they were worth $719,800 in 1983. The first quotas were set in 1973, owing to the increase in price and thus in market pressure; maximum harvest was set at 250,000. Subsistence Eskimo and Indians have greater fishing privileges, a factor that causes tension in those who make a living off the back of a salmon (Bulkis and Barton 1984).

Salmon used to be unbelievably abundant. A person could pull a hundred pounds of fish out of any stream to feed his farm animals fish a couple of times a day. The fish were so abundant that one could yank them out with a fish hook as fast as one could yank. Fish were bank to bank.

Consciousness of limited numbers comes slowly in a land of vast space and rampant individualism:

> I thought of all the luxury-loving females that were dreaming and scheming of the day they would have a mink coat. Not one in a million had an idea of the heartbreak and work it took to drape a swirl of prestige fur on their lovely shoulders. I thought about a cute red-headed friend of a friend, Grace, who lived in New Orleans and whose acquaintances teased her about her mink bar-mop. She could trail a stole through a plush lounge with the best of them (Harbottle and Credeur 1966).

A gallery owner acquaintance of mine in Denver, generally intelligent and well-informed, sniped at a well-done display about wildlife killed for fur in a glass case at Stapleton Airport: "This is just all a hoax put up by radicals to raise the cost of fur," she said angrily.

The river is restless now; it constantly shifts its rhythmic slap of waves. A deep rust, it floats over patterned glacial pebbles. It has no bed but murmurs over a dent in land. Changes its mind visibly. The angle of the sun changes it from bright turquoise to black-brown in moments. The land is young, joins the water as uneasy newlyweds in an arranged marriage.

I admit to an Emily Dickinsonian character: the twitch of minutiae is as moving as volcanoes and tsunamis. The outer margins of life, like the Southwestern deserts, and the northern tundras, where the greens are never crude and robust, draw me: the subtle ranges of grays, lavenders, oranges like flute scales in Oriental quarter tones, where one sits through long, quiet observations.

/ August 14:   Eagle Pass, Summit

The White Mountains are raw, flat, vast in scale, yet so minute in plant detail that human proportion is denied. This Mountain of Eagles forms its own weather, orographic uplifting. Mist surges in fat greasy sheets, creating rivulets down the windshield without rain. One-hun-

27

dred-mile-per-hour gusts are interspersed with a steady forty-mile-per-hour blowing. Stiff tundra plants vibrate about four times a second.

This is no ordinary wind. This is wind that can compact snow so hard in winter that ten-ton trucks driving repeatedly over it leave only slight tracks. This wind exhibits a character of its own and brings with it its own set of physical laws, as if from a grander planet. It is the big bully brother of the katabatic winds we hear on the Front Range of the Rockies, the avalanche of warm dry air that hits the plains so hard at times that it knocks over Air Force Academy cadets like twigs. With both arms I hold on: almost rips the door off. Glaciers hover a mile north, unseen in the mist. Powerful funnels of gray goo allow only occasional glimpses of the soil-scallops.

Solifluction comes down these hills in scallops like hoary velvet curtains rimmed in dark green of foliage feeding off the seep. How a solid actually behaves as a liquid has always entranced me: glass, a liquid? A potter on the wheel understands how to make stiff clay reform to the beautiful amphoras of her will by using time, not strength, to realign molecules. Solifluction is a form of mass-wasting that includes landslides, rock creeps, rockslides and mudflow. The thin topsoil behaves as a liquid, flowing down too slowly for the eye to perceive. Upon the land's first emergence from the sea, this took place massively. One patch creeps much faster than the next. Slowly the soil is stabilized by permafrost and by vegetation to become the sort of soil found in the Lower Forty-eight.

Like few soils we know below, this one is suspended in water, a slinking beast of the rocky surface, forming striking patterns of vegetation. Often it does not disturb the shallow roots of arctic plants but moves them downhill with it, as an animal with its fur.

Flowing down in lobate forms, like lava cooling at its front edge, it may turn to mudflow in the middle, or be covered by clumps of flora in distinct shapes on its surface. It forms oblong polygons due to the dynamics of rock suspended in water, accentuated with dark vegetation at its edges, as lyrical as Brahms quartets.

Scientists and explorers have trouble defining edges because nature is not made up of edges. The Arctic is defined geographically as being north of treeline, but treeline in central Canada plunges downward.

They try temperature: 50 degrees F (10 degrees C) in July defines an isotherm, an imaginary line that delineates plant life, since plants are finely attuned to conditions up here. I am amazed to find the British Isles as far north as Alaska. No wonder that island nation produced the great explorers of the world: who wanted to stay home?

Unlike England, whose Robin Hood forests are percolated by warm ocean air currents, the harsh topography here is created by the rapid uplift of land in northern Canada after the retreat of the last ice dome (which is still melting). Glacier Bay in southeast Alaska was not open a century ago, but now it allows sightseeing well up into a labyrinth of fjords. What John Muir recorded during the first decade of this century was quite different from the exposed slopes seen now. During the uplift as the ice disappears, the Pacific Plate continues to slide under the continent. An ongoing geomorphic process of land-wasting is visible in strips and scars, an earth-moving trolley sluffing mountains downhill. I can feel the movement underfoot. No sooner has water broken down the rock than an active layer of unconsolidated soil moves down the permafrost by convection of the freeze-thaw cycles. The stunning patterns, such as regular stone and mud polygons (stone circles), lie as inexplicable as Druid circles.

The churn of earth, an actual boiling motion caused by the constant freezing and thawing, is called congeliturbation: from two Latin words, *congelar* (to congeal) and *turbation* (as in turbo). The idea of gelling adjacent to the idea of constant movement makes this an ideal word for the Alaskan continent.

The landscape colors I so admire are vascular plants, the first to establish themselves on congeliturbated soils—extremely slowly. At first they dig in their heels in the relatively stable furrows and pits between polygons, creating reticular tapestries of color. The middles of the polygons are devoid of plants, owing to the rapid churning. Slowly the vegetation creeps toward and claims the center of a polygon like a chess strategy. A protective mat eventually covers and slows down the freezing/thawing process, only to be thwarted by another set of laws: updoming in the center of the turf hummock. A final hardening of the plastic core of the tiny plant hummock deactivates congeliturbation. Then, organically rich, deep furrows harbor new plants too fragile to root on the tussock alone. Next, willows lay the groundwork for larger plants.

Lemmings, hoary marmots, pikas, voles come in, spread seeds, and become morsels for the larger predators. Eagles, hawks, and owls follow, introducing nitrogen in their excrement, thus producing more plants, and thus more lemmings. Here, an eagle glides unceasingly on an updraft with a mere twitch of feather.

The wind is harmful now, curtailing plant growth. In the lee of rocks and tussocks, the mechanical abrasion of sand and snow is abated. Protected cone patterns form as wind howls past obstacles. If I stayed here long enough, a miniature garden would grow in the wind-shadow of the truck.

In sleeping bag, I write what I thought the tundra was before arriving here: brittle in air, a land locked with ice. Underneath snow, dwarf rhododendron, narcissus waiting to be eaten by marmot. I expected to see flocks of arctic terns along the famous 20,000-mile migration to the tip of Africa. I had imagined the prolific lemmings running over my feet like pet guinea pigs, each pair producing forty to fifty new lemmings a year. I expected to stumble across the snowy owl nesting on the ground and to watch the grizzly eating everything and anything until disappearing into its hole high in the mountains. Instead, such life, though abundant, is dispersed over vast miles, most of it doing its best not to run into me.

There are parallels here to that other edge of life, the warm test tubes of tidal pools. Whereas here life creates itself in spite of elements, there in the interlace of rock and sea exist the perfect yet highly improbable conditions for life to begin. Something glows, becoming organized. A turning up of the lithospheric burner toward pudding, and one of us, without a need to breathe oxygen, smears through the electrical-chemical slurry into being.

Whenever I need a soul-absorbing landscape, I go to Earth's extremes and watch the politics of survival. Phenotypic versus genotypic change. An ability to change immediate and seeable traits based on my environment versus inherited ones. Perhaps I take for my role model the phenotype, the weird one, the one knocked over the head with a low-flying quark and changed, the biological nerd that goes limping, three-legged or seven-toed, into the next era. That's me, we each say. That's why I'm so odd. I'm beyond all this . . . this . . .

I gaze upward.

The night is filled with connect-the-dot mythology, many, many more heavenly bodies, and closer to the source up here than I have ever seen. My natural instinct toward observation, toward collecting, sorting and naming, falls away and I hover only a fraction away from primitive man's awe.

4

Breathing for the Planet

/ August 14:   Porcupine Drainage

I walk up toward Mammoth Creek, under dark clouds. A car from
Washington State stops to see if I am all right. Odd, a woman out here
with no vehicle. In spite of the insistent south-southwest wind
in my face, the walk does me wonders. The time lapse movement of
clouds, dark-bellied cumuli being mushed ahead by the wind, ragged
swirling bases, signaling imminent precipitation.

I think of this:

WIND AS BREATH

There are two skills that have taught me that observation and breathing are one and the same: Zen and scuba diving. One a concrete sport,
the other a spiritual path; it is odd they are similar.

Scuba taught me to see slowly and thoroughly, to move little to
conserve oxygen, to absorb the oddities of the underwater universe.
The less you move, the less air you use. The less air you use, the
longer you can stay out. And stay out is what you passionately want

to do, because few of the forms follow any of the laws of gravity that are familiar. Instead, forms spread and pulsate, float, change color, transmutate, as if demonstrating the Hindu notion of the transformational nature of matter: Shiva's dance manifest right before our eyes. I love the sway and pulse of the waves in the dusky blue atmosphere a few meters under the surface of convex waves. In the mere slip between surfaces, the entire physical universe inverts and becomes weirdly beautiful.

It is slow, slower than slow, as time heals itself of our frantic pace—that is, until a moray eel strikes out at my father, photographer and fellow diver, faster than the human eye can follow. Due to rules of underwater breathing, it's hard to giggle in a regulator.

Primitives equate breath with life. In Zazen, the meditation form of Zen Buddhism, one breathes deeply instead of chanting, filling one's lungs entirely with air and pausing at the hiatus between intake and outbreath to accept all into the blood. This serves not only to relax and invigorate but also yields a transcendent high as the body is given the unique chance to fully absorb oxygen. The scuba manual, too, advises one to breathe calmly, deeply and slowly.

Here the white anemone, the windflower (Greek: *anemos* = wind) oscillates in the wind. The earth is breathing through its lithosphere and into its upper atmosphere, a concept presented by James Lovelace: the concept of the planet as a conscious entity, carefully tuning its heat and oxygen to evolve a greater complexity of life on its surface, balancing oxygen constantly with carbon monoxide (W. Thompson 1987). The key to ice-climbing, to carrying heavy loads uphill, to traveling on snowshoes, to backpacking: breathing.

Breathe slowly in and out with every several steps. In this manner backpackers may peak when they are in their fifties, as opposed to participants in faster sports, such as foot-racing or football. It is the art of breathing.

Breathing. Once an asthmatic, up here I feel the planet breathing for me.

The wind up on the tundra: the distribution of seed, the aeolian fans of loess. The birds' use of thermals and updrafts to fly effortlessly: hunting, migrating. The primitive who was found by the anthropologist one morning at dawn spitting on his hand and blowing toward the sun. It was through breath that the soul entered the body, and through breath that he blessed the sun each morning.

/ August 15:   Mastodon Creek, near Central, Alaska

Woke up in a drumming rain this morning, worried about the New Orleans wetlands and the oil industry versus the oyster industry. A billion acres of oyster swamplands lost to the construction of the oil industry, an area the size of Delaware. Nonrenewable swamps never to be returned to oyster farming lost at the rate of one football field every 61 minutes. Death to the shellfish industry, life to the oil industry. Why am I thinking of oysters as I walk, soaked, through this pitted landscape, a land stripped down to river bottoms, of heaps and pits of gravel?

I am thinking about oil versus oyster because this new sort of confrontation is the style of the future, of humanity coming face to face with the limitations of Mama Earth, in which two legitimate concerns come to loggerheads. It is the conflict of an epoch's end: of dinosaurs versus mammal adaptation strategies, of humankind versus the rest of nature, in which humankind cannot win. Stephen Jay Gould is downright cheerful about it in one of his essays for *Natural History* magazine; these catastrophic wipeouts, and thus changes in organisms on a cyclical basis (tied in with the Supercontinent Cycle theory), actually are positive. Instead of the Darwinian wedges of animal species becoming entrenched forever, a periodic wipeout is healthy, creating room for new species.

Humankind's out, and something else is coming in. So, cheer up, Susan, and step on the Cretaceous pedal.

/ August 16:   Central, Alaska

Population 600 summer, 150 winter. Large pickups are parked akilter
in the Central grocery store and bar lot, with bumper stickers reading
THE HELL WITH THE LOWER 48, three-tiered gun racks, dangerous-
looking protrusions welded to front and back bumpers. Signs on
buildings warn against environmentalists (tree-huggers), governmental
agencies, and their employees.

The man I am supposed to meet wears a gold caribou on his bare
chest. He is handsome and in good shape. His chopper has just been
shot full of holes in the bush, but the sheriff isn't concerned. "No one
was *hit*, was they?" he asks the pilot.

"Weed growers or illegal operators?" I ask, but I reach a closed
door. Gold Caribou doesn't want to talk about it. The noise of a
helicopter overhead—he hurries to meet it. I'll go to the bar later
to find him.

Meanwhile, I'll bone up on mining law history and begin to understand its original intention: to encourage settlement of the West.
To push expansion into Alaska, which we bought from the Russians
in 1867 in a political maneuver against the British. The 1872 mining
law is a vestigial fragment of land law from the nineteenth century,
designed to encourage economic development and pull natural resources out of the land as quickly as possible. Because Alaska was
perceived as a vast wasteland, the law encouraged unregulated
exploitation.

Any person who found what he *said* to be a mineral deposit on
any federal land could stake a claim simply by filing in the local court-
house and posting a notice. By marking the corners of his claim with a
pile of rocks it became his, along with free access and any necessary
use of the surface for mining and consequent development. The only
criterion to be met was to prove he had done at least $100 worth of
exploratory work (without necessarily finding anything) on the land a
year. The law allowed miners to gain ownership of any federal land by
obtaining a patent, the only criterion for which was to show he had
spent $500 in working the claim. The patent, or title, could be pur-
chased for as little as $5 an acre for a lode claim, and only $2.50 for a

placer claim. That was some bargain even back then, and the price is still the same. Unlike homesteaders under the Homestead Act, which resulted in agriculturalists bunching up next to one another for safety and company in an urge to create communities, miners created a patchwork of individual claims that dot federal lands to this day.

In contrast to the more updated laws concerning our fossil resources, the gold and silver mining laws stick out of the land like porcupine quills in a dog. With fossil minerals, the land is leased and a substantial royalty is paid to the federal government; the royalties are supposed to go back into the maintenance of public lands. The greatest trouble with this mining law is its lack of environmental protection, although recent regulations require better water purity and land reclamation. The miners fought this aggressively up here.

There is irony: the old law of 1872 does not help the miner's cause either. The small size of individual claims, plus the casual manner of staking them, leads to counterclaims, confusion, and no small number of dead bodies.

Not only does the 1872 mining law give away federal lands at $2.50 an acre, but wealth, in the form of gold or other minerals, can be taken from the land at will. Under the new, stiffer reclamation laws, many individual miners are slipping over the border to mine in Canada. Alaskan citizens scream about the manpower and raw wealth fleeing the state, as well as the country.

I take a deep breath and enter the bar; this is not always easy for me to do alone in the boonies, but this bar turns out to be an underground historical cache full of a clutter of memorabilia, pulsing, blinking, swirling beer signs, signs advising women not to wear certain items of clothes. I feel relaxed. Two very dirty guys, ragged from working mines, saunter in with severely used bodies.

" . . . '84," he is saying, "my license ran out on my rig. . . . Never *did* get my pilot's license." He is flying his companion into the Yukon wilderness tomorrow. The bartender shoves them beers without asking what kind.

"Government's done a lotta damage up here," the other says. "They put us little guys outta business. All these regulations mean only the megaliths can come in and tear up the land, faster and better.

They got the big smartass lawyers'll tear up them environmentalist assholes."

"Goddamned Sierra Club. They got this water regulation passed where you gotta return the water to the stream cleaner than it ever was, only they didn't get the streams all sampled before us miners got in 'em, and so they lie and make out that all these streams used to be real clear. So now there's laws that we gotta put back the water *cleaner than it was before!*"

"Goddamned motherfuckers from the goddamned Lower Forty-eight ain't got nothin' to do with us, and if I meet one I'd just as soon . . . "

"Yeah, we oughta sell *them* to the Russians."

"Yeah? The goddamned Russies wouldn't have 'em. Do you realize how bad Washington D.C. red-tape fat-assed bureaukercy'd mess up their communist government there?"

I smile, thinking of who originally sold what to whom, but dwelling on subtleties is dangerous to one's health up here.

In the late '70s there was a movement afoot in Congress to reform the original 1872 mining act. The Mineral Leasing Act of 1920 converted the oil industry to leasing from owning, and the old mineral act needed the same sort of change. It covered a wide variety of mining types, without distinguishing between them, and provided no land protection whatsoever. Just as the regulation was about to be passed, it mysteriously disappeared, a foreshadowing of the Reagan era practice of selling off national resources for short-term economic gain.

Highly toxic results of historical practices are now showing up in the rivers and groundwater of Colorado, leaching out of ancient slag heaps. Cleanup will demand astronomical amounts of taxpayers' funds. The old miners with pick and shovel, thin cable and bucket, have long since disappeared into the ground, along with any sense of financial responsibility.

How to protect the environment and, simultaneously, to protect the renegade character, the individual operator? Deviation from mainstream culture is a vital asset to humanity. The deviant offers alternatives, inspires, gathers the wealth at the edges of frontiers. Most *Homo*

sapiens desire closely knit, highly reinforced common morality systems, which consolidate into tighter and tighter systems until those
systems deaden at the center just like the lichen. Rebels come along to
blow open the escape route. We need the renegades. We once were a
nation of them.

Meanwhile, here comes my friend with the caribou on his chest.
His handle is Mad Wrench. Mad Wrench isn't happy with me; I'm
asking too many questions. But I can sense he likes being near a
woman, likes my attention. I like being near him. He emanates masculinity. He is all brown and tough. Soft-spoken, gentle. As a renegade
from the confines of the Lower Forty-eight, he is an archetypal Alaskan character, whose inner-being I must understand. He doesn't much
want to, but after two beers he begins to speak. He doesn't understand
what the purpose of my writing project is. I tell him, "That's okay, I
don't either." He can smell an environmentalist ten miles away, he
claims. His eyes have depth and intelligence. I cross and recross my
legs and fiddle nervously with the wisps of hair around my face.

He works now as a mechanic for other people, but is getting antsy
to be out in the field again, working for the BLM, flying people, is the
pits: everybody's a chief. Forest fire fighting: flying through smoke all
day in highly dangerous conditions doing the same route over and
over.

"I like Alaska; it accepts Alaskan characters," says Mad Wrench,
"it puts up with me. I have lack of respect for authority and give them
many reasons to fire me. They don't. Alaskans should be governed
by Alaskans. Many of the laws from the environmentalists are well
founded but lost in the translation. Alaskans should be administered
by Alaskans. Now we got too many people down there in Juneau
pushin' pencils. Alaska's a jar that's got resources in it which the
masses down south want to control. The Environmentalist Cartel
System, the damned tree-huggers, so full of misconceptions . . . trying
to find something to pick on us with . . . "

Suddenly, he is hushed by the sound of his own voice. "I got a
bad outlook on life. You probably don't want to hear all of this dark
stuff." He pauses, saddened, waiting for my denial. I don't respond,
lost in my own thoughts, staring through him, through his rugged

physique clouded by what he has seen in Nam.

Mad Wrench is truly an Alaskan soul, and I must understand him to comprehend Alaska. I catch his eyes sizing me up sidey-ways. I half expect an invitation that I only half dread, but it never comes. Turns out he must go back to base camp with the helicopter crew. He is shyer than I expect.

"I was in L.A. and got arrested by this bastard airport cop who chased me into the crowd, said I was a terrorist or somethin'. People on the airplane had been buying me lots of drinks because I was a hero or somethin' back from Nam. Oh, yeah, I was a little blitzed but not much. This bastard cop grabbed me and called for support to pin me down. All those people lookin'. Cost me thousands in court costs. I'm no terrorist! I just don't fit in in the Lower Forty-eight. My brother died just as I got back from flying helicopters in Nam. Dove into a swimming pool head-first into the shallow end. I survived a horrible war; my brother didn't make it through a senior party."

I am looking at him. I do not see the angry character toughened beyond sensitivity he intends me to see. Rather, I see a cautious tenderness, a reaching out, a love of intense life, a love of things and people. "So what about getting shot at in your helicopter?" I ask.

"Goddamned chickenshit shot at us from the back, where we were blinded to him. If he had any balls, he would have shot from the front. Don't know who he is, nor why he did it. Just that he's got no balls to shoot from the rear, whoever he is."

"Or she."

He looks at me. "She?!"

"Well, that would account for the lack of balls," I say. We crack up.

/ August 17: The Arctic Circle Motel

Perched eight miles up in the mountains from Center, Arctic Circle is at the brink of goldminers' territory, the famous Birch Creek. Isolation and toughness, however, do not make for a lack of colorful culture. I am drawn immediately toward the Victorian hotel/bar/pool/ everything building. In fact this building is town. Belying a rough exterior, inside is a different world. Elegance and overstuffed chairs abound. Fine old photographs document local mining history. Loads of books. Well-crafted woodwork and porcelain bowls depict an eighteenth-century English countryside. Each motel room is decorated pleasantly with a different theme. I smell food. *Good* food.

At the front desk, as ornate as anything else in the Victorian lobby, is the female persona of Alaska: Corrine Jones. In her seventies, she stands at the registration desk holding court over a tall young man who obviously admires her. Bright-eyed, sharp-witted, she chain-smokes over a half-finished sweet roll.

Age and health up here do not obey the laws of the Lower Forty-eight: life makes rigorous demands. This creates a lack of middle ground: no comatose masses barely able to cope with the physics of the family home, let alone the complex decisions involved in the democratic process. There are the young and very tough, and the old and very resilient. Here I seem to have one of each.

I swiftly whip out my investigative reporting skills and dive into Corrine's character, but she, just as swiftly, outmaneuvers me with a huge pile of magazines. It seems that she was the editor and business reporter for the North Slope for years, and is not about to have her own interview tactics used on her. "Read these," she instructs. I eat, return to my pickup, and read for four hours.

Corrine, it turns out, lived ten years up at Prudhoe Bay. She writes vividly and abundantly of her experiences there in *Our Alaskan Business and People*, the magazine she edited for years:

> Men and machines worked in sub-zero temperatures to extend a gravel causeway to stranded barges in Prudhoe Bay. The barges were part of a contingent that arrived in early October and froze in place before they could be unloaded. The 5,000-foot causeway extension, operated by Atlantic Richfield Company, is necessary to unload modules, large buildings containing facilities essential for the development of the Prudhoe Bay.
>
> Long before the actual work began, there had been three desperate weeks of testing. Those were days of try, try, try again. Sometimes a

glimmer of doubt may have plagued the planners, but their combined thinking and engineering equations found the answer. Arco's designers conceived a six-ton basket and Frontier people built it from iron and 3″ and 4″ pipe. The crane operator maneuvered the basket under each ice cube cut by the Ditch Witch, laboriously lifted the nine-ton mass to be dropped with a thundering crash on the build-up of chunks along the route.

That floodlighted area, on the ice itself, was an awe-inspiring sight. Never to be forgotten, the languid motion of water slopping forth and back after releasing the ice to the grip of a crane operator's basket, was unbelievable. Thick, it looked like cream, like simmering gravy. There was a gruesome quality to that slow fluidity. It didn't splash. It surged. And, as the Ditch Witch saw cut a swath about eight inches wide, the sludge hung to the chain and dripped in globs.

Corrine whets my appetite for the mysterious North Slope, for those magnificent struggles of men in machines against insurmountable odds.

I ask her my ever-driving question: How does she survive up here in the winter, mentally? She tells me about the car starting up at 20 degrees below, responding, as most Alaskans do, to a metaphysical question with a concrete situation:

"I was stuck out there where I am building a cabin for three days once, couldn't even come into the hotel to work. I loved it! Just stayed in bed and read for three days. That is the most delightful thing on Earth one can do." Aloneness is not, apparently, an issue for Corrine; but then Corrine is no ordinary woman. She is instinctive, like an animal that lives and breathes wilderness, changing coloration, metabolism and activity as naturally as does a marmot in hibernation.

Once again Corrine sends me away, tired of my questions. So I head toward food smells. During a hot lunch I overhear a heated debate:

"I hear there might be oil 'long up this way," says one man.

"I'd like to see that," says another, "to see about 150 big National Army oil rigs up and down here. They'd probably build a pipeline and run it right into the main pipe."

"Yeah, but if they did find oil right this very minute, it'd be five years before they started."

"Five years, is about the right time for the A-Rabs to have another rebellion, isn't it?" Laughter.

"They can't afford to rock the boat now: they own too much of America."

"The last oil boom, it got so crazy. Prices shot way up. Boomers from Texas and Arkansas came up and took all the money back down there. I'd rather pay high prices at the pump and at least be able to sell my house in Anchorage. I paid quadruple what it's worth."

"They're not going to pull another boom and bust routine on us so fast."

"Maybe. We got no sense of history. People's already forgotten the last a little under a decade ago."

Could these be the same men who hunt caribou, whose existence or pleasure depends on the calving-migration territory they want to get oil out of? Each spring, 150,000 porcupine caribou travel to the coastal plain of the Arctic National Wildlife Refuge to calve. Their selection of ground is very narrow, owing to the clouds of mosquitoes (the caribou must be near the Beaufort Sea, for the breeze), the closeness of the Brooks Range, the availability of food, and predation danger. Grinding machinery intruding into the pristine calving ground would eliminate this herd; the central herd's options are much greater, and it is on the larger herd that the oil industry's positive argument is based. The naval oil reserves, called Pet 4, already cover a majority of the coast of the North Slope; it is ironic that they feel obliged to take a last small percentage. The Arctic National Wildlife Refuge was created by an act of Congress in 1960 to protect the area's outstanding wildlife. In 1980, it was doubled to 18 million acres through the Alaska National Interest Lands Conservation Act, and eight million acres were closed to all development.

Now Arco and Exxon covet the calving grounds only 75 miles east of Prudhoe Bay. This coastal strip was not closed, because it is said to sit on top of one of the richest oil fields, a claim that simply is not true. At most, the available oil from under the Refuge would supply oil for the country for about nine months at the cost of destroying epochs of evolutionary balance.

The plot thickens. In 1981, then Secretary of the Interior James

Watt attempted to pull a fast one on Congress by assigning the required Environmental Impact Report 1002 not to the National Parks or Fish and Game guys, whose goals presumably would be responsible toward wildlife, but rather to the U.S. Geological Survey, an agency whose sole purpose is to assess and encourage use of the nation's natural resources. He and Reagan killed negotiations with Canada for a treaty to protect caribou calving grounds.

Meanwhile, in a very CIA-type maneuver, the Department of the Interior held secret meetings with Native American corporations within the wildlife refuge to develop land trades: "megatrades," or "Project M," as it was called in the secret documents leaked to Congress. Many Native Americans are subsistence-level hunters, whose survival depends on caribou. Entirely subversive to the democratic and legal proceeding of Congress, the shit hit the legislative fan when it was purposefully leaked out: Congress passed a bill disallowing any land swaps, especially behind its back (Kizzia 1986).

The oil industry has dreams and plans. In 1979, Elfen Enterprises very quietly applied to the federal court to open the process for a pipeline grant. A Washington reporter's curiosity was piqued; he found that Elfen Industries, which represented several large oil companies, wanted to build a pipeline from the North Slope down through the Midwest, with a direct line to every home in the United States, and it wanted to do it without the knowledge of those troublesome environmentalists.

Lunch done, I return to bug Corrine once more. She is so intensely alive, her spirit comes buzzing through her eyesockets like electrical current. At 10 a.m. I take leave reluctantly of Corrine, who seems embarrassed by all my questions. Fascinated by her stamina, I want to know more. As a decoy, she tells me of the vivid history of mining up Birch Creek Road.

Her ploy works. High noon. I find myself out the last road high in the Birch Creek mining territory winding twenty miles up and down ridges. It makes all concessions to land, twitching up suddenly, plunging down, a hairpin second-gear turn in the hungry jig-jags of tire tracks. Along the way, the giant machines of small operations squat on their haunches like metal insects: Cats, backhoes, shovelers, cranes. So many fortunes rusting away. A bright blue Chevron oil can sits on one side, fifty gallons and a spigot. Underneath, gas cans tilt in mud, bright orange ones, rusty old models, each with its insect proboscis pointing heavenward. My journey ends suddenly in deep mud settling ponds.

The streams are chopped and criss-crossed by dirt tracks. Most of this valley is raw gravel laced with house-sized settling ponds. After the earth is bulldozed and sluiced, the dust syrup must be transformed into clear stream water for the fish. During the surge of gold mining in the early '80s—3,000 claims a week—this area went virtually without enforcement of environmental standards. Now the lower courts are enforcing standards rigorously, to which a miner said:

"What's a few goddamned fish mean anyway, compared to all the gold we can take out of here, and make the country rich?"

In the case of National Wildlife Federation versus Robert F. Burfort, director of the Bureau of Land Management, a suit involving more than 7,000 mining claims on 120 million acres of wilderness, the federation claimed the miners' land use was "inconsistent with the original withdrawal of land classification" (Bradley 1988). Interpretation of law that pertains to Public Trust lands is the environmental Lebanon of the future: What *is* the greatest good for the most people (to say nothing of animals)?

Up either side of the bulldozed valley rise lush ridges full of birch and aspen. Their reflections sink like white silk banners into the rust-colored settling ponds. It is balmy, unusually hot under a pure blue sky. No one is here.

Pipes strewn about like pickup sticks. Orange markers flutter. Where are all these miners on a prime workday? It is too hot to be soaking in the hot springs that come out of the ground at 115 degrees. This is reminiscent of Baja California: building materials and equipment left in awkward stages of progress while the owner scrapes for enough money and time to continue his dream.

Placer mines, from the Spanish word *plasser*, meaning "where gold comes out of the gravel" (Kopvillem et al. 1985), suffer under strict new standards. When silt covers up fish roe, oxygen deprivation decimates whole subspecies of fish. Miners soon will be required to leave part of the stream channel open for fish. Authorities in Canada had

been ignoring vast fish depletions because of the Yukon's $30 million
gold industry, but its second largest industry, fishing and hunting, is
being depleted instead. It is estimated that 16 percent of miners may
be forced out of business by the strict implementation of reclamation
law, so Canadians are seeking compromise.

Our Environmental Protection Agency writes in "Mining Wastes
in the West," a 1987 fact sheet, that:

> A hard rock mine generally produces large quantities of wastes. In
> addition to the overburden of soil removed during the mining operation
> itself, there may be large piles of tailings, slag heaps, and flue dust from
> the benefication process. A large portion of mining waste presents little
> risk. . . .

But some do, the fact sheet continues. Sulfur, in the form of metal
sulfide—fool's gold—oxidizes to sulfuric acid, creating acid water,
which in turn leaches other metals from the rock faster. When this
acidic and metallic seepage is released into the environment, chains
of other chemical reactions continue for decades. Contamination of
water runoff from mine sites may have a dramatic impact on fresh-
water communities, plants, and livestock downstream. Environmental
scientists cannot estimate the full extent of damage, since it will be
insidious over many years to come. Fish damage, in particular, results
from high acid runoff, toxic materials, and high sedimentation. Sometimes fish are able to sense and to avoid such areas, but other fish
become smaller and smaller, until they disappear altogether.

Cadmium, arsenic, lead, and sulfur send toxic water to humans
and animals below. Once again, there must be found a balance between pulling metals out of the earth and allowing life to perpetuate
itself.

A peregrine falcon passes overhead with a curious cry.

The road shoots up the escarpment from the mines toward the
Yukon, rising high above the dendritic stream system flowing down
toward the Yukon in Yukon Flats Park and Preserve. The air is
pristine.

Far overhead, many hawks rise on thermals with the slow turn of a
knife peeling an apple.

Somewhere behind, dynamite blasts, very muffled. I welcome it: it makes Earth seem immense, because sound seems to expand exponentially over the distance it travels.

In 1893, Pitka Pavloff and his brother-in-law, Cherosky Demoski, struck color (gold) on Birch Creek. The two, of Native American and Russian heritage, had long searched for the yellow, pliable metal. Before the river froze that winter, they established a camp called Old Portage above Circle City. The surge of prospectors came like locusts in the spring of 1894, covering these hills between Birch Creek and the Yukon River; the supply centers of Circle City and Center boomed. Pavloff and Cherosky's claim on Birch Creek provided them an excellent living; they raised huge families, many of whom still live and play important roles in Alaskan politics today.

WE RESERVE THE RIGHT TO REFUSE SERVICE TO ANY GROUP OR
GOVERNMENT AGENCY THAT THREATENS THE WAY OF LIFE IN
CENTER AND THOSE STRUGGLING TO MAKE A DECENT LIVING
Sign in bold letters at the
Center Bar and Cafe

Balanced on an old-fashioned red plastic drugstore stool, I eat the "Famous" Yukon Rush Burger so large I can barely hold it with two hands. The ubiquitous television is on during the soaps. An old man comes in; he is delighted, thinking that because I am at the bar I am set up for therapy. The bar is the farthest point from the television. It is raining hard, and I stuff on dead cow muscle to get me through the 16 miles of the Pinnell Mountain loop. The foot trail crosses the flanks of Porcupine Dome, traversing 27.3 miles of high alpine ridge-tops above treeline. It promises to be rugged; I will need a full three days to cover it all. Twenty miles in one day in the Lower Forty-eight is challenging but possible for me. Tundra is exhausting. Alternating bog and scree demand constant concentration on feet. The wind sucks off one's life juice slowly. Smaller distances are greater in Alaska. I triple my normal hiking time estimates.

Pinnell Mountain, 4,721 feet above sea level, is the southwest flank of Porcupine Dome. It was named by Lt. Commander R. Darling of the USC & GS for Robert Pinnell, who was accidentally killed on July 17, 1952, while climbing the dome, according to *Alaska Place Names*. The same reference says that Pinnell River, however, was named after Jesse Pinnell, a miner from Nome, at about the turn of the century. Of course, it could be pure coincidence that two men with the same name ended up spontaneously on the topography at different times. That's what I enjoy about Alaskan history; it's still being invented.

I sleep at the trailhead this night. Wind howls as the sun goes out in the White Mountains, thousand-foot rolling mounds trending east-northeast through middle Alaska. One story has it that they were named by miners for the handsome limestone outcroppings. Of course, a local story has it that a miner named White was the namesake.

I do not believe I will sleep, but sleep comes—in huge dark green drapes of solifluction. There are so few mornings in the city I awake so excited to be alive.

I wallow in being here, amidst vestigial fragments of evolution saved from massive ice scrapes where the glaciers were not. On high arctic steppes, I want to flirt with 18,000-year-old flora and fauna. I want to cruise around a corner into a peaceful herd of arctic yak or steppe bison, or observe a ground sloth's long claws and cumbersome movement.

At 3,300 feet, bushes are jittery with wheatears, brown buntings, swallows, juncos. A marsh hawk slices two air masses, delineating the edge between them. The elegant scallops of soil drip down thick as homemade chocolate syrup on cold ice cream.

We have too few words for green. There are many greens: the pearly malachite layers of creeping berries, a verdancy of brand new lichens, the translucent beetle greens of old medicine bottles, glaucous slopes of low willow, deep army green of brush, and the light reseda of newborn groundcover. Greens resonate down through parabolic curves to the base of the hills. Each vertical trickle of stream beginning acts as a knife drawn up through the pattern of dark/light meringue forming the break lines between scallops.

Stegosaurus-shaped shadows cast in dark zinc follow the angled crenelation of ridgetop: this toothy outline is repeated with great exaggeration on the bottom side of the shadow. Within them the mind does not perceive the deep rock gullies, the inverse crags that appear as flat areas of no sun. These shadows soften the mountains; it is as if they are melting under some great force. They are.

Gentle they are not. Covered with slabs of ill-formed volcanic stone, even the established trail tips and rocks. Hot-compressed stone in powerful wavy layers hides complex origins. Over each summit the stone stutters, shattered as glass, heaps of frictioned surfaces covered with bright green and jet black lichen. Immortal stains, each individual lichen plant may be more than 2,000 years old. At one time, they dominated the world and now are the final organism seen on the way to the North and South poles. They are beginning life again through improbable combinations of carbon, hydrogen, oxygen, salts of potassium, phosphorus, sodium, calcium, and sulfur. Over bare stone thallophytes splay their tapestries of color: red where the birds shit, orange where animals pee, pale green, blue-gray, and black as a black hole.

Most humans shun this tentative earth skin. It reminds them of the time before they existed . . . or the time after.

Three miles away, the opposite mountain appears as an etching, and the next mountain after that a fray of wet watercolor into dry. The sharpest crawling forms are Persian calligraphy, Farsi, made of bare stone left open to the sky, the last raw stone stumbling down the steppe. Larger shapes look like continents pulled apart and pushed back together.

Gray characters surrounded by the red-rust-orange of heathers in moisture-soaked crevices are like a wild child's first warm gurglings before it forms sensible syllables. Rugged tundra is blessed: it will be a long time before it is turned into the flat profanities of parking lot or the overenunciation of English garden.

Flatness in this country is an anomaly. The few flat areas, such as the shelves of mountain shoulders, offer up unexpected uniformity of hue. Nothing is normal—there is constant surprise. The human eye loves these "random" needlepoints of purple-rust, rust-gold, gray-greens, because it evolved along with these patterns in another millennium. We thrill to these archetypes of Earth as it organizes itself further and further from chaos, through gradual experiments of evolution. The human eye came out of the sea looking for patterns: the mottled morsel against its mottled background, dinner camouflaged à la underbrush. The art of discerning pattern elevated itself, became in and of itself pleasurable, released itself from the struggle for survival, and was called "art."

Eyesight was one of the last faculties of the brain to develop in us humans, yet there it was, in with the crustaceans, sniffing and shifting, later scratching and mobilized, sorting out information in its primordial split-level. Food or danger came, not in terms of interdepartmental communiques, but in visual patterns of color and movement. This does not denigrate our deep response to beauty, but rather raises the question of why it isn't there, when it isn't. An essential part of the brain, dead.

I believe that our salvation as a species will come through the revival of the sense of beauty, our wanting it above all else; through it a vital need to preserve nature arrives. Through this beauty sense, we will find intolerable gravel-scraped streams and oil-humped shores.

Up here it is easy to observe the exhilarating push-pull balancing act of Earth: the ever spiraling growth of rock-to-flora-to-fauna and from fauna back to flora, life ordering itself right under my nose: an exquisite flight from chaos beginning in soil. Familiar plants from the Lower Forty-eight here are adapted to oligotrophic soils: they lack the nitrogen on which plants depend, nitrogen fixation by bacteria is lacking, and decay is slow. There ain't much to eat. This becomes apparent in exuberant growth around animal dung and in Eskimo ruins. Eutrophic habitats, such as owl perches, raw humus, lemming bones, can cause a hummock to form 25 inches high. This, in turn, attracts more lemmings and lemmings' burrows, in which there is more dung. This lusher vegetation then attracts ptarmigans, which leave behind ptarmigan dung (Porsild 1951). Seagulls, falcons, gyrfalcons, peregrine falcon, create flowery red lichens (*Caloplaca elegans*) on cliffs below. Musk-ox and huge geese leave meadows luxuriant in decaying bodies and dung.

Plants under the snow cover begin to sprout green, forming miniature igloos over themselves, the greenhouse effect. Plants protect themselves from desiccation of the howling wind. Lack of birds means seed dispersion problems. What must it be like to be whipped in high winds, crushed by snow, while remaining glued to one spot one's entire life?

Amazing strategies! Genetic dwarfing is the most obvious. Plants I would recognize in Washington become hand-lens size up here. This, combined with the pulvinate habit—being cushion-shaped or bulbous at base—creates within the plant its own microclimate and reduces abrasion of snow and wind (just as in the deserts). Protoplasm is the fluid that makes up all plant and animal life, formed of water, proteins, lipoids, carbohydrates, and inorganic salts; keeps it from freezing. My theory: it is like salting the highway. An increase in membranes, phospholipids, accompanies hardening, which means plants may survive at –50 degrees centigrade. Just as individual plants may change form to suit their situation on a window ledge, a scrub pine may pull in its branches to protect its seeds in a tight whorl of cones and sling branches around itself like feather boas, twisting many times. New growth often is protected by dead leaves, or plants may lurk down in rock depressions. I am suddenly homesick for a desert full of scales and shields and pricks, of growth with death on the outside, for soft wind vortices depositing snowflakes and minerals in leafy interiors.

I am forced back to the pulvinate microcosm of the truck: winter is in the gray breath of the sun. It is no longer summer in mid-August; lit-up seed-pod fibers turn sullenly to snow sparks. The wind picks up an eerie low moan through the mountain-sized harmonica and blows the sun's low angle.

/ August 18:   Of Time and Space

Yesterday's storm strips morning radiant. Membranous clouds stretch back into summer, and flocks of wheatears sweep by, handsome brown patterns on their backs. I sit looking up the bell-form *Psilocibe montana*, when a large four-wheel-drive pulls up. An off-duty game warden, originally from California, steps out, giving me one swift glance. He walks out manlike and stiff-legged to glass tundra for meat. I discover that he came up here seven years ago as a conservationist against all shooting, married an Eskimo, and became a subsistence hunter for his family. With two jobs, two children, and studying for a masters degree, he does not make ends meet.

My curiosity about the Eskimo is piqued; the taciturn man begins to speak. "There has been a tragic gap of an entire generation," he says, "due to methodical destruction of their culture by white man, church, and alcoholism. They are poor in white man's terms. My wife's generation has begun to reach back to the grandmothers' traditional skills and language. Each year she returns to the village to tan hides, learn sewing, and prepare food for the winter. She still loves that thick chunk of whale blubber with the black skin still on it." He wrinkles up his Anglo nose involuntarily.

Of the federal government he says, "Those guys still do not hire the Native Americans up here because they are not on white man's time schedule." I am reminded of an intelligent state employee guideline in New Mexico: Native Americans are allowed leave for all their dances and ceremonies, even though these happen with unpredictability in terms of our Roman calendar.

In the Coastal Salish on Vancouver Island, as well as in the Hopi Pueblos in northeastern Arizona, time and space are interchangeable, not only in grammar but in thinking. Similar to nuclear particle formulas in physics, in which time and movement through space are represented by the same vectors, in Hopi or Northwest Native experience one may go backward in time as well as space. Space is spoken of in terms of time (such as three days' travel), and time is spoken of in terms of space (such as three orbits of the moon). That expanded eye, or vision-thought, on extensive pack ice is profoundly different from our whiteman linear thought. Vision-thought is a way of knowing, and then describing, that evolves from our ways of moving through time and space. Reference of nouns to positions in space may, in other contexts, refer to positions in time. Both time in crossing and the actual distance through the howling whiteness relate to nearness, visibility, or the experience of getting there. Also as in contemporary physics, the quality, location, direction, and speed of a moving particle can only be expressed relative to another, not in terms of stationary points, not on a rigid grid or calendar. This is distinct from the Anglo way of seeing, which operates around absolute points of reference: quartz clocks, Big Ben, latitude and longitude, poles, Greenwich Time, et cetera. We probably made up absolute time at the same time we made up an absolute God and elevated a monarch. A Native Alaskan's relativity is closer to the way the universe works. It operates mysteriously well in his vast expanses.

"It was ridiculous to attempt to pin Native Alaskans down to reservations in the 1920s, to certain spots on the earth which emphasized our way of thinking," he said sadly. To attempt to comprehend this sense of time and motion, I close my eyes, and open them as if anew on a world I had never seen. I then define all about me in terms of water, fire, dwelling, and the direction of the flow of water. The direction of the mountains. The number of days to travel to the next place. The sense of life being cyclical, repeating itself, and I but one small being in a timeless flow of such beings. Up here, I have become extremely aware of celestial bodies and weather. I calculate my actions by storms, by the size of the moon, by the northern lights. Although I will never have the privilege of perceiving the world as a Native Alaskan, it is beneficial to try living time before the time when time only went forward.

/ August 20:   Coming Off the Mountain

My eyes are painfully dry. The Fish and Game man dissolves in distance. A potent image: the man, a minute dark fleck of dust on the lens of large binoculars, absurdly small, then disappearing. The last of him is a glint of his rifle, a metal clink in vast gray.

I walk right into rock ptarmigan on the ground in perfect camouflage against mottled stone. Even after I see them twelve feet away, I can't keep the birds in focus. Each turn, each spin on heel, there is another chortle warning me not to step on them. In winter they become snow-white with scarlet combs over the eyes. Rock ptarmigan and the rarer white-winged ptarmigan prefer these stony territories, while the larger willow ptarmigan are down among the willows and brush. They presume me to be as harmless as I am blind and clumsy.

No caribou. An eerie paucity of four-leggeds. A dearth of marmoty things. On the other side of Pinnell Mountain, more mines strung out along impossible dirt ribbons. Five forest fires burn along the Yukon River. Nobody lives out there, just somebody supplementing his or her winter table with BLM firefighting budget.

I make a classic bad decision when I come out: instead of taking care of my physical needs immediately—hunger, dehydration, wind and sunburn, tired leg muscles, sore and rubbed feet—I set out in the truck for a hundred dirt miles to Fairbanks. The city would cure all these troubles. I wouldn't have to lift a foot. Famous last wilderness words.

Five miles from the trailhead, another flat tire. It requires all my strength to loosen the nuts, only to find the back bumper too high to thread the jack handle in the holes under the truck to lower the spare. Jump up and down on the bumper; no dice.

Lie underneath to align the jack handle through the holes. No luck. Meanwhile, I am too hungry, burned, and filthy to think. Frustration and belligerence are modus operandi. Tire has come all the way off the rim and flops about like a black calamari.

The first big pickup to come along carries two Athapascans who know less about cars than I do. Not that having European blood means evolving with a mechanical sensitivity by any means. Mine is wrought, wrestled, and wrangled by rote, not intelligence. Their solution: jack up the truck precariously in order to get the spare out. "Height won't help!" I snap emphatically, but there is no explaining. One hooks his humungous jack under the thin sheet metal of the decorative outside of the truck. I knock his hands away just as he begins to crank it up. Now I have two problems: a stubborn male *and* a stuck spare.

Two young miners, who have just struck a huge gold nugget and are in fine form, stop to help and are able to lower the bumper by force. Now I have five problems: two stubborn males, two drunk males, and a stuck tire. I then lay under the body, while the one threads the jack handle, me guiding it as I beat on the ratchety device that has frozen shut. "When intelligence won't work . . . " I shout, wielding the hammer. Ancient road dust pours into all orifices on my face. At times I remember to appreciate the mechanical insults men must face throughout life.

On the way out Steese Highway I pass a skinny hillbilly soul with his thumb out. He has just stepped out of the nineteenth century wearing a droopy felt hat, a plaid shirt, and a worn-out face, although he is only in his twenties. I pass on by quickly, never picking up hitch-hikers, but something in his sad face . . . a poignancy: a buttonhole photograph, circa 1860, moving and talking. This willowy Lone Miner is for real. He is the color of rock, having been vulcanized and glaciated himself. He is not only the salt of the earth but also the gold, the uranium, the cadmium, and the zinc. He has dressed himself from the bottom of a sluice box. The opportunity for an in-depth interview with a captive study is irresistible; and I am cognizant of the reciprocity of the universe: four people have stopped to help me. He is in need after his first emergence from a back-in-the-hills-for-four-months-at-a-time placer mine. Not only is he willing to talk, he is desperate.

I forget all about my hunger and windburn, at once absorbed by his speech. He lectures about mining, how miners are so stuck in their ways that they refuse to buy new machinery or use scientific knowledge.

" 'N ev'ry cr'k," he says passionately, " 'n on ev'ry small acre of land, thar's dir'ctions," meaning that each claim contains a unique set of directions as to how to work it. Baudelaire said the same of poems: each poem contains within it an internal set of directions for how to read that one particular poem.

"Even th' color and shape and feel of gold is dif'rnt in each difr'nt crik," he is saying animatedly. "Look here, ya c'n tell a difn't nuggit fr'm each dif'nt streamb'd. Why'I c'n tell by jes the feel 'f it." In terms of the description of resistance to change and lack of scientific knowledge, I feel he refers to himself.

He's broke, no vehicle, living off of someone else's land in a shack with his five beloved sled dogs. The owner of the land puts him up there all year to do the required $100 yearly "assessment" that is the only prerequisite for retaining the mine claim. In exchange for all this free prospecting, Lone Miner is to receive whatever gold he is able to find by hand, which, of course, is none.

In the winter he traps "as humane as pos'ble." He hates to kill animals. He mines in the winter by building fires on creek ice and working down into a hole in the frozen creek and earth. This is done way high near the stream's origins, where it is easier to reach the gold: it is not under the hundred feet of frozen muck that must be bull-dozed away below. "It's ev'n easier than summer, 'cuz in summer ya got all th' roarin' water t' cont'nd with, and winter, jus' froz'n."

"Doesn't it take you an awful long time to gather wood under all that deep snow?" I ask, being a woodcutter myself. "Well, it'st s'm time, but i's w'rt 't." He doesn't seem to have articulated to other human beings much. He tells me how gold sinks down to the bedrock, and how "th' b'g guys rip b'ck th' top lay'r to r'veal th' perfrost so th't 't can thaw, 'n th'n dig down till they h't b'dr'ck—wh'r th' gold h'a got to." Sometimes they go years with no pay dirt, yet the government is still cracking down harder and harder with regulation. Next year, a miner won't be able to use the creek water for washing, only pumped-up groundwater, and that will push many more small miners out of the business. It is the small guy that supports Alaska and brings in real revenue to the state. Big operators are all from somewhere else, he tells me disdainfully. To him, it is as if the federal government is doing everything it can to destroy Alaska's great individualistic characters.

Lone Miner has life honed to its most abbreviated form: minimum task, minimum possession. Modus vivendi: Nothing, just be there. When one's luggage is lost, one can live with so little, the clothes on one's back and a book to read. Normally, we are desperate not to be stripped of our ruse: the importance of ownership, the ritual of rou-tine. Lone Miner lives up here year-round; he never lights a fire in summer because he is used to the cold. He only uses one pot to cook in. Often cooks right in the can, so he doesn't have to wash dishes. He loves his dogs mightily, so he doesn't need friends. Never lights a lantern at all, until this last week, when his mother blinded him with her flash camera.

He has not seen his mother in six years. Just remarried, she has come to visit him with his new father. They've come up from Texas "t' fetch h'm." He is invited to go down and learn knifemaking in Joshua, Texas. He reveals to me with great pride his father's beautiful antler inlay work and the sharpness with which the knife snaps in and holds on to its sheath. He snaps it any number of times, fondling the knife with the delight of a child.

> He who knows he has enough is rich.
> Perseverance is a sign of will power.
> He who stays where he is endures.
> To die but not to perish is to be eternally present.
>
> Lao Tsu, *Tao Te Ching*,
> translated by Gia-Fu Feng

Monks, miners, Alaskans. The *Tao* was written around the sixth century B.C. by Lao Tsu, and probably folk-written many times after that. He was on his way out to the mountains, disgusted with civilization (I know the feeling), when a gatekeeper at the Mountain begged him to write down his great wisdom before he disappeared. This paradoxical book of less than 5,000 words is pure wisdom for living simply and close to the earth, dealing with the harsh elements of life.

Find peace in your own forty acres, says Lao Tsu, and do not wander. We move on constantly, to the next state, the next bar, the next home entertainment center. Where our internal equilibrium centers once were there is now a psychic television beeper. The children and college students I taught had internal television beepers, so it was difficult to teach the slow, meditative sort of observation most conducive to art. Once, while I was supervising the student teachers teaching Saturday morning art classes to children at Pennsylvania State University, I had a Japanese gentleman working under me in a masters program in art education. He had his training in Japan, and had already spent many years teaching young children. As I walked down the long corridor of the building, most classes were noisy and exuberant. The more physical the work, such as clay, the greater the bedlam. Yet the children were learning and loving it. As I passed this gentleman's classroom, it was absolutely silent. The first time I heard this silence I rushed in, wondering where the class had gone.

There were thirty 9- and 10-year-olds in utter concentration, entranced with the simple object in front of them: a sliced open red cabbage. They were slowly, slowly following the lines of this vegetable with their eyes as their old-fashioned nib pens recorded it, unseen, on paper. This was Ippon Sen, or one-line drawing. I was later to learn that he was teaching not merely drawing as we westerners do, but also a form of meditation.

I have seen this sort of concentration in subsistence hunters. Hardly moving a muscle, they watch and listen. In not moving there is movement. In stillness there is the beginning of All Things, the vast patience of subsistence people living off the land, for whom every object is of great value. The Eskimo traveler reads unbroken whiteness as we read a book.

Here, this flabbergasting child/man who sits beside me in his miner's feltdroop moss green hat, his dirty old pants, unshaven, has achieved what most of us could not. He can stay in one place throughout the harsh winter and find contentment. He values and is proud of his life.

Boredom is a thought-structure born of the industrial revolution, born of the time clock and of the split between work and leisure.

I am reminded of another folk story that probably has its origins in the *Tao*: amidst the government's great modernization of the irrigation system, an old man was found to be dipping his water out to the field by hand, bucket by bucket. The state came to him and said angrily, Why do you not do this in the modern way, that way making more profit and having more leisure? He said that this was the way he enjoyed doing it.

Lone Miner and I enter a long, narrow, low-ceilinged bar where he makes his phone call to reenter the world of sun. He disappears. I

57

stand in this long cavern of knotty pine alone, except for one other blithering soul. The bar is cluttered with memorabilia, signs advising one not to avoid sexual impropriety and alcoholic overindulgence. A biker and his lady enter. The bartender, a standup comedian *au jus*, begins his routine: he pulls small gadgetries off the wall: twisting cubes, wood-spitting rubber bands, three-dimensional puzzles, all of which keep humanity from going mad in those empty hours between jobs and lovers. I am reminded of the Rocky Mountain oysters in jars on bars all over Iowa, the purpose of which was not so much to eat as to shock young women-poets who, unsuspecting of their nature, ate them. I ate them heartily, enjoying them all the more for knowing they were testicles.

Comedian/bartender selects for me from the wall a beautiful brass instrument. He is an astute judge of character, for I couldn't be more fascinated. Not only are its curlicues of French horn evocative, but I am a collector of folk instruments. There are three spigots. He hands it to me very gently and I turn it around in awe.

"You mean you haven't seen a ptarmigan caller yet?" he asks. As this is ptarmigan-hunting country, I shake my head abashedly. "This works best in the snow, when the birds are all white," he explains patiently. "A long puff on this will guarantee you the sudden flash of white ptarmigan.

"Here, you try it. This valve down is the male, this one down is the female, and all three down is the mating call. You should blow very hard because there must be enough air to vibrate the plates inside."

I am enthralled: How could such a beautiful French horn–type tube make a sound like the quibbling chortle of the talus slope chicken? I take a deep breath, open all three valves at once, and blow with all my might.

Instantly I am covered with a coat of talcum powder, all in my hair and over my face. Drying a glass with a deadpan face a good distance away, the bartender says, "Now see, didn't you see the flash of white immediately?"

5

Frozen Deserts/Burning Seas

/ A Day in Fairbanks (72 degrees out)

GRIT-YOUR-TEETH-AND-DO-IT LIST

>Change oil, get rid of old oil
>Price out new windshield
>Check out why camera timer doesn't work
>Groceries, water, film, paper towels
>Call the folks, mail letters
>Do laundry, take shower, clean back of truck
>Dry-clean ski jacket—disgusting!
>Fred Meyers: oil, filter, fuel filter, air, batteries
>Eat at Greek place
>Research at U. of A. in the Alaska Room
>Buy a thingamajig to fix the whatchamacallit

I hate these city/supply days. They remove me from the magic of vast wilderness and thrust me onto hot, aromatic asphalt and confront me with strange human beings who may or may not wish to help.

RANDOM THOUGHTS

> The placer miner is a rare species to be preserved. He should be on the endangered species list.

> Travel is the process of training self to be vitally curious about everything.

> Overheard: "We've been superbusy with all these fires up here."
> Response: "It sure gets short this time of year. No more survey work, no more government work."

> If given a choice between shooting a bunch of wildlife and one hunter, shoot the man.

/ August 21:   First Day on the Haul Road

The 414-mile Haul Road begins off the Elliott Highway 70 miles above Fairbanks and travels to Prudhoe Bay on the Arctic Coast, making it the northernmost road in the United States. I cannot get permission to travel the upper part of the road because my writing is connected with no university and no industry. I will see how far I can get. The first 211 miles are open only up to Disaster Creek near Dietrich, and for good reason, since there are absolutely no services, no houses after Dietrich. A broken-down vehicle is truly stranded. It may cost up to $20 a mile to be towed back. My vehicle has been thoroughly checked out, both here in Fairbanks and before I left Seattle. Huge eighteen-wheelers, which travel up there at the rate of one every five minutes, are inadvertently dangerous. Some are overtly dangerous. They aren't allowed to stop for any tourists and don't want to. All very good reasons not to go.

So I go.

The real name of this highway is the Dalton, named for arctic engineer James William Dalton, who was involved in early exploration on the North Slope. It did not even exist above the Yukon until fourteen years ago and was completed in only five months, a spectacular engineering feat, but also yielding a "Road from Hell." The road is only twenty-eight feet wide, visibility zero on the twists and turns. The only way to get assistance in an emergency is to CB the State Trooper, who also serves as the Fish and Game Warden, and so is out in the boonies a lot. I have no CB, just good running feet. In all the years and thousands of miles of back roads I've done, I've only been stuck once, and then I jogged eight miles out. The two retired Forest Service characters I found simply picked up the back of the truck and swung it around where it should have been.

I get my first taste of Haul Road driving: a long strip of road that is floating wet. It takes all my concentration to keep on track, and there is only one real track, and that is on the wrong side of the road. At each hilltop, I pass over twelve-inch-high lumps of gooey mud with a slippery base, in case an eighteen-wheeler is on the other side. Beaver Dip and Roller Coaster are aptly named and plunge into 600-foot-drop valleys and straight up again. The mud engages my wheels, steering becomes water ballooning. Big rigs charge downhill to build momentum for uphill. All the while, the steering wheel is playing Russian roulette.

So I want to meet the person who masterminded this monstrosity of a road. Later, I get my wish.

The following interview was conducted with Steve Matthews, Haul Road director while it was being built, after I returned from this trip, on November 11, 1988, in his home near Portland, Oregon.

/ November 11, 1988:   Interview with Steve Matthews

So full of energy that he cannot sit still, bright, blue-eyed Matthews describes his patchwork job career: licensed to fly commercial planes; licensed as a multi-engined aircraft pilot; licensed to fly very large cargo planes; a welder on the top secret Guppy Project, which created space age jets sold to the French; an emergency medical technician;

a tow truck driver; a mechanic extraordinaire (my judgment); an ambulance driver; an advanced emergency coordinator; chief of police in Winston, Oregon; a very active father to his children; and, last, responsible for ninety-plus employees while building the Haul Road to Prudhoe Bay. It was perfectly logical that he ended up there, he joked, as the head of one of the most impressive road engineering feats around. He had not completed high school.

Being director of the Haul Road meant being responsible for all pump stations, for the search and rescue missions, for the many small airports in far-flung stations, such as Stevens Village and Fort Yukon (roadless) up the Yukon, Bettle and Barrow and Wainwright airports. He was responsible from Nome up the West Coast all the way across the north coastline to Canada, down the eastern border to the Alcan Highway entrance, and west to Fairbanks. In other words, he was in charge of and responsible for half the state, which is equal to a third of the Lower Forty-eight in area.

The nearest radio-phone connection was down in Gobbler's Knob, so that he would drive several hundred miles on unfinished gravel road just to communicate with headquarters. The state issued him a 1979 Bronco with 400 miles on it. At the end of one year, the odometer read 132,000. In a prefab house with no communications and a 12kw generator, he lived for a year with his wife Gloria and one very unlikely dog, a snow-white miniature poodle. The only serious accident to the toy poodle came not from the many predators in Alaska but from his master's hand. Steve was tossing stones one day from his yard and beaned his dog. The beloved pet lay unconscious at his feet. It recovered, but the incident accentuated the isolation of the place: what would happen in the case of life-threatening flu or a broken bone?

On days off from driving miles and miles, or flying to remote areas, he and Gloria would take the 1½-inch gold dredge in the back of the truck and clean out the state's culverts for them: a culvert serves as a perfect sluice, and the work proved beneficial to both state road conditions and their own pockets. Other days Gloria would fish while Steve sat with rifle, watching for grizzlies.

It was an extremely difficult year, one in which truck drivers attempted to run him off the road and kill him. Matthews was the highest level of state authority physically present on the scene, and the truck drivers had a legitimate complaint: the original Haul Road was an underfunded, incomplete deathtrap.

Matthews worked against extreme elements and human problems to complete the Haul Road as quickly as possible. The State of Alaska would not fund the road sufficiently, despite the fortune it was to make off the oil royalties and leases. He worked without gravel, digging it from the ditches with inadequate machinery against incredible odds. The unaltered tundra wilderness loomed immense and unlikely toward far horizons for many more miles than other countries have borders.

The greatest challenge was the bogs: Steve described entire Caterpillars disappearing down into the black muck. High-centered, they would spin their tracks and dig themselves deeper. There was no beast of burden big enough to pull them out. The men could only stand helplessly by and watch the tens of thousands of yellow-colored dollars gurgle out of sight.

The second greatest challenge was high water: the logjams behind bridges could take out the pilings in a matter of hours. The culverts would fill with flotsam and jetsam and drown the road.

The third greatest challenge: the weird frost heaves, a science-fiction phenomenon that cannot be grasped by the normal mind. In spring, when weather warms to a balmy 20 degrees below zero, the ground heaves upward. The moisture within its gooey center may not be frozen and can swallow trucks. It is believed that the mysterious holes that extend below the boils may be the results of geothermal activity.

They made the road only twenty-eight feet wide, so that when a seven-foot-six-inch-wide eighteen-wheeler passes another, there is only room for a mirror vibration. It is for this reason that noncommercial vehicles, particularly recreational vehicles, are *verboten* on the Haul Road. At the large dip, Beaver Slide, when one driver sees another truck barreling down the opposite side of the two-mile roller coaster, he knows that the momentum of each reaches an uncontrollable crescendo at the bottom. It seems that the Alyeska Pipeline Company neglected to put in the water-wicking protective shield on this section.

Then there were state politics. Alaska's underfunding of the Haul Road endangered lives and equipment. Matthews' bosses occasionally were beheaded when the angry truckers demanded a sacrificial victim. Grave charges. Trucks rolled off the stretch between Elliott Highway and the Yukon River with stunning regularity. The Kamikaze Highway, it was called. Instead of following a straight track, as it does today, the road swung around each small mountain, a feather in a whirlpool. Truckers at one end could not enter the twenty-eight-mile stretch if there was somebody coming from the other end because there was no passing and certainly no turning around.

Breaking down is disastrous because one cannot pull off, and one's rig soon is the same color as the mud around it. In spite of blinkers, it can be rammed by moving vehicles who perceive it to be part of the landscape, which it soon is.

There is the story of the guy whose brakeless rig started rolling backward down a long steep stretch of highway. He thought to himself, before it got going too fast, "I could stay with it, and guide it, risking death in case it swerves off the road." He elected to jump, and suffered several injuries, including a broken arm. The truck flew backwards down the mile-long steep grade, continued up the other side, and came to a slow halt, perfectly aligned with the road.

Matthews started out late one night from Dead Horse, after having a good dinner with the workers in the cafeteria. For some reason, he checked neither the time nor the mileage, and drove off into the dark swirling snow in winter. Darkness being abundant means something different up above the Arctic Circle. He drove hours and hours, creeping along at 4 to 5 miles per hour, and still he did not reach the next pump station. A thermometer rigged up on a stub of the antenna was reading fifty below, not a temperature one survives in very long. He was driving in his parka because the snow was filling up the flat spaces inside the cab with high crusts of snow. He came to a stranded trucker whose tow was coming for him. The trucker did not know where they were either. He continued on. Slowly it dawned on him that at minus fifty degrees, with a wind-chill factor putting it at minus eighty, he would not even be able to get out to change a tire. Heat would be sapped from his body so fast he would last only minutes. He turned carefully around and returned, checking his watch. Four hours to return. The odometer read 13 miles.

Another time he became mired, pushing too much snow in front of the Bronco. At the base of Ice Cut, on the way to Prudhoe Bay, he sat at the base of the steep cut for three days, eating from his wooden food box, idling the engine to keep the heater going. He was down to half a tank when he knew he would not last the night. Although an aircraft directly above, with which he was in voice communication, flew through a clear blue sky, helicopters could not drop down through fifty feet of ice soup to rescue him. There was a building, but the energy required to dig out the snow in front of the door might have finished him off. He sent a final message to his wife.

He was thinking about death. He was thinking about his own death. The idling engine was eating gasoline faster than he had calculated. He was not a romantic about death, but there it was, clear and cold as a glacial interior. Had he not been in contact with the airplane overhead, he might have been losing his mind. He got out. He looked around through zero visibility. Five or six large cement weights, Roman archways used to hold down the pipeline under rivers, were holding down the metal building. Matthews, director of the Haul Road, superintendent of the upper half of Alaska, an area as big as or bigger than most countries, tender of the most complex and life-giving equipment in America, thought about burning down the building. He thought about his own death. Then he found the fifty gallons of gasoline someone had stashed inside one of the arches.

Then there were the bears.

The Haul Road has more grizzlies than men.

One Caterpillar operator was grading the road on a beautiful spring day. The sound of the Cat's engine hung like audible honey in the air. The road was neither dust nor mud, but pushed on smoothly under the blade. All was right with the world.

Then for some reason unknown to him to this day, he glanced back over his shoulder. He was going forward, so to look back was not natural. There, climbing up the Cat's track, six feet from his left shoulder, was a huge grizzly. There is the legend that loud noise and the smell of man scares off the griz, but there it was, clawing right over the track of one of the noisiest machines made—for hors d'oeuvres.

The man jammed the Cat into reverse, knocking the bear off for an instant, but for an animal that can move yards in a matter of seconds, this was not buying much. The operator thought for sure he had bought it, jammed the Cat back into forward, drove up to the side of his pickup, jumped in and drove off, leaving the Cat still lit up on the road. That was enough Haul Road for one guy.

Steve Matthews continues.

Yet another huge grizzly was asleep in the sun beneath a roadsign reading 45. Now, in the tundra there is nothing around with which one can compare size for scale, so for a photographer this situation was ideal. He halted, Bronco still running, ready to floor it, clutch in, in gear. The groggy grizzly cooperated, a photographer's dream, his sweet gigantic head, the size of a lawn mower, resting on sweetly crossed forearms like a family dog. Matthews snapped away. He was delighted. But then he wanted a picture of the grizzly *standing up* beside the sign for size. He spoke to the bear gently. No dice. Bear was sleeping. He grumbled and made noises at the bear. No dice. Bear was resting. Finally he reached his arms out the window and with a giant gesture upward made a roaring sound. The bear did not rise, but shot from a full recline straight at the truck. Matthews jammed down the accelerator and sprang the clutch out. The truck leapt forward, but the bear hit the back wheel with such force that it swung the heavy vehicle entirely around in a circle, leaving it facing in the opposite direction. Matthews sped out of there, knowing that if the clutch had not engaged or had engaged and killed the engine, the bear would have come roaring in through the window.

The Yukon Bridge is a magnificent piece of engineering spanning a wide, tarnished breadth of water. From the south one comes upon it suddenly, having climbed in second gear over the lip of a bluff. The ride down is quick and stunning, disgorging one out over a quarter-mile of water. One is tempted to stop in the middle to ponder the powerful fist of river.

If one does stop and get out, one is monitored, watched, hauled off, and checked out by an armed guard in a white vehicle. This oil business is war. Security on the Yukon Bridge is elaborate enough for a 007 movie. No one can cross without being visually monitored and asked by loudspeakers what she or he is doing.

Matthews, at this junction of the interview, off-handedly mentions five more slings for five more pipelines that pre-exist under the Yukon Bridge. They were put there when it was first built. My eyes open wide. Oil companies make their plans faster than a speeding Congress.

"You know what a Christmas tree is?" asks Matthews, knowing that I don't. When you fly at night over the vast North Slope, over supposedly empty plains above and below the Brooks Range, for miles and miles you would see this eerie glow. Every three square miles there is sunk a capped oil well, thousands upon thousands of them. The environmentalists will let them sink wells only at given intervals, to protect the surface and to diminish impact on wildlife, but out from this one pipe go lines in many directions, at angles underground. An inverse Christmas tree.

They are *active* wells. Electronic gauges surveyed from the air read out abundant pressure on most of them. That is land full of oil. "Don't let the oil engineers kid you. We are swimming in oil," says Matthews.

"Kid" is not the verb that comes to mind.

"They are not running more pipelines now because they've got to get the Oil Cartel in the Middle East stabilized with their prices, able to hold back, thus driving up the price here. They will then create an artificial shortage, driving the price up enough to make it worthwhile to bring massive amounts down."

I am fuming: think to myself, *They've already got control of most of the northern coastline. Why do they have to go after the Wildlife Refuge as well?*

Matthews hastily moves on without me; I am foaming through the corners of my mouth. He is now drawing me off on my favorite topic, wildlife, of which he is an astute observer:

"Fifty to sixty feet on either side of the highway melts first because of the layers of dust and snow: the dirt heats up the snow nearest the road first, and the waterfowl just teem to either side of the Haul Road. They aren't way off on the tundra, as one would suppose, but right on top of you. And that, of course, brings predators. Wonderful predators: the white wolf, the red fox, the cross fox, and in early spring, the bear cubs."

"I hear that truck drivers shoot them from the cabs of their trucks," I say.

"Yes," says Matthews sadly, "it is strictly forbidden, but how do you enforce it?"

I am thinking: five more pipelines. Perpetuates our dependence on hydrocarbons. A society fueled by fossil fuel: nitrogen oxide, acid rain, destruction of the ozone, greenhouse heat-up, and a wheat belt moving up into Canada. A baby poisoning its mother.

Matthews' voice is continuing outside of me. He describes the conservationists' high standards: how even a simple oil drip from an engine, let alone a pool of oil, can result in substantial fines. I think of all those Cats out there humming, the pickups, the bright red Alyeska trucks, the purring generators, the whacka-whacka helicopters, the light planes, the eighteen-wheelers hauling in more vehicles, the backhoes, the dredges, the drills, the entire great mammothian, megalithian gurgling mass of internal combustion, going to sleep, dripless and pure in the crystalline evening.

End of interview. Back up to the Haul Road.

/ August 21:   Arctic Circle

I pass the Arctic Circle, the line above which the midnight sun rolls across high tundra, infinitely grand topography. One cumulus the size of Kansas boils dramatically overhead. The gleaming pipeline, suspended above the permafrost here, follows the land, a slug of black sludge moving rapidly through a Rousseau painting; the wolf leaning up against the Dall lamb, and the wolverine lying down with mountain goat kid, and the caribou calf and the mountain lion together; the moose cow and the brown bear shall feed; their young shall lie down together; and the lynx shall eat lichen like the musk-ox. We shall not hurt or destroy in all our magnificent tundra; for the earth shall be full of the knowledge of the Environment as the waters cover the sea (from Isaiah 10:17, via Alyeska).

Fifty-foot granite tors protrude straight up, fingers of Earth gesticulating toward heaven. These odd forms are left after solifluction pulls earth downhill from them. Close up, they are very rough in texture, as in stone that has not had time to cool and crystallize, and are covered in black lichen, which appears dead but is just resting.

Deep water beneath each rock: the entire tundra is abundant water on top of permafrost, which here could be 700 feet thick. In Barrow, the northernmost village in North America, it is 1,300 feet thick. It ceases only in response to Earth's heated core.

It is hard to comprehend this as desert; with annual precipitation of only 8 inches a year, its vast sogginess is lush with life. Black spruce are scarce now, although they can survive with a shallow root system. Birches and larch cover most of Siberia, which is deep green and dotted with thousands of lakes, yet has less precipitation than the Sahara.

The paradoxical Arctic. A frozen desert full of water covering an ancient sea deposit that burns. Home to 900 species of vascular plants, owing to the moisture on the surface. When the permafrost ice is sliced, as in a road cut, it is an ice of no air, as in the blue cores of glaciers. The core ice of glaciers is ten times as dense as refrigerator ice and is classified as rock. Tourists consistently wander past warning signs and under the hard blue arches at Kenai Fjords National Park in Seward, thinking it is like ice cubes, not stone.

The top layer of permafrost, the "active layer," freezes and thaws. It snap-crackle-pops with ancient atmospheres, as gases are released at ten times that of surface pressure. Yet another form of harmful environmental impact comes from huge Japanese barges sent over to our bays to harvest and cut up icebergs. It seems that it is "in" to listen to these ancient fizzles at cocktail parties.

PROSPECTOR'S CAMP

I make camp on the beaver ponds at an old prospector's camp, which boasts the lowest recorded temperature for the lived-in United States, minus 80 degrees F on January 23, 1971. An old track leads down to and across the river to Bettles, an isolated village. The ubiquitous camp robber, the Whiskey Jack, is darker than his Lower Forty-eight brothers in crime. He appropriately wears a dark face mask. He attempts to raid the food box while I am sitting here, and the clatter of his feet on metal brings him within inches of me.

I ask myself, Would a real naturalist strangle a bird? He walks on the tailgate: clatter, clatter, scratch. I wonder if they would be good to eat if I strangle enough of them.

There is a huge splash in Claja Pond: it must be a moose, so I rush out in the drizzle. Instead, ten grebes have bellyflopped on the beaver pond all at once. The sun is behind them, but with their red-shining necks and dark brown heads, I suspect they are red-necked grebe. The fact that this coastal bird's wintering grounds are inland lakes forebodes winter's coming, although I had hoped it wouldn't. Although seen in Southworth in Puget Sound, this is a bird special to the taiga, its odd shape congruent with the arctic atmosphere. A sharp, snake-like head and neck joined to a lozenge-shaped body is ideal for spearing fish in dark arctic waters.

Above Claja Pond sits a lived-in trailer: I cannot resist a snoop. The trailer is named "Nomad" and appears innocuous enough, but I am unprepared for the picture on the door: a gorgeous brunette with eighteen-wheeler-sized mammary glands. This does not bother me until I get closer and see her fingers exposing her vaginal opening for all to see. I jerk my head away. This isn't even *Playboy* sex, but pure aggression against female as object. Although I should be incensed— and I certainly don't condone sexual exploitation—instead my disgust turns to grief for all the lonely men up here and the system of oily work that entraps them.

/ August 22:   Coldfoot, Alaska

Population between 18 and 70, depending upon season. Around
1899, a town sprang up at the mouth of Slate Creek and bore its
name. In 1902, it was just a gambling den, a couple of roadhouses,
two stores, and seven saloons. About a decade later, the miners
moved on up to Nolan and Wiseman, villages just north of here, and
Coldfoot belonged to the ghosts.

Coldfoot is the site of the 1900 gold stampede at Slate Creek and
home of the 350-mile Coldfoot Classic Dog Sled Race. The gold
dreamers, it is said, would get up as far as the Koyukuk River, get
cold feet, and retreat.

It is late morning. I tell the burly gas attendant that he lives in a
grand spot on the planet.

"Yes," he snarls, "*if* they would quit regulating us and let us live!
There is all this big beautiful land out there and they don't let us work
it. The regulations-makers down there in Washington don't understand that we have to make an existence on it. I have this job but
nowhere to live. There is no land available for us to buy just to put a
cabin on. We all live in trailers like gypsies. The goddamned senators
don't understand . . . goddamned federal government . . . goddamned
Juneau. . . ." I am backing out as sweetly and subtly as possible.

Richard Mackey, owner of the Coldfoot Gas Station Kingdom,
asks me if I am having a good time. "Yes!" I gush, "I love Alaska."
He is pleased with my answer; he advises me on places to see and
camp, and suggests a ride over the Brooks Range.

"Or you can drive on up Slate Creek quite a ways when it isn't
raining, and hike out in endless wilderness from there. You are also
welcome to sleep anywhere on this property—probably over there
with the trailers." His eyes are intense blue, as if he alone carried
enough life for several men. Later, I was to learn that he, and later his
son, had won the Iditarod, the famous dog sled race across Alaska,
and was quite well thought of across the state. For such a man graciously to stop and give information to a stranger gave me a clue to
the Richard Mackey legend. According to one story, Mackey was
awarded the Coldfoot lease when a state official demanded to know

where he could get gas services around the middle of the Haul Road. Mackey laughed uproariously and pointed to a large mudhole, saying, "Right over there. At least that's where the government promised to build us a village-supply post, but it's never quite gotten to it."

At that time, a rig had to make it 340 miles from the Yukon River up to Prudhoe Bay with no gas stops, no place for a good hot meal. Mackey opened his all-in-one service island, but because it was not federal the government supplied no housing or land for housing. The airport, the motel, a friendly restaurant, the bucket and sponge available to anyone desiring to know what color his rig once was, make quite a kingdom, indeed. Everything one could want on the road. Well, almost everything.

I have that delicious anticipation of going where few people get to go, farther north than I've ever gone, and over rough and dangerous road. Gassed, washed (the truck is black, it turns out), fed, talked with, informed, I turn up that long dusty ribbon to the northernmost realms. It is good, and all's right with the world. Seventy miles up the Haul Road to Antigun Pass a blonde wolf is carrying the leg of something. She flees when I stop, used to truckers with guns. A red fox flows across the road in front of me. To either side are copious *Coprinus comatus*: shaggy-maned mushrooms, white missiles rising from subterrestrial silos. Slowly the Brooks Range builds before me, lofty angular sediments earlier deposited as sea on the Alaskan continent. Pushed inland by a convergence with another mysterious continent, this lower Brooks Range rock rises perpendicular to the earth.

The checkbooth man asks me to stay and chat. He introduces me to Wayne. Wayne is an engineer with "The Company." "What company?" I ask. Wayne doesn't know. He signed up in Houston, Texas. Really good money, though. "Don't know my employers," he says animatedly. "They just pay me. Wizard of Oz at the Gates of the North hiring company." Gate man checks me out: Yes, I can change a tire (been practicing). Yes, I can survive to minus 30 degrees. Yes, I have water. No, I am not insane (one tiny lie).

Sunset. The steep shadow of the Brooks Range peaks. Out east over the Chandalar Basin, a spacious basin 20 miles wide at the top of the world, an immense rainbow's end is immersed in the valley and vaults twenty miles into the sky. Then a second, and a third, each reversing the order of color, expand exponentially until an eerie glow buzzes through the immense space. Lavender and orange permeate the entire atmosphere; each mist droplet is charged and incandescent.

The Gatekeeper of Oz officially warns me to turn around. He cannot legally prevent me because I, representing the People of the United States, own this land. He does not let me through officially, but knows I am going. "Only one other woman has come up here solo," he says, "but she was driving a fancy sports car as a publicity stunt from the tip of South America."

My windshield had just been broken by the first eighteen-wheeler whose driver smiled at me. One inch higher and I would have had to alter my bra; one foot higher and I should have had to learn braille.

Tomorrow: Pingos! Salt playas. Other wonderful and weird forms water takes up here! All await me over Atigun Pass and beyond, on through the lake-spotted plain of the North Slope—essential nesting grounds for all the Americas—on toward the North Sea. Rhythmic ice-filled mounds rising to announce a change of vegetation. My eyes wallow ecstatically in an unknown land.

/ August 23: Atigun Pass Camp

My camp is of glorious dimension. High enough to see great distance in all directions. Due west it plunges down to a stream. To the north, a high promontory bright red with bearberry. Northwest, a vertical gray wall dotted with Dall sheep. I will live here for five days and must conserve drinking water (use melted fridge water for dishwashing). Stream water, one-half-hour down and longer up, and must be boiled for five minutes, compliments of giardia.

Giardia, so legend goes, began in the '60s in my home state of Colorado when backpackers came back from Russia and deposited the critters near Aspen. Even at 10,000 feet, the giardia cysts can live in the ice. Moving through a fecal-oral route that can come in a high mountain trickle from marmot, it survives in a cyst stage up to two months at 17 degrees F, and for one month at 70 degrees F. Exposed to boiling water, it survives two minutes or more, depending on the altitude (atmospheric pressure).

Since it came over from Russia, it has followed aspiring skiers back to New Hampshire, New York, Pennsylvania, Utah, Oregon, Montana, Washington, and California. I am always surprised by longtime campers who blithely say, "I've always drunk water right from the stream and will continue to do so," as if change in nature was not possible. The consequences are serious.

This pathway north is an icy test tube for viewing the clash of man and nature. Humanity's instinct not just to survive but to increase is as strong as a spruce's roots penetrating basalt. Human instincts produce self-perpetuating habits, in and of themselves rewarding: for instance, what might originally be practical turns perpetual: the pain of martyrs, the pleasure of aesthetics, the arguments of philosophers, the unrestrained growth of religions or monarchs. Growing for their own sake, detached from the original need.

Third day out, too much health food grains and soups, I hear voices. Overriding Consciousness is saying:

"Ah, we came *so* close this time with mammals."

"You mean because of brain volume in *Homo sapiens?*" snaps E., testily.

"Okay, okay," says O.C., "so we forgot to give them wisdom."

"Nor any overall awareness of the entire system and the complexity of Ourself as one Organism," says Big E.

"But we gave them a highly organized system of government for that: democracy, Rockbrain," whines O.C.

"Didn't even organize them as well as ants."

"All right, we screwed up again. Let them blow it up, ruin it all—we'll begin again right away."

"But what about the radioactive lithosphere? Or the indestructible polyurethanes? And where do we dump the chlorofluorocarbons?"

"Some volcanoes will exchange the surface with the interior, then an ice age or two. . . . "

"But how will we ever develop wisdom?"

"Got me!" says O.C.

The pipeline snaps along beside the road, silver, thin, and fascinating, sag bends dipping first below ground and then above, a reptilian Slinky. The technology is rather elegant: picking up the colors of nature, it sings in pizzicato counterpoint to the mountains.

Pipeline personnel in their bright red trucks are relaxed and friendly. This is a jubilant example of environmentalists having done their job well and of engineers responding brilliantly: The pipe of the underworld, it disappears under the caribou, then flies with the sky deities some twenty feet in the air. American ingenuity at its best, a technology to be copied by other nations.

But Alyeska has big plans, technology gone mad with its monarchy. An English king once described himself as the phallus of his people; here, there is 700 miles of it down to the sea. Technology begetting technology. Some fanciful technological mythologies have been created by the oil industry and evolved to self-perpetuation up on the Beaufort Sea. Allow me to tell a few:

Once upon a time—in 1979, to be exact—there was thought to be 320 trillion cubic feet of gas and 40 billion barrels of oil under the Beaufort Sea. Global Marine Development was busy growing a mythical beast: the hovering barge. These football-field-sized barges would hover seven feet above the sea ice or the tundra. Self-propelled on an air-cushion system, they would weigh 3,000 tons and support 250-ton cargo, or 10,000 barrels of oil. They would move along the ground by winches, wheels and paddles, drilling holes down into the sea and the tundra. And the Canadian government plans an entire fleet of icebreakers with 150,000-horsepower engines which would require 17,000 tons of fuel a month to drive a conventional steam turbine. At a cost of 300 million 1977 dollars, these air cushion icebreakers would crumple the sea ice under their weight.

Yet another fantasy technology was reported by the Smithsonian (Boslough 1981): a 15.2-million-dollar rig to float over land and sea, capable of probing 4 miles down. It would cost $100,000 a day to run. Men would sleep, eat, play, and work on board, earning $70,000 a year. It was to probe the oil-rich area in the Beaufort Sea just east of

Prudhoe Bay, prime wildlife calving and nesting grounds. The Anglo Energy Company built one such drilling unit in Edmonton, Washington. It rose fourteen stories high. Broken down, it would be hauled thousands of miles by 125 trucks.

On the steep slope up Atigun Pass I climb, gathering shaggy mane mushrooms, and find strong evidence of a moose orgy. The blue Kentucky-type grasses look silly, out of place, but they were sensible to plant on the upheaved turf: one could not make this back into tundra, could not return it to fragile heaps of rock and moss and grass hummocks. Instead, pipeline botanists began with the second skin that forms on solid ground. The caribou love it. They dig in the pipeline soil cover with flexible bivalve hooves designed to dig through snow for their winter food, lichen.

I have entered a land of magnitudes, not only in size but in quality of light and staging of stone: the Brooks Range.

THE BROOKS RANGE: EARTHWARP EXTRAORDINAIRE

Each mountain range penetrates one's consciousness in a distinct manner when first encountered. I, to this day, remember vividly my first view of real mountains. Near my thirteenth birthday we drove westward in a covered (station)wagon named Moby Dick, the Great White Chrysler. I had seen picture postcards, but did not believe that such an artificial landscape could exist: Who would believe such an absurdity of vertical blue zig-zags? It was early morning. We had slept fitfully in a bad motel in Kansas. When we began, there was nothing at all on the western horizon.

Then suddenly, bam. On the horizon. That low purple zig-zag, just like in the postcards. And slowly, slowly they rose. I sat in the back-back of the station wagon with my eyes glued to the front windshield. The mountains continued to grow, swallowing more and more of the blankness that Kansans call sky.

The zig-zag swallowed more and more, took on detail, but mostly remained a deep purplish blue, which I could not believe. After all, those cards had been doctored in the darkroom: thousands of lies sent home from the glorious West. No, this did not, could not exist. In postcards I could see the edge of the blue where it did not match up to the form below. But these! These "Rockies" were BLUE! A deep royal blue, a blue of deep ocean in sun, a blue as in a Night Watch plaid. And so they rose upward to fill a third of the sky, and to fill the next two-thirds of my life with a richness, a texture, and a *raison d'etre* I cannot imagine having developed anywhere else.

The Brooks Range is a thick gruel of mountains from 4,000 to 9,000 feet high, interlaced with glacial valleys that demarcate the North Slope from the Yukon drainage below. Named for Alfred Hulse Brooks of the Alaska Geological Survey, they were the Rocky Mountains until 1826. The name was a misnomer, as they are entirely distinct from the Rockies of Canada and the Lower Forty-eight. Mighty rivers dip southward through Paleozoic rock, the gray shale of deep seas, and through river gravels and shallow carbonates of organic material.

ATIGUN PASS

AVALANCH AREA
DO NOT STOP NEXT 44 MILES.

Dark soup again, so dark I cannot see past the black hood of Die Fledermazda. Beside me, the song of a braided stream, which starts an inch below the top of the pass. The fog is rolling over, constantly revealing and covering steep unstable shoulders of talus. Hard driving, socked-in fog and steep drop-offs, a thin coat of slip-mud underneath the tires. There is a golden glow from the groundcover as if lit from underneath. At the top of Atigun Pass, the Continental Divide, I watch the water go in two opposite directions. Below, tiny men moving slowly as if on Pluto, reinstalling a section of flawed pipe.

This area is extremely dangerous for the pipeline men. Buried in insulated concrete cribbing, the pipe penetrates part of the mountain on the steep slope. Many peaks in the immediate area exceed 7,000 feet, only 130 miles from sea level.

PURE ARCTIC TUNDRA

Since visibility is zero over Atigun Pass, I retreat and plan a hike just south of there up Table Mountain: a moody elemental walk straight up its steep slope, hopping from one mud boil to the next. Four miles up, made it to the first shoulder, which I perceived to be most of the way up. Later, from Atigun Pass, I was to learn it was barely a quarter of the way.

From it: such a thunderstorm display! Not just one, but many of them at a great distance, roiling themselves over peaks from far west, Gates of the Arctic National Park and Preserve, crashing like surf in the north, threatening from the east. Yet none approach the wide Chandalar Shelf. Thunderstorms, like Dall sheep, prefer not to leave their steep mountain slopes for the open. Rain squalls hit on and off.

I love potent storms as much as any beautiful natural phenomenon. It is seeing diagrams of Earth's patterns of energy release, from oceans, sun, mountains, and atmosphere. Thunderstorms restore the center of the continents with water requisitioned from the oceans. They return to earth a negative charge that has slowly dissipated into the atmosphere. This is why the air around waterfalls and after big storms smells so refreshing: negatively charged ions. I seek telltale paths of immense storms, those that leave scars across people and landscape, not for the love of destruction, but to be reminded, ultimately, of what is in charge.

Cumulonimbi here are magnificent, towering giants that reduce mountains to small muttering tooths. They extend eight miles straight up into the troposphere, that part of Earth's atmosphere between the ground and the stratosphere. Alaska is particularly good at overloading air with great amounts of water, powering it up steep slopes, so that these cloud beasts develop in time-lapse motion. Today was terrifying and thrilling at once; like prey, I had to keep a sharp eye on the circling storms.

Growing up the daughter of a pilot, one learns about the turbulent interiors of these clouds full of strong electrical fields. Each thunderstorm becomes an entity of its own, developing its own charge, a negative one at its base, which we feel in our scars and bones. In the high puff pastry and anvil tops there is a positive charge. The land and the atmospheric beasts become so charged that they create nasty exchanges between heaven and earth that terrify humans.

Metaphorical spears shoot out of God-fingers with awesome randomness, killing one, leaving the next unharmed. Their paths can carry 200,000 amperes, instantly heating to millions of degrees the object of their affection, which expands, then explodes (Schaefer and Day 1981).

Lightning shoots across cultures as spiritual illumination, the descent of power from heaven to earth. Krishna holds the *varja*, the thunderbolt that holds both destruction and refertilization: their balance means eternal transcendence. Our national symbol holds lightning in one talon and peace in its other, the Seal of the United States. Apollo's arrows are lightning as well as rays, and symbolize piercing masculinity, the benefit of mankind and also the scourge of war.

In a balance that provides scientists of the U.S. Forest Service with an ideal metaphor for lightning-produced forest fire, the Tibetan God Dorje's sceptre (thunder) symbolizes virility/power (method) in balance with the feminine (wisdom). The result of a good balance is paradox, the act of compassion, power in passivity. Translation: natural burns are good if they are allowed periodically, not suddenly after many years without a fire.

Thunder mumbles low in the distance. It could easily be the voice of divine anger or the fecundity of the sky god made audible. Humankind has so long attempted to repeat that sound and to channel its dangerous power: bull-roarer, the dragon, the hammer, the drum. After one of those god-awful job aptitude tests in college, in which one's life's work is determined by entering little blackened dots into numerical slots (Would you rather go to a movie with good friends or clean doorknobs?), I decided it would be best for me to become a Siberian tribal shaman. I could have danced to a drum made of sacred skins and forest bones, translating, through rhythm, man's tongue to summon the spirits. Instead, I just sit in the cab watching the rain pelt.

Exhausted after the tundra haul, I shall never move again. Until, against the dark gray stone wall, white dots are moving! Dall dots! One-half-mile along a precarious edge I move until they develop legs. Sheep legs! A little closer and they have heads and are grazing pastorally on a green shoulder of mountain. One up on the ridge has run down and appears to be "playing" frantically with the others, butting them into a knot. How odd: this play among adults who should conserve precious energy for winter.

Closer. Look again. Can't believe my eyes: a dark figure lumbers after them. A wolf? No, too large.

Bear! Huge white slash down its side and a muscular hump on its back. Grizzly! My hands shake.

Bear! My circulation stops, adrenaline zings out to my fingertips and toes. Not out of fear, but out of respect. The white slash and the muscular hump chant grizzly. The magnificence of the beast at the top of the food chain, Elder Bear to Native Americans. There is, they tell us, a human inside of each bear, who is here to share his wisdom and power with us. This is true, absolutely. Only now it is through scientific terms.

The largest land mammal on our half of things, 9 feet high and weighing more than 1,000 pounds inland (1,500 pounds where they are able to eat salmon), they are the smartest predators on land, smarter than foxes, wolves, or coyotes. They also are powerfully fast, fifty yards in three seconds. Their moods are powerful and change from aggression to whimsy in a matter of moments.

The bear galumphs after the sheep clumsily; his feet sink into the mire between tufts. The bear circles around, unseen by the sheep. The chase is on! Sheep and bear do not see one another. The leader on the rise walks cautiously to the depression where the other three are. The bear galumphs across more tundra above them slowly. The guard sheep spots him and there is instant movement of all toward the rock precipice, walking steadily to conserve as much energy as possible, yet fleeing. The entire chase seems to take place in slow motion, each animal carrying out a role vital to survival while conserving as many calories as possible. They step over sheer cliffs, cliffs too steep even for my rock-climbing buddies. An older one now places herself behind the youngest of the seven, to encourage it to keep up and to keep an eye on it. How intelligent they seem compared to humans, who leave kids alone in cars.

As they traverse, I look for a sight of the bear. Finally, just on the horizon, a tiny speck, the arch of leg and body as he takes one long last longing glance and disappears over the knife edge of the ridge.

As in most of this journey, I feel elation and heightened awareness, not fear. I restlessly look around me constantly. Literature warns that people who have high-range hearing loss are most vulnerable: they do not hear the twig snap that is the difference between life and death.

For centuries, human fear has shot grizzlies for the hell of it. There are only 900 left in the Lower Forty-eight: the last one in California was shot in 1916; in Arizona, 1935; in northern Mexico, 1957. In 1968, many died at the hands of Yellowstone Park rangers after the deaths of two young women in their tent. At the same time that year I was a camp counselor in the Sangre de Cristos, New Mexico, seven miles out in a wilderness camp with twenty-nine eleven- to thirteen-year-olds. A crazed black bear carried off our food locker. My fellow counselor lay in the dark, clutching a five-inch hunter's knife to protect the children. We watched as the bear picked up the heavy metal locker like a toy and reduced it to splinters with singular blows of his two arms. The trigger in Yellowstone was a sudden change in policy: closing the garbage dumps to the garbage-dependent grizzlies. Forgetting how to eat berries, bears found campers were faster—and fatter.

The sheer cirques and valley walls come alive with white dots moving, always moving. By the time my eye learns how to see them, I have spotted more than eighty. I try to imagine how frightened those four must feel: the loss of precious feeding ground and time; to stand now on a steep scree, balancing, watching, always wary.

Legend says the grizzly taught humankind everything we know; he was Brother Bear. Just as it came time to disclose the secret of hibernation, we grew impatient and killed the bear. Now we must remain awake throughout the long, cold, dark winter in dank houses (Thomas 1988). Humans have only a weak second-best: marijuana, a type of hibernation. Athapascans speak of Winter Bear who, forced out of his sleep in early spring by hunger, is a very ill-tempered beast, indeed.

Alaska, Siberia, and Canada are the last land of grizzlies on Earth. They need more than a thousand square miles of wilderness to exist, fifty square miles a day to feed. At night they may travel eight miles to new territory for food. Unlike the black bear, who is more of a vegetarian and whose flesh tastes sweet and rich, grizzlies are omnivorous. John Muir said that to grizzlies the whole world is food—except granite.

As a young girl I had a fantasy that a bear husband would drag me to his cave and I would become his She Bear, reverting to the wild. Unlike the adversarial approach of my young "mountain men" friends, I saw the Great Ursa as lover, not as adversary. John Donne once described woman's reaction to Death as Lover as her longing for the ultimate lengthy embrace. My fear in the wilderness is substantially different from that of men I have known. I feel part of the long continuum of life and death. I mostly fear to be disconnected—no husband, no children, no family.

I think as the hunter, too, crawling into his bear skin and wandering in his bear mind and bear body, crossing steep scree, the pads of my feet sore on the volcanic stone. There is nausea in the pit of my stomach; muscles ache with it. I will sleep deeply (not really hibernate) without urinating or eating beginning the end of September, a month away. Just one fat-sheathed sheep could make all the difference. Now I must come out of my hibernation prematurely and scavenge the steep winter snows. I hurdle through tundra in the dusk, seeing in my brain's eye the blood-twitching red meat, the delicious fat hanging in drapes from the inside of the skin. I feel my powerful jaws crushing down on the skull with delight, the brain squirting out, protein rich caviar, that greasy thick wool in my mouth.

It is not just the meat I enjoy; it is the chase, the exhilaration of moving over the land. That metallic sting of fear again and again.

The temperature drops from 48 to 38 while I watch. It begins to rain steadily, filling depressions. Bear! Symbol of resurrection, from his cave in spring. Symbol of Russia. Tied in with initiation rituals of young girls, with the Dianic Hunt of the Night (Greek), and in Japan with benevolence and wisdom. Life at its finest: meeting the Magnificent Bear.

I will come back greatly changed, looking to predators for my answers. To the bald eagle, with seven-foot wingspread and eye seven times keener than the eye of man. To the peregrine falcon, who flies at 180 mph. To the osprey, who hunts by diving headfirst into the sea. Even to the tiny territorial shrew, whose heart beats a thousand times a minute, and to the water shrew, who eats constantly or will die.

The attitude of humankind toward predators is still in the Dark Ages. According to the Alaska Department of Fish and Game, even with no legal aerial shooting last year 1,064 wolves were killed, an increase of 39 percent over the year before, the highest kill in the last ten years. Still, there is not enough focus on and money for enforcement and prosecution; illegal killing is regarded by some with a twinkle. The killing of wild predators is tacitly admired. Fall 1987: 6,000 wolves in Alaska, down from 15,000 less than a decade ago.

NIGHT

By lantern light, I reawaken the stream pebbles I gathered at the top of Atigun Pass:

1. One conglomerate with uneven chunks of jasper, rose quartz, obsidian. The matrix is gray.
2. Two metamorphic river pebbles with white streaks all the way through: quartz intrusions going at all angles to themselves.
3. Dark gray slate, thinly layered and partially metamorphosed. Some hard nephrite mixed in with sedimentary rock, cracked with the uplifted dome of Brooks Range, like a dried mud cake punched up from underneath. Through every hairline crack squeezes quartz. Gypsum veins cross the quartz, perpendicular: one thousand feet of seawater condensed to two inches of gypsum.

The keys to continents right here in my hands! Each pebble has gone through many changes, moving here from other continents, going down inside the earth and coming back out again.

Parts of these pebbles moved about as animals in the sea, then were molten myth-globs inside the earth bearing the weight of high mountains.

Walking on the top of the tundra is walking on the back of a bear. Its muscles ripple. One sinks in. There is no question in my mind that it is entirely alive: sucking, swirling, unpredictably certain. Covered with silver fuzz in tiny lobes all over, like lace, it glows lighter than the sky. When walking the tundra, silver moss means "a dry place to put one's foot." A brilliant crimson moss cradles streams and means a place to get one's knees wet.

/ August 24

This morning I solve the mystery of the mud boils while incarcerated in the truck by rain:

Mud upheavals occur at consistent intervals, support my weight. My legs, if stretched, would just reach from one to the next. If I flew along, the left foot would just be landing on one as the right foot left another. It becomes not only an efficient method of tundra traveling, but also a game of strategy. My mind leaps two moves ahead, always positioning for where the next foot will land. Yesterday, it was a confusing but interesting mind tease to figure them out. They were not animals' burrows: they were too even, and no animal of that size would live down in the wet, cold swamp water.

The mud actually boiling. When the upper layer freezes from the top down and squeezes the soil against the permafrost, it comes "boiling out" at regular intervals. Although slower, it is no different from this thick Knorr asparagus soup here in my camp pot. When saturated soils are squeezed, masses of silt ooze toward the areas of lowest pressure, forming cells of circulating muck; on gentle slopes above timberline, the soil whirlpools vertically.

Soil formations here suggest Druid cult and ritual, as in the power of water over stone, prehistoric Celtic Circles. Stone rings, stone nets form in response to the intense frost action. Stone rings begin as the frost action pushes up at an epicenter, moving the stone outward; the nets form in rhythmic patterns of freezing and thawing. Ice wedges form polygons. Stone tussocks, stone garlands, stone stripes alternating with vegetative bands all come from this constant movement of ice and gravity. Patterns of lichen indicate stabilization. The shape of land here creeps, ripples, sussulates, and crawls as if alive. It is. Higher in the Arctic, ice wedges become rhythmic and organize themselves with the grace of trabiculae in geodesic domes. The forces of ice organize into breathtaking staccato patterns across the northern slope.

The rain lets up a bit; I leap out of the truck. For some strange reason, I lean down over the door and catch a glimpse of a bizarre creature. My heart almost stops; I know what it is, but it is so alien. It is a creature that is in all of our lives, yet we seldom see it. I freeze,

so as to not frighten it off. It is the colors of the tundra: reddish epi-
derm, green eyes, rust-colored fur. The body is covered with a wool
also of tundra camouflage: reds, lavenders, greens, and golds. I stare
at it in shock for quite a while, and then begin to truly see it, as if for
the first time.

In spite of Liberation, women are still defined by their exterior
countenances; even our worth is defined by it. We spend lifetimes
staring in mirrors, smearing overpriced petroleum byproducts into
our pores and lashes and lips and eyes in hopes of attracting a more
attractive, richer mate. In hopes of gaining each other's approval. In
hopes of finding the magazine visages staring back from our mirrors.
It is such a face I have looked at for thirty some years.

Not this bright new creature I see in the driver's mirror: a wild
animal, a *real* animal. I study its distinguishing markings. Its lips are
bluish-lavender. Its skin is windburned, tan with reddish abrasions.
Its eyelashes are little, nonexistent, its eyes a mossy green intent with
wariness and curiosity. Oddly, it has become part of the tundra, part
of this environment in response to its ecosystem. It is animal once
more.

A weasel slinks across the road: brown on top, white on the
bottom (camouflage in water for animals looking up), low and long.
Slowly, the hubris of the Santa Fe art scene wears off. The fine crop
of myopic egos fallen away from the genuine and original shamanistic
impulse we call art: the first call for humans to dance. Art mitigated,
sliced off in tiny jugular fragments, shrink-wrapped and sold.

I ponder animals who have lost their wild nature. Like the raccoons on Vancouver Island. I listened, one evening, to the constant
clicking in their windpipes, little furry murmurs as their sweet black
hands came over the tailgate. Adorable black masks designed as
perfect begging tools. People being bitten often while hand-feeding
them. I was lying down when one of them catapulted itself into the
back of the truck. Before that, I was tolerant, watching them stand at
the tailgate with their black hands moving nervously over the bumper,
boys at the bar: "Please, sir, just one more drink before I go home?"
Shame! With the sea right there and such abundance of food in the
rainforest. What are they doing here, hooked on the same junk food

that hooks humans? They are fascinated with my face and look me directly in the eye. They have lost their wild nature.

When one catapulted himself over the *closed* tailgate, I was up with a frying pan and notebook beating him out. Little bastard!

Yet it is we who are wrong. I was seduced by their clicking noises, the low throaty gurgles that give the feeling of constant chatter. And amused when this turned into hostile growling and hissing when one happened upon a bit of dinner, and ran out of the pool of lantern light. There was the humorous and unavoidable comparison to human sibling rivalry.

It is for odd reasons we respond to different animals differently; because of evolutionary adaptations, we love kitties, shoot wolves, hate weasels, and attribute wisdom to owls. Animals with frontal searching eyes are perceived as lovable: those sweet masqueraders with their delicate black hands resting so plaintively on my bumper/bar, with those little digits that could easily deal cards as they suit themselves up for human charm.

And what's in a voice?

In the voice of crow and Stellar's jay, so grating. Or in the clackety ratchets of chickaree squirrels, or in the whines of begging gulls. The eerie vibrational warbles of coyotes and wolves, so welcome, yet sending adrenaline tingles out to limbs. The low grunts and barks of bears, at once so endearing, like old men we have known, yet so frightening in the power behind them.

And why is the white sound of ocean, stream, and rain so soothing to our human psyche: the white silk scrim-stretched across consciousness behind which Shiva dances. A white sound punctuated by a noisy cacophony of waves and boulders. Or the visual thunder of one thousand jet black crows landing at once on golden snow. The sudden swirl of black angels in Milton's *Paradise Lost*, Satan's swarm wafting over the horizon.

What of those sounds and visions from ancestral memory?

My feet take on their own consciousness, separate from me, and act as animals springing over the mosses and tussocks. The forms of submerged mosses are repeated in the vast dendritic drainages of the Brooks Range above. Nothing on the human scale in tundra.

That is not true. There are several things of human scale: wolf, bear, loneliness, and fear.

The sheer multiplicity of things! Vast night skies hold more stars than a hundred ages of man have seen below, catching their light in a net of longevity, juggling about crystalline deities. Strange deformations of sound, warped as in circus mirrors. Silence. Then the slither of predation behind one's back. Tonight I have, most clearly and literally, an immediate sense of sailing through space, crouched, clinging to some ultimate time kayak.

Today I found antlers on the tundra where someone had placed them in gnarled logarithms. I go to sit now, in the dusk, on the bank of the Sukasan River. Tired bones. I feel happier at this moment than I ever remember.

A strange bird cries, watches for the river water to go backwards. It does; an eddy upstream holds a fin.

Tributaries come down in deep Vs of army green, glittering like children. All around an air crisp with brutality.

On a muddy river bank, all night long loud clacking outside. Bear or moose. Finally, I slip out to investigate. The night has become viscous, like black bean gruel. Across the roaring river channel, horse-sized slabs of stone slap down onto the river. The Brooks sediment returning to sea.

/ August 25: Coldfoot Restaurant

The names on the coffee cups on the pegboard read: Flash Gordon, Silver Long, Snake, Big(heart) John, Oregon Logger, Sam, Hard Rock, Slam Down, Halfreak, Nice Car Driver, Used Log Truck, Rock Dog, Toklat, Trapper, Dutch, Joe, Big Jane, Dogma, Outlaw, Streamized (fish), Irish, Fingers, Arctic Fox, Pump Runner, Hips, and Miss Long Pistons.

Truckers sit at the central table and talk accidents and weather. An exotic breed, they do not deem it necessary to fit norms. Their character, though, comes off sharp and amusing. Their words run together. They talk a harsh line and drive a harsh wilderness.

I sit and monologue with Ol' Slimy Yellow-eye and his cohorts, the hashbrowns. What happens to these men when there is no more wilderness to conquer? I ask. Is there life after the dragon is slain?

"Shit, no!" answers the egg, "you just go home and stare across at the Little Princess who is in a terrible mood from having been locked up in some damned tower for one hundred years."

"And where does *Dragoni vulgaris* go from here?"

"I don't believe they survive in captivity," says the egg.

I think of the packs of arctic wolves, in which only one dominant pair get to mate; the rest are the biological reserves who step and fetch it for the mother and new pups. The mating goes to the smartest and the quickest. Here, we neuters and drones cater to the oil mammalia of the energy-crazed beast below.

Up here, eating habits change profoundly. Vegetarian for years, I now crave meat: big bloody pieces of it. The ornate tinned fish I have hauled from the states below hors d'oeuvres me to death. Give me bloody hunks of dead raw muscle. I have begun to look upon the deer family hungrily.

Coming over Atigun Pass, the guard rail is ripped with impact. Some places it is gone entirely. I realize how safe and anal-compulsive our Lower Forty-eight is. We don't even have to shift gears or steer, as little glowy bumps on the lane edges guide us. We don't walk or even open doors. The life juices of Mother Earth, namely Alaska, flow into seeing-eye triggers that operate our every move. Bionicination. Voracious for fuel. Fossil fuel. If we were the embryo, we would be devouring our own egg sack; but we've already been had, and we now devour our mother.

Oblivious to what's under the hood, Americans power off down the freeways. Now, up here, this is driving! Every pore is driving. Is listening. Is straining. Is looking out of all sides of the head at once. Watching for large rigs coming. A nation of blithering cars in a headlong rush toward safety. They will soon issue insurance at birth for every bump, scrape, or bad feeling the individual will get. Pain-killing substances for marriage, birth, taxes, and death will be issued at birth. The unfortunate infant that cannot pay will be put to death: life would be too dangerous.

(Later, I hear a piece on the "Weekend Edition" of National Public Radio in which Susan Stanberg interviews a young woman with a newish Subaru. The two "car guys" on the third line advise her to get a new car, for, horror of horrors, she has been out in the "wilderness" of the Adirondack Mountains (i.e., her hotel didn't have color TV) and the head gasket broke. She had to be towed more than sixty miles! Two other minor things have gone wrong with the beastly car. Well, if she ever looked under the bonnet she might have seen oil slipping out early enough to fix it for about $40. I would add to the advice of the two garage men: I do not believe such a person should leave home at all.)

TOWARD PRUDHOE BAY

Prudhoe Bay lies enticingly on the Beaufort Sea, the farthermost border of our country: 70° 22′ N, 148° 22′ W. I am only 20 miles out but short on gas. I do not want to be caught and fined for driving the Haul Road without permission to Prudhoe, so I stop. It tortures me to stop so near, and yet I have heard of the gigantic garbage dump I would see should I proceed. A scientist who works for the Company on the North Slope has told me, "When Prudhoe drillers move on, we will be the owners of the biggest junkyard on Earth. It is not true that the Eskimos haul off all the barrels to recycle: they sit in huge rusting heaps, leaching oil and metals onto the tundra. Although there are $110,000 bonds posted for Alyeska to clean up and remove wells after they are done, it will never happen: each well would cost half a million to remove. Toxic waste is being poured into the permafrost, and EIS is requiring weak provision for its cleanup. Twenty-five-thousand-gallon spills happen not infrequently and are no big deal." (My source desires to remain anonymous, for his job's sake).

Named in 1826 by Sir Franklin after a place in England, Prudhoe is the heart of the Naval Petroleum Reserve #4 (Pet 4), 51.8 million acres of prime wildlife habitat and 14 percent of the state's total land.

President Warren Harding established Pet 4 by executive order in 1923, following reports of oil in the new territory. Maybe the vast wasteland was good for something after all!

Multiple jurisdictions and land tenure claims pose difficult problems for federal management of such lands. The boundaries of Pet 4 are yet in dispute, over the two-mile buffer zone around it, because neither the Navy nor the Department of Interior is clear whose responsibility it is for surface resources administration and for the vast petroleum reserves. No one is clear, legally, over the claims of Native Americans, and the Native Americans themselves pull every which way: while one group was adamantly fighting Reagan's greed for oil in the Arctic National Wildlife Refuge, a clandestine Eskimo group was making deals to trade prime caribou habitat to the federal government for oil-leasing.

The land status of the Arctic National Wildlife Refuge, the region's second largest withdrawal, is no more certain than that of Pet 4. As of 1989, there is still great pressure for a natural gas pipeline to cross the refuge, traversing from Prudhoe to the Mackenzie River Delta of Canada. Environmentalists as well as Native Americans are frantically challenging the legality of another destructive gas corridor along the Canning River southwest of the refuge. Years hence, our descendants may look back at our shortsightedness appalled.

In 1986, Congressman Morris Udall, Democrat of Arizona, and John Seiberling, Democrat of Ohio, and James M. Jeffords, Republican of Vermont, introduced legislation to protect the wildlife between the Brooks Range and the northern coast, particularly in areas adjacent to Pet 4. Caribou calving range there is extremely limited by snow depth, food availability, predation, and migration patterns. Pipelines through this fragile area would threaten not only land mammals but also the wildlife dependent on the coast of the Beaufort Sea: walrus (recovered from threatened status), seals, bowhead whales (endangered), ducks, geese, swans, loons, snowy owls, eagles, gyrfalcons, peregrine falcons (threatened), muskoxen, and countless others. Cecil D. Andrus, former Interior Secretary, wrote that "we decided that the known wildlife values in the refuge outweighed the *possibility* of a petroleum strike there. The highest and best use of this land is not exploitation of its finite resources, but perpetuation of its renewable resources" (*Wilderness* 1986:4–5).

The battle goes on. According to *Congressional Quarterly* (First Session, 1987), Reagan's Interior Department estimated that the refuge sits on top of the richest oil field left in the nation. They already have sunk wells every three square miles on the west side of Prudhoe, and those wells have enough oil potential to produce at any moment, once the price of the gasoline is driven up. This last year, a fight broke out when the Interior Department sneakily divided up land to companies on Native Corporation land for imminent development, once it slipped past Congress. George Millery, Democrat of California, chairman of the Interior Subcommittee on Water and Power Resources, let out a howl: the Interior Department was pre-prejudicing a decision that Congress was to make!

Then Congress balked. The executive branch was playing fast and illicit by beginning to allocate oil resources even before Congress had voted on the *appropriate land use for the greatest good of the people.* Congress further found that the Department of Interior had acted to allow study for oil potential before any environmental impact statement was made. This was in blatant disregard of the seasonal intensity of life; i.e., essential calving grounds and an important world rookery had not been considered. The "if-you've-seen-one-arctic-tern-you've-seen-'em-all" mentality aside, there was realistically only a 19 percent chance that oil pure enough to be worth drilling for would be found. Congress retaliated, holding its own against the most environmentally destructive administration in the history of the nation.

According to scientists, total impact on wildlife continues far beyond the first obvious disturbances:

The environmental impact on the tundra that results from drilling and building activities is added to actions of the past and foreseeable future. Such drilling activities result in cumulative damage from individually small but collectively significant actions over a period of years.

The tundra over permafrost is a delicate balance of shallow lakes, wetlands and higher ground, laced intricately together and controlled by frozen ground. Each component of the tundra is vitally important to wildlife. Flooding and thermokarstic action—the artificial melting of ice wedges—caused by roads and building pads block the essential flows of water and destroy the natural heterogenous mosaics of microsites vital for waterfowl and shorebirds. The melted water absorbs more heat, causing more melting, and keeps expanding the thermokarst.

Aerial views show much damage along the older roads of Prudhoe Bay. Over the 500 square kilometers of Prudhoe oilfield, there are 350 kilometers of road, 21 km² of gravel-covered tundra, 14 km² of unnatural flooding. The pattern of disturbance is seen over 29 percent of the total area.

We must study entire land and river system functions and how biological diversity and movement corridors for animals work. We do not know this. We should not build until we have a thorough scientific understanding, and then only within carefully prescribed guidelines to save the tundra.

Right now, according to biologists who requested their names be withheld to protect their jobs, we Americans are the proud owners of the largest junkyard on the planet. Barrels, equipment, defunct wells and cement pads are not cleaned up, capped or removed. It cuts too much into profit, even though the state often bonds companies to remove wells.

The Department of Interior's proposal to lease 1.5 million acres of ANWR for oil is based on *two false ideas*:

Myth One: The nation must depend on fossil fuel.
Myth Two: That environmental impact will be minimal, owing to experience gained at Prudhoe Bay.

I hike up mountains rising at impossible slopes with critical-angle talus. The north side of the Brooks Range pulses gray/white/gray/white from ancient sea deposits. I ponder what cyclical changes created the handsome patterns: a sea rising and submerging repeatedly? On this northern rim of land, billions of barrels of Cretaceous creatures were trapped slowly by a landmass moving west over the top of Canada, piling up here. I have stopped to rest. Up a loud stream with tall shrubs, I sing at the top of my lungs for the bears. First, "The hills are alive with the sound of music," which clears out the area for miles around. To give the bears a break, I sing Janis Joplin's "Oh, Lord, Won't You Buy Me a Mercedes Benz." Just so the bears won't be confused by urban images, I make up my own:

Oh, Lord, won't you buy me real good tundra boots.
Walking on tundra, Lord, I must have a screw loose.
So mold-form my feet, Lord,
To those of a moose.
Oh Lord, won't you buy me some real good tundra boots.

Still no bears. Nor any other animal, for that matter.

I squat by a rock that has a large black pool where it bunts its shadow. This is the ice lens phenomenon, a natural thermokarst, or melting, sideways instead of underneath: ice wedge in the warm August sun. This pool does not "teem with life" as would any desert pool. Just a bit of oxygen-deprived algae floats over silt at the bottom. A dead heather reaches out across it, its black leaf-packed arms like a body traced on a sidewalk. The warmth produces a greenhouse effect around the rock, but this pool is a pool of deadends. The rock, the Oz of all this, is an ill-formed conglomerate.

I am prostrate, examining the lichen dance across the hard stone, breaking it down in some biochemical Hava nagila, when suddenly there is a great roar.

I flip over. Above, the steep slope has just disgorged boulders in great pink rockslides from a gray stone face. These rock showers reveal unoxidized granite, as well as surfaces not covered with lichen. A method of dating has been developed to determine how long stone has been exposed. The Australian Roland Beschel first measured the movement of ice by comparing undated thalli, or rounds of lichen, which grow at a known rate of speed, with those of a known date, such as those on tombstones. Exquisite flowerlike concentric lichens continue growing for centuries, dying at their centers and producing outward. These organisms have been found to be 4,000 years old, some of the oldest living critters on the planet, and so offer a continuous time line against which to measure the movement of ages. The retreats of ice from peaks around the world are amazingly coordinated, in Africa, Greenland, Italy, and the Stubai Alps. Even the northern and southern hemispheres are synchronized, demonstrating what a finely tuned whole entity our Earth is (Richardson 1974).

VITAE EN EXTREMIS: HOT DESERT/COLD DESERT

Tundra is desert, at least in terms of rainfall. Whether cold desert or hot desert, life thrives near the scarcest commodity: water in the Upper Chihauhuan Desert, protection and nitrogen here. Water, water everywhere here, but less than 10 inches falls from the sky in a year. Life explodes in the shadows of rocks, where there is protection. Life explodes under raptor nests, where there is nitrogen. Life explodes up through a muskox carcass, where there is fertile soil. Here humans exist only by the fragile grace of artificial systems. Although the Inuit technology is amazing, it still is only the edge of life on the tundra. It reminds me of the Tohono O'odham at another edge of existence in their land of less than 10 inches of rainfall a year in the Sonoran Desert.

Distance in deserts expands exponentially. Perhaps it is attributable to the lack of human-sized objects: only the vast rolling mesas or steppes punctuate a horizon of *terra incognita*, which makes one small. Or perhaps it is the harsh elements that distort one's perceptions. Normalcy is a thing easily forgotten, a fragile husk that blows off the edge of Earth. This is truly a different reality.

Mechanical sounds from rock, water, air, and beast seem to simulate one another. The creek that pours over stones a quarter-mile away also could be wind, coming up to me here in rhythmic lunges. Or is it an engine on the road far below? Tiny gray birds chitting into the bushes sound like rocks hitting together. A peregrine wing close by startles me, sounding like a food blender's pulse button way out in the middle of nowhere.

Visual and auditory parallels make no sense, unless one wanders through the inner structure of the universe: the physical plant. Masterful engineering, time and trial, screws things together and apart according to unviewable laws and the electrical glue of atoms. The way sound travels, the way minerals reflect color, the way an organism moves, assert uncanny parallels freshly seen up here.

94

There also are discontinuities.

The sharp tooth of the mountains does not fit the sinuous curve of river; nor does the pipeline, in its angular twitch, fit with either of them.

/ August 26:   Jim River, Down the Haul Road

Anyone who thinks all rivers are brown or blue is not looking. I sit at the Jim River where bears lurk. Water rushes by black and creamy. Tar waves send off white sparks on their crests. The sky just cracked open.

I pass the Arctic Circle, at 66 degrees 33 minutes north, above which is the land of the midnight sun. Two more lines, Tropic of Cancer and Tropic of Capricorn, are drawn at 23 degrees 27 minutes north and south, which also happens to be the angle of the ecliptic, the angle at which Earth's axis is tilted relative to the sun. Without this tilt, Persephone would never have been abducted by Hades, so that Demeter, in her grieving, could strip the earth every six months.

Earth's axis does wobble two to three degrees every 40,000 years, give or take the overtime in soccer games, and appears to be related to the ice ages as well—and to the Supercontinent Theory. Occasionally, the poles flip-flop entirely, the south becoming north and north south, but I hope this does not happen soon: I'd have to adjust my dashboard compass again, which is constantly changing its vast amount of inaccuracy up here anyway, owing to my closeness to the pole.

Ptarmigan fly swiftly through tangled black spruce with white bodies, black wings, never missing their ptarmigan-shaped openings. The intense yellow of willow, the burnt red of resin birch emanate heat onto the all-gray-scale. Grays are executed as in a Renaissance painting, in which tonalities are laid down first, then hues added in thin gels to create translucent volumes. Color is the frill overlying the substance here, the exaltation of chiaroscuro. A skilled artist loves executing chiaroscuro because it brings the full intellect into play.

At the Yukon River, a young boy crosses in front of me with a red wagon. On it is all his hunting gear: a wooden rifle, snow shoes (no snow yet), supplies for the winter. Sad, deep-set eyes. I decide to see if he will allow me into his world:

"Looks like you're all set for the winter."

He looks at me suspiciously. He knows that I know it isn't winter yet.

"What kinda animal you going to shoot?" I ask, pointing to the gun.

He waves it at me, annoyed. "I ain't gettin' anything." He knows that I know a wooden gun can't shoot. He grows more suspicious. This is a child who does not usually speak to strangers.

Later, after my shower, he stands staring at me for a half an hour as I carefully put *Aloe vera* lotion on the parts of my skin that stick out. Later, loading up my Coleman with ice, I feel his eyes again, just staring and staring at me.

At midnight, I park against a red-barred gate below a Headache Bar. The Headache Bar stands just below the height of the Pipeline and is designed to stop a trucker dumb enough to sabotage the pipe. All night the alders rub on the body of the truck like a wild animal. Something large and feline mews. It seems also that I hear a Highland Scots female voice singing near the streams. The truth lies not in auditory hallucination, but in the fact that the Scottish voice exists *a priori* in these high streams, and young maidens have but to open their throats for it to pour out.

6

Return to Civilization

Let us go then, you and I,
When the evening is spread out against the sky
Like a patient etherised upon a table; . . .

   T.S. Eliot,
   "The Love Song of J. Alfred Prufrock"

Coming out of the wilderness is falling down through layers of
garbage, Alice down the looking glass tunnel. Things float by, also
falling: cumbersome RVs, cute signs, children, herds of them, trash,
picnic tables. It becomes summer again. Back through November and
into a sizzling hot fall, as if one could fly backward through time,
exchanging energy for chronology like poker chips. There is a price to
be paid for descent, as any average Greek god can tell you. Here come
the safety nets, the webs of wire, the résumés that nail your self-worth
wriggling to the techno-industrial cross-beam, the time schedules, the
stress-related diseases, the qualifiers, the nay-sayers, the government
regulators, the guarantees, the bloody guarantees.

/ August 30:   Angel Rocks

On Angel Rocks trail I have seen something so odd as to be miracu-
lous: a great white beard of mushroom, an invention of surrealists.

Hericium ramosum. At first, I couldn't even comprehend it. Thought my vision was blurring. Then I drew it, photographed it, cut it, handled it, cooked a bit, and ate it. Tree ears, *Auricularia auricula,* animate dead wood with golden plates, dusty white underside propagating itself. At first the river was white water, then slowed to a fat slug of a pond behind beaver dams. I sat for a long while to identify mushrooms; a fishing weasel ran up the bank and over my leather sneaker carrying a fishy morsel in its mouth. He barely paused to collect this odd sight and smell, then disappeared back under the beaver dam. Now 1,000 feet straight up to gothic granite spires recently exposed through solifluction. I attempt to climb one; although technically an easy ascent, the exposure is too great for climbing alone.

This is a unique flora island, the remnant of vegetation that covered the interior 10,000 to 20,000 years ago in the Pleistocene. Violets, sage, poppies, arnicas, dogbane, saxifrage, and broomrapes bloom on this hot dry side of the mountains. I think I've been dropped into the Desert Southwest. The first wave of Siberians from the Lena River Basin would have seen such plants dominating the continent during the Algonquian Migration 23,000 to 35,000 years ago.

10:17 PM: JUST NOW DARK

Rain in the night is seductive. I find it so difficult to go to sleep here because there are so many things to do. I move sun to sun. My journal lies writing itself in my brain's dusk. The nature of journals is finally dawning on me: how to use it seriously. The nature of the journals of Thoreau, Edward Abbey, Samuel Pepys, da Vinci, Michelangelo, Delacroix, or my mother scribbling away in southern New Mexico, hunched over some poor unsuspecting beetle. Reading the raw materials of creative lives gives me courage. The creative process always requires leaps of faith in one's own capacity. Journals act as rope bridges or, as in mine, a free rappel, over chasms. They heighten curiosity. Going to sleep is hard on such rainy evenings when there is so much learning to be done, so much to be written, so many specimens curling their unique chromosomes about themselves to fall asleep.

It is a curious fact that a predominant leisure activity of tourism is learning. Tourists all over this continent, gleaning odd and wonderful bits of information about blue glacial ice, or Captain Cook's thwarted Northwest Passage, or the nature of the water shrew. There must be an instinct within our evolution that rewards the human organism for learning about its landscape. There is a Kutchekutchin word, a dialect of the Tena, whose meaning has been twisted in English slang to mean "stupid newcomer to Alaska." Actually, it speaks of the principle of migration. *Che-cha-ka* translates as "one who comes in the spring hungry and leaves in the fall fat." If this is translated to "one who comes here hungry to learn and leaves in the fall, full and satisfied," it is an apt and flattering description of tourist migration.

/ September 1: Richardson Highway

On the Richardson Highway southeast of Fairbanks, the land ripples by in low, dry non-browns and non-blues like Nevada. Too low to touch snow. Donnely Dome rises singularly, a volcanic plug punched up by the weight of the Alaskan Range on the bottom of this continent. The Alaskan Range rises majestically and abruptly in spasmodic white peaks. Wind is rough, gusts up to 80 miles per hour. The tundra ascends imperceptibly. The pipeline joins the road.

THE PIPELINE

Started November 16, 1973, through presidential approval, the Alyeska Pipeline Service Company built 800 miles of pipe across Alaska and 360 miles of road from the Yukon River to Prudhoe Bay. The first lengths of pipe went down in 1974 and the last in spring 1977: an unbelievably short time. In March of 1975, pipe was laid under the Tonsina River, an engineering feat, and through the earthquake-prone Alaskan Range; all pumping stations and the Valdez Terminal complete. June 20, 1977: the first oil left Prudhoe Bay and arrived July 28 in Valdez. The first tanker of oil left port on the First of August, 1977. One-and-a-half million barrels a day slog through the 48-inch pipe under pressure in a race with time.

The wall of the pipe varies: .462 to .562 inch of insulation with 4-inch fiber glass bonded directly to a galvanized steel jacket. Depending upon the terrain and wildlife, it is either elevated or buried. Under and over it move moose with 80-inch antlers, black bears, wolverines, Dall sheep, wolves, and bison reestablished from Montana in 1928.

Wind sings through the heat dissipators, tall radiating gills above the pipe. Eerie. Architecture from another planet, whose dominant species lives underground after it has spoiled its atmosphere.

Where the soil nears thawing, which would turn permafrost into deadly mud wallows, a complicated system of insulation and pipes extracts extraneous heat through the vertical supports. Anhydrous ammonia, a liquid with a low boiling point, rises up to radial-finned radiators, condenses and moves back down the insides of pipes in a thin film. As beautifully engineered as it is, the pipeline is not without serious flaws. In 1976, there existed x-rays of 31,000 damaged welds, only 2,600 of which were repaired. Our Secretary of Interior, Thomas Kleppe, was busy saying, "Not one drop of oil will flow until the pipeline has been thoroughly tested and we are assured of its integrity." Alyeska Chairman Edward L. Patton (a good name for a pipeline general) said, "The welds are equal to the highest quality ever produced."

Meanwhile, near quake-prone Valdez, a seven-foot rip was appearing in a normal pipeline pressure test. A pipe built to withstand 1,189 PSI burst under only 187 PSI. This was "explained" as human error, thereby vindicating the pipeline technology itself. This "explaining off" by the human error factor is befuddling. An evangelistic Faith in Technology, itself flawed, always nullifies the effects of human beings. "The guy was tired . . . the guy was distracted . . . the wiring was confusing . . . the engineer was drunk . . . or else it would have worked perfectly."

Very little oil spreads a very long way in cold water; a boat spill in Kachemak Bay spread 30,000 gallons of diesel fuel over two miles of water within the hour. Kachemak has a rich marine habitat, which not only substantially supports the population around Homer (tourism and fishing) but is one of the most beautiful spots on Earth (Hanson 1976).

There! A tiny lake at 65 miles per hour, a simplified image is burned into my retina: two black silhouettes of northern shovelers on a deep red lake. The red mountain terraces are caught and recast in the red mirror.

The Alaskan Range bulges upward through the sedimentary layers, showing pristine colors in plant dyes of Navajo weavers: heather, lavender, sage, rust, dusky blue, and cochineal. Just a decade before Alyeska executed its final weld, the city of Valdez was destroyed by earthquake. What the quake did not flatten, the flash mud flows from ice dam breaks did. What the glacial water did not get, the tsunami did.

It is thrillingly steep here. I can hear the oil mump along like a heartbeat every five seconds. Zinc ribbons are buried along with the pipeline, sacrificial anodes to draw off corrosion to itself. The zinc, more vulnerable, is attacked first and spares the steel. Anhydrous ammonia slurps and giggles its way up to vaporize and down to condense below.

/ September 2:   Gulkana Glacier

Terry, a cook at the Summit Lake Cabins, has promised to introduce me to his Samoan friend from Hawaii, a subsistence hunter who lives on his mining claim. That means he can hunt and trap year-round. The claim can only be reached by boat across strong current. For four hours we sit on the edge of the river and watch the world glint off it. The smells are so strong, smells of a muscular wildness enticing us from the far side of the water. The sky is expanding, gleaming after two days of heavy rain, and orographic clouds bloom years into the heavens. Whether we cross or not, I am ecstatic in this moment. Two Frenchmen cast off in a flat-bottomed craft, also for a mining claim way upriver.

Terry is longing: next summer, instead of being a cook in a lodge, he is to help run the mining equipment twenty-four hours a day, four hours on, four hours off.

"Isn't that kind of exhausting?" I ask.

"Aw, naw," answers Terry's Tennessee drawl, "it ain't workin'. It's just ridin'." Three-wheelers and four-wheelers tear up the slope over impossible terrain, sometimes so steep "you got to throw your body up over the handlebars to keep from flippin' over backwards." His friend scrapes roads and mines all over his secretive patch on the river, Terry boasts, as if raw land were intolerable.

The Gulkana Glacier glows from underneath the clouds, nacreous and luminescent. A peregrine falcon hunts small songbirds, letting out mews of disdain as his prey proves too facile. The reddish breast glows, its wings like knives. A sharp cry: the joy of capture.

/ September 3:   Denali Highway

I awake to a landscape resounding with metallic shots. The entire 135-mile stretch called Denali Highway is prickled with sniping. Fall has raked the landscape. The Denali "highway" advances through the rubble of glacial retreat. I have slept fitfully all night on an esker, the negative inversion of an under-glacier river. Made of unsorted rock, as if thrown together by a bulldozer, the 25-foot eskers snake through the land like immense mole trails. Kettle lakes shroud themselves with leaden sky. Sun is a white lozenge through bitter clouds.

Fall here is red. September First is blood red. Rusts, rouge, wounded leaves. Roses, berry reds, and fiery reds of willows. Crimson red berries. Vermilion. Even the rubescence of blood is not one singular color but changes through oxidation.

Everything is frozen this morning. Ice crystals in the water jug. Stove must be put between my legs before I get up. All over loons cry. All is gray and blood red. What I expected to be wilderness is an urban hunters' realm. People parading up and down it, guns erect. In subsistence hunting, there is some balance, but this city hunting is insanity licensed. A mockery of the ancient balances of predator and prey. Men who purchase meat in supermarkets riding four-wheelers, three-wheelers, motor boats, horses, sedans, and four-by-fours into the wilderness to practice a prehistoric barbaric instinct.

I overhear someone boasting of heat-sensor technology he developed based on his experience in Vietnam.

GRACIOUS CREEK, DENALI HIGHWAY

Three flat tires later.

The day is not going as planned. A handsome French family from Ontario pulls up to help me change the first flat, only to discover one of their own. I now help them change theirs with my tools, and we sally forth at 30 miles per hour to a defunct wooden mansion, once a roadside inn. Their van has a second flat. Fifty miles out from nowhere, no means to fix it. So we throw one of their tires in the back of Die Fledermazda, leaving resourceful Gilane and three children to entertain themselves in rain, in mud, in the middle of nowhere.

Jim and I now tiptoe forth in Die Fledermazda, the volcanic debris they used to pave the road caustic against our ears. That is how I came to be sitting in this chintzy cafe, soaked to the gills, waiting for a dubious hamburger, and listening to a young Black stand-up comedian, alias "waitperson." Since they don't see too many women here not attached to an Alpha Male, the performance intensifies. There is little progress made on either my truck or Jim's van tire; levity must substitute for efficiency.

This cute young guy is telling his hard-labor buddies about fat urbanites who fly here from all over the country:

"Unguided Moose tour only $750. Take you out in a plane and drop you in the middle of nowhere. Shit-fuckin' nowhere!" Much giggling, and I find myself giggling also, even though in a stench of a mood. "Guided Moose tour is $1,000, just for a couple days. Then there are these motorhomes with portable satellite dishes which rent for three hundred a day, or you can buy into one for only $400 a month. I know a broad in town who lives in a shack so she can make payments on her hunting motorhome at $450 a month." He takes a breath and I take the opportunity.

"I need a glass of water over here real bad," I gasp. I am exhausted from changing tires in the rain and have not eaten—cold, wet, dehydrated.

This turns out to be a straight line for one of the funniest pieces of body language I have seen. A giggle wells up through my foul temper in spite of myself. He must come all the way around the bar to get to my table, foot dragging, schlepping, growling and scowling, complaining loudly, until he reaches me. Instantly, he becomes obsequiously cheerful and subservient. I suppress my grin like a thumb on a volcano.

I order, although quite flustered at his act, dignified as a drenched person can be, once again playing the straight man. Before the end of my order he is displaying exaggerated impatience with me. As he disappears into the kitchen, I make the mistake of adding, "Could I have that rare?"

"*Rare*," he roars, returning from the kitchen. "Did you hear that?!" he explodes to the cook. "This *woman* has a *special* request." His hand thwaps the grease-infested sign above the door of the kitchen. It is pouring sleet out, gutting the sky. The sign reads:

THIS IS NOT BURGER KING.
YOU GET IT MY WAY OR YOU DON'T GET IT
AT ALL.

He cackles a grand stage cackle and disappears into the kitchen.

I pull my wool shirt and raincoat up around my head and go back out to the garage where the young mechanic is pumping gas, talking on the phone, doing everything but fixing our tires. Jim, quite good-naturedly, seems to be helping him. The van tire, it turns out, is unfixable. They try one more time to get it on the rim using all eight hands and feet. I am doubtful. I back Die Fledermazda as close to the garage as possible, and the young guy says, "Oh! You want *me* to put it back on for you. That's extra." The rain is pouring. "No," I say testily, "I'll do that. I'm short on money." He laughs at me. "For *you*, its free," he grins. I don't know what is joke and what is not, and I am growing dizzy from not having eaten.

Back inside, no hamburger. I read maps and write several pages in my journal. Finally the comedian waltzes out of the kitchen singing jauntily with my hamburger platter cavalierly high on his splayed fingers. I am a perfect straight man when my blood sugar is down. A sitting duck. He bows low as he serves it. I say, "Do you have steak sauce?"

"Steak sauce?" he roars. "Hey, Fran, this gal wants *steak sauce!*" Dramatic pause in kitchen. "We got any *steak sauce?!?*" I jam the food into my mouth with both hands, quite grateful for his humor.

/ September 4:   Near Nowhere, Alaska

Yesterday was long and grueling: we did not find a tire until Cantwell, twenty miles north of Denali National Park. Cantwell is a whistle stop on the great Alaskan Railroad from Portage on the Kenai Penninsula to Fairbanks. Jim and I did not return until eight that night, having left at eleven that morning. He turned out to be a fascinating companion, a corporate executive capable of making large salaries. He has business brains galore, but stops periodically throughout his life to try new endeavors or to take six-month-long trips. During these trips he educates his offspring, explores, lives intensely, and decides what he wants to do next. His three children, Gabrielle, Miguel and Katherine, already are lovely, distinct human beings who assert themselves and pelt me with adult questions.

Miguel, 13, asked where I had been and where I was going. They sold their home, cut all ties, and now the five of them live out of a small, well-designed van.

Jim eventually was able to buy one good tire for his van in the last garage open during Alaska's hunting season. There were no tires for my size of truck. "They don't much stock tires for toys in these parts," Jim teased me.

We had a wonderful day looking for tires. We discussed fervently
Native Americans and what our respective governments are doing to
help them revive their languages and culture. We spoke of art, muse-
ums and cultural anthropology, good places to travel in the world.
We argued passionately (as the French do so well) about the function
of art in pretechnological cultures: Jim said it only developed after
people had enough to eat. My opinion—the correct one, of course—
is that art is as essential as food because it is the spiritual and cultural
glue of a tribe—or a nation.

DARK: SUSTINA NON-LODGE

The Sustina River, from the Tanana word meaning "sandy water,"
flows alongside us in the dark. We return after dark in the pouring
cold onslaught to the Sustina Lodge, and all pile in the van. Gilane,
Jim's wife, has befriended a state senator who is a man of many
talents, one of which includes fixing flats. He runs an airplane ferry
service for hunters at $200 an hour. "Why mend tires at $5 an hour,"
he says, "when at $200 I can fly." He is no longer enamored of
hunting and would prefer, instead, to sell shares in Save-A-Moose or
Save-A-Caribou companies to the Lower Forty-eight.

"What about those with little money?" I protest.

"For limited budgets we have a 'Save-a-Ptarmigan' special."

"How would that work?" Gilane asks seriously.

"Each stock owner would receive a picture of their particular
animal and a hand-scribbled letter from the moose or whoever, saying
how he was doing."

"And," I continue, "that he was of mixed heritage, but now thanks
to the donor, he would have enough to eat, and not ever get shot at."

"Thanks to you," continues Gilane in a low, distinguished Moose-
voice, "I have now been accepted to Harvard in Law and Animal
Husbandry."

There is the story that turned the state senator around on hunting.
He was hired by a scientific outfit that came to study why only eleven
out of twenty-eight moose pregnancies produced calves. The locals
preferred to think it was wolves, in order to justify shooting predators. Scientists attached motion sensors to each new calf, and as soon

as the animal had not moved for a certain period of time it was assumed dead: this allowed immediate helicopter surveillance. The imbalance came as a surprise: grizzly bears attack mothers with young calves. The scientists then removed some grizzlies and partially restored the balance.

Gilane relates this story:

The state senator, as a result of his participation in the scientific surveillance, came to value each individual moose. "I take these guys from the big cities out and fly over the moose. We look down, and I say, 'There's your moose, fellows!' Little do they know how hard it will be to get it, let alone haul it back several miles on their backs to the landing strip."

When I ask Jim and Gilane for their last name, it is Eagle! I finally have found the True North American Spirit and it is Canadian. French Canadian, no less.

Someone tells me not to wear my white wool cap, that in spite of a bright turquoise raincoat I resemble a caribou's ass. My face has been compared to many things before, but never a caribou's ass.

5:58 a.m.: One last pure vision of the Denali Highway as I flee the volcanic-glass paving; two giant-antlered caribou stand breathing fog nearby in the slow-motion hush of early morning.

/ September 5:   The Forks Roadhouse

Nine men drink instead of hunt in a roadhouse twenty miles south of the Denali Park boundary. I have been enticed up this long rocky rut, twenty miles back, by the thought of solitude. Silly me: during hunting season? Instead I have found a picturesque old roadhouse/ bar; inside I find the well-oiled Hunter. Denver Broncos tromp Seahawks: I should feel something; one is my home state, the other my adopted. Instead I view the huge screen as a primitive would: orange and green blobs bounce up and down. On the road, I stop and stare at a four-wheel ATV with a moose head mounted on the handlebars as if it were bionic. The hunter is delighted at my attention and asks if I would like him to take a picture of me with it. Its nostrils flutter still, giving it a living appearance.

After coming out the west end of the Denali Highway, instead of going straight to the National Park as planned, I have been forced south to Anchorage in search of that elusive species, the tire for small pickups. I have driven, foolheartedly, without a spare up this winding road of rock.

The amount of garbage on the roadside increases in inverse proportion to the mileage to Anchorage. The Alyeska Haul Road had been immaculate: not even a cigarette. Denali Highway had been good. Now the debris.

I believe that we will not last as a species. I sometimes wonder whether any ecological political action is anything but an absurd postponement of the inevitable. Just as at the end of the Cretaceous Period, when a thick layer of volcanic ash covered the planet and snuffed 80 percent of its lifeforms, the Holocene too will meet its end in darkness. Whether it be acid rain, nuclear winter, or simply the demise of Earth's resources is academic.

With luck, it will be one of nature's quicker disasters.

BOOK TWO

Fleeing to the Wilderness
on Silk Threads

7

The Art of Conducting Oneself

You cannot stay on the summit forever;
you have to come down again. . . .
So why bother in the first place? Just this: what is
above knows what is below, but what is
below does not know what is above.
One climbs, one sees. One descends, one sees no
longer but one has seen. There is an art of
conducting oneself in the lower regions by the
memory of what one saw higher up.
When one can no longer see, one can
at least still know.

Rene Daumal,
Mount Analogue

/ September 8:   Palmer Lakes Valley

One day of errands in the crowded city has sent me fleeing back to the wilderness, this time south to the Kenai Peninsula. I turned back west along the south side of Turnagain Arm, reaching the village of Hope, and was there given the advice to take the right fork of a gravel road up to the Resurrection Trail. I, of course, took the left fork. There is one other human here, and that is one too many.

The two of us have climbed to the second highest cirque of the U-shaped Palmer Lakes glacier valley twenty miles in. As the Alaskan land is wont, it goes from sea level to matterhorn in a matter of miles. Last night a solid freeze; thin-aired morning heats up quickly. All around is a symphony of falling rock clatter. The night was absolutely clear, with a thousand more stars than the saber-toothed tiger saw. The night itself shattered cold around the crest of the day.

And what a day: the sun swabs off the membranes of cloud through the valleys, which all morning have revealed and concealed towering spines, ribs, and gothic spires. As we climbed quickly up, the fresh sting of air was pure exhilaration. The number and pitch of rockfalls is various. I collect cacophonous jeuvenations: some slide with a rustle; some pluck themselves high-pitches like silk threads; some like caribou on trails; far above, on the shoulder of a matterhorn, is the deep rumble of death's hooves.

I cannot see them. They are too quick and camouflaged against their stiller cohorts. Even when the sound of stone houses rumbles down the mountainside, my head whips around and I am left with only a few susurrations of stone on a snowfield. I feel so tiny, a one-minute egg on the wall with billions of organisms laced together as "graywacke," the womb of the sea gone stone-cold and hard.

Small trails move up the canyon walls like shoelaces: back and forth, up from mine hole to mine hole, bleak enticing eyelets. We climb a half-mile up the steep wall on a road built to haul metal parts. My companion climbs back into one hole a quarter of a mile deep, despite a crumbling granite roof, in the belief that surely a railroad track could not be all wrong. I point out to him how long this hole has been defunct, at least thirty years, ten years before he was born. He has a keen instinct toward death, one of those individuals of our species who would fall to the wolves. He gobbles things out of tin packages or chain-smokes. I feed him healthy food, and he is mine forever.

He leaves me alone and goes back down the mountain.

Pika whistles pierce the air like auditory atl-atls. Mountainsides are zoned with strong paint-by-number patches: army yellow, deep green, brilliant blood red of a ground willow, snow patches catching the sun. Snow is scalloped in rhythmic depressions begun in the first day's melt: they glitter. Rock tracks spread evenly and parallel down each of them, as if raked by a ridged tongue. I remember bears and weasels sliding with joy on a glacier in the Olympics and smile. Castanets followed in their wake.

The critical-angle talus shivers straight up to undereaten cliffs. The cliff layers ripple upward to an unstable arête. I sit attached precariously to a bare hump of glacial-scraped rock, which rises straight up from a turquoise cyclops. To one side, a white artery pumps off the glacial lip 100 feet above me, pounds down to rock 300 feet below. It forms a stream through army camouflage caused by the green molasses of active solifluction. Vertical strips of yellow willow follow streams down through green drapes of the solifluction: gold metal ribbons holding up theater curtains. I examine half-inch-high forests: heathers, rough lichens in their myriad of dendritic and coral forms. A miniature world made of chartreuse leather.

To be solitary here is to become poignantly aware of the state we all arrive in, all leave in, and, in between, live in.

Clouds churn by in time-lapse motion. Snowfields float as flat shadowless shapes above the articulated jags of cliff walls. Leftovers from earlier times, they are trapezoids gone wild and unlikely.

If one were to cut a dress from them of red silk, one would have the dimensional form to fit exploding gases.

Air here is absolutely pure; it smells as it did before technology was born. Garrulous cumulus are boiling by, lightening and darkening the ragged sawtop. I freeze/roast/freeze/roast. The toothed gray arête could not look more lethal: a chart of the saber-toothed profit-and-loss cycles.

The serrated tops scrape slowly westward, or is it quickly? In whose time do I speak? The stone is leaping from its frozen torte. The gaseous whiteness is spiraling around the matterhorns in jerky time-lapse, the television's weather satellite pictures. The lichens in rubbery golf tees are funneling moisture downward, and one-sixteenth-inch orange television receptors are dropping white spores. Simultaneously, a last tectonic plate is crashing into the North American continent, pushing up Los Angeles into a suburb of Hope, Alaska. It is not clear whether pollution increases or decreases the drag.

In whose time am I here?

The iron element of humankind stands for a fraction of a second, a hurdy-gurdy operation, shiny new faucets, pipe joints rusting before one's eyes. The six-inch pipeline that once channeled a "Giant," the stream of water under pressure that could kill a man, lies in fragments: a snake who met a reptilophobe with a hoe. The sunrise on the gray lake filling a miner's hole slips through the coin slot from pewter to brilliant blue. Sunrise comes at six minutes past noon in these steep shadows. There is no lake as beautiful as a tarn, the lake at the origin of glaciers: still, pure, cathartic coin-shaped eyes of Earth, polished *ojos de tierra*, quicksilver potatoes in the morning, azure tunnels at noon, black shining eyelids in the evening, with pieces of moon stuck in them. Lonely up here at the beginning of Earth, of gaseous masses just this instant congealing. One has the immediate feeling of cascading through plasmic space over the sharp edges of cirques, alien, silent, and awesome.

I must return . . . back down to Hope for food, batteries, shower, company.

/ September 9:   Hope, Alaska

A local cafe is a town newspaper in three dimensions. The living tabloid I sit in is a narrow pink trailer, the locals' favorite. Hope, as do many of the small towns here in Alaska, has a vital sense of community. The morning's chit-chat before each one goes off to mining, carpentry, mechanical repairs, or correspondence school studies is not only an information exchange but is essential to the community organism, sort of a communal pep rally.

"They still trappin' bears up here? I entered every game lottery there was for $5.00 an area. Fish and Game keeps your money. Bet they make a mint. I didn't draw a single animal in the lottery, so I'm out a bunch."

I remember the conversation in non sequiturs because all such conversation exists in non sequiturs, like particles from space flying in

114

from places we who live in glass cloud chambers know little about.

"Yep, bear-baiting. Because of the Koreans and Asians . . . the gall bladder's an aphrodisiac to them. They'll pay 60 to 100 dollars for 'em. The claws'll bring in another 20. Meat just lies there and rots though, and those black bear are pretty good eatin'. Brown bear, all greasy like a wolverine. They jus' let it rot. Can always tell where they're trappin' too. Don't know why the Fish and Game don' smell it clear fifty miles away. They put out slop pails of rotten meat."

"Yeah, I remember when they made [moose] cow huntin' legal. The logic was 'some of 'em gonna die anyways,' why don't we just let some guys shoot 'em. Of course, that was wrong thinking. The ones that were dyin' were way th' hell out there in the bush, starvin'. The ones they shot were right down there by the road cuz they were the younguns that hadn't learned to hunt for themselves yet. So they not only cleaned out the cows, but the young strong part of the herd. Neither caribou or moose ever been seen in any number for years, and used to be that 20,000 be running through here in the spring and fall. So many they'd be grazing right in town."

"Yep. Reminds me of a really sick story my mom likes to tell. Well, she moves down here to the Kenai a long time ago, when I was born. She goes and has six children, all boys, of which she is really proud because they need a lot of men down here. Now my father has gone off to the Aleutian war where they cut off the Japanese supply line. They just kept comin' in waves and waves to get slaughtered; they'd rather die than be captured. It was really ugly. Meanwhile we concentrated the Aleutians and the Kodiak Island peoples in camps so that they got TB, and many never returned home. That was for their own safety. Finally my grandmother came down to visit and saw all of us kids at once for the first time."

"What'd she think?"

"She just huffed, 'War fodder!' and walked away. My mother's never forgiven her for that."

There is talk of a log cabin roof-raising on Tuesday. They all say sure, we'll come.

Hugh is a man of God who has successfully soldered together an ecological consciousness with a joyous way of life.

"God," he says of all the wrong hunting, "is holding everything in balance. Nature is a fine teacher," he twinkles, then quotes: "My children perish for a lack of knowledge."

"Well, why th' hell's He takin' so long to teach 'em?" quips another.

Then there is the story about the woman tourist (I'm sure for my benefit) who was so stubborn about her opinion and so determined she was on the road to Anchorage that she wouldn't listen to the locals.

"No?" she said, sure that they were messing with her mind, "I *know* that this is the road to Anchorage."

She drove right off the end of the campground road, which leads down into Turnagain Arm, to crash on the beach. Totaled her car. She came limping back to town to find a room and a tow truck. There is no tow truck in Hope.

High above the tidal flats of Hope is a yard so full of neck-high sedges and fireweed that buildings and old cars appear to be sinking into the earth. Two ancient trucks have the elegant lines of beluga whales: a burnt yellow 1938 Chevy and a 1940 fading red Chevy. Two malamutes, who would love to have my throat, lunge in a thin wire yard. I stoop low to knock at the back kitchen door of the sunken house, and Emma answers. Her voice is so low-key, it is as if I am an expected neighbor she has known for eighty years, come to borrow a cup of something. Emma herself is about 80, a handsome woman with hair swept back into a silky white bun.

Emma came here all alone on February 2, 1930, to be a nurse in the Anchorage hospital. A woman whose husband she had nursed invited her home to visit in the isolated peninsula seven miles across the way from Anchorage. No phones. No electricity. No plumbing. A boat came for her, and off they went over the wild tides of Turnagain Arm. She had no idea where she was going.

Once in the plain log cabin, she remembers, "All these young men came pouring out of the kitchen." She chose Carl. "Why Carl?" I ask. "He was the youngest," she answers with the deadpan logic of animal husbandry. They married in 1934.

Five-year-old Carl came to the Kenai Peninsula in 1913 from

drought-driven Texas. A man named Matson had appeared down
there with whole Mason jars just chock-full of gold. Then it was only
$16 an ounce, so a little pill box would do today at $340 an ounce.
They landed in Seward and had a two-day dog-sled ride over to Hope.
The sled that came for them had only three or four dogs, certainly not
enough to pull a whole family. Carl's aunt, a cripple, needed to ride.
His mother was in long skirts, and she would walk, then ride down
low to the ground where her skirts filled up with snow. They came
34 miles the first day to a roadhouse. Sort of. There weren't any real
roadhouses in those days. You would just stop at an old man's cabin
and he would be really glad to see you.

"How did you come to this beautiful piece of land?"

"Ol' Man Wolf, he came in 1895. He came up from Cripple
Creek."

"Colorado?" The connection sends chills through me. I did a lot of
time around Cripple Creek, absorbing the hardships, the stories of the
first miners, searching for metal rifle butts and whiskey bottles, enjoying the vivid ghost towns they left behind, storing up stories of their
sudden deaths. As a kid, I sort of expected to come up on a pit mine
and find the miner himself, gray and leathery, with pick still in hand.

"In 1914 Ol' Man Wolf sold us this here homestead he had. He
died and got buried back there just beyond the yard; that's where him
and my mom and dad are buried, right out there. Ol' Lady Wolf sold
us 160 acres for $300. The land used to extend down to the bay, in-
cluding where the Discovery Cafe [the pink trailer] is now."

Carl Clark fumbles through an archaeological pile of books and
magazines beside his chair to find a scrapbook, and I have time to look
around the living room. Frozen somewhere in the early '40s, there is
an intoxicating smell of molds and lives being lived. From the ceiling
hangs a single dusty polystyrene ball covered with satin and red
sequins on long pins. There are two sofas, both well-worn. One is
brown plaid, the other plain brown, that sort of stiff fuzzy material
that scratches, with the hand-crocheted afghan draped on it. Sunlight
barely makes it through the heavily draped window.

Carl Clark has found the scrapbook. His knotted hands thump the
pages in emphasis, as if to wake the dead. Faces as real as fresh bread

and buttons stare out glazed by the camera. Carl is saying:

"1946. The Ladies of Hope." Women stand clustered together in styles that do not look out of place today.

"1895 . . . oh . . . *this* is Charles Davis who flew planes during the war." I realize he means WWI.

"Back then," his hand thumps the picture of a younger self holding on to a Giant, "we didn't have Cats to bring down the dirt. We used hydraulics, which brought down water from three high creeks at 125 pounds per square inch. These were called Giants."

A sunrise. "This here is 1916, 1917. Can't remember." I smile at his sharpness of mind. I can't remember between a 1988 and a 1986 color transparency.

He shows me pictures of the mines where he worked. "I got my fingerprints on most of those rocks all around here," he grins.

"Used to be that you didn't need any money. No bureaucrats. Then all you had to have was money to dig your grave. The mine made money for two or three men and their families. But now you got all these pencil pushers and payments since we got statehood. I was against it, you know. Now you got the hospital to pay. Back then, if you was really hurt, you might get hauled all the way to Seward. You might just die."

On the wall behind his chair is a photograph of Carl with his arm around a moose, as casual as if it was his wife. "Who's that?" I ask.

"Oh, he were as loyal as a dog. He'd a-come running whenever I called and would follow me around like a pet." A pause.

"Then he died." For the first time, Mr. Clark seems genuinely to mourn. "Dogs chased him and his legs went out from under him on the ice, and blam! He went down so hard it broke up all his innards."

I move back into the kitchen, and Emma clears a small space for me on the linoleum. I don't put down my notebook: the accumulations of the ages, laminations of smoke and grease. Every nook and cranny is piled high with significance. Emma loads, chops, and carries her own wood for the immense six-burner cast iron stove with a warmer on top. "This is where I spend the winter," she gestures toward a high stool. Carl must have felt wonderful entering this kitchen of warm smells, busy importances, children, food and cooking on his returns from days alone out in the mines or in the forest, hunting.

I have been allowed by Carl to trespass into the past. He sits now oddly transformed, waiting for a trajectory from long ago to pass through on a beam. He moves in and out of his immediate presence, suddenly struck by a light beam from 1933. His face instantly animates.

I leave Hope and the Clarks, headed south and west for Captain Cook State Park. I am aware of a distinct difference in myself. My senses have changed profoundly in just one month of being alone. At first I am aware of it in eyesight, which has become keen, aware of slight movement. I am seeing far distances without the binoculars. Yet, physically, I see no better. I discern subtle patterns against pattern: a marmot no longer appears to be a rock.

The sense of smell is acute, even though my own body smells more and more like a wild animal. I smell for animals, for water, for fresh plants. The woods become odiferous codifications. And hearing, never very acute for me, awakens with the slightest rustle. A sense of *air pressure* allows me to know what the weather will do without looking up. Air temperature and moisture combine to press a topographical map directly onto my nervous system. As a myriad of unusual minerals in berries and mushrooms enters my tongue, the sense of taste is heightened. By avoiding the terrible crap America eats, which deadens the senses, taste buds are intensely aware of new subtlety, new tastes whose origins are untraceable yet wonderful.

The world has become vividly alive.

The day begins and ends, a great masterpiece. The night is essential with constellations and the aurora borealis.

In yet another roadhouse, I overhear the following:

If you shoot a moose and miss and the bullet hits Dead-Shot Annie's radiator instead because she's driving through the bush where she shouldn't ought to be, who is responsible?

Is the designated sober driver liable if his drunk passenger opens the door of the pickup at 50 mph to get in the back to take a leak, and falls out and gets a concussion?

Sign in restroom at Roadhouse Cafe:

PLEASE INFORM THE KITCHEN
WHEN YOU TAKE A SHOWER AND WHEN
YOU'RE THROUGH OR YOU MAY
FREEZE YOUR ASS AND BURN YOUR TITTIES.

/ September 11:   The Kenai Peninsula Continued; The Eagle Pondered

Before dawn, the cries of strange birds draw me down the steep mud cliff through thick brush to the waters of Captain Cook Inlet. I can almost see the giant wooden ships of the British creaking their way up this sound to Turnagain Arm, joyous in the prospect of the Northwest Passage. A slippery fine silt appears dangerous, so it is with head down that I flush a bird of prehistoric proportions: its wingspread shadow is over seven feet. The silent shadow has square wing tips with distinct digital feathers twitched separately for navigation. Not a sound: no swish of wing, no cry of distress, just a silver economy of movement.

Only by its wingtip could I recognize it as the bird of Zeus, the feathered embodiment of a god entering our temporal field as a VIP. The codified eagle has nine tail feathers, the number symbolizing decadence in Christianity. I am reminded of a passage in a book written by a woman living in the bush in the middle years of this century; she is worried about the survival of her small pet dog in the wilderness (Harbottle and Credeur 1966):

> We spend many rounds of ammunition trying to shoot eagles but they are an almost impossible target and we got very few. They are not protected by law in Canada as they are in the United States, but they are well protected by nature. They can fly very high and very fast. They have strong wings and claws and can swoop down and scoop up a small animal with lightning speed.

I have been crawling through thick bushes high above the water, trying to find my way out. Finally, the silty embankment extrudes my own shadow out along a tangled ridge to the sea. The beach is palpably black. Black black. As the sun hurtles over the ridge, each round black stone casts a shadow two and a half times its length, creating a staccato of tiny pyramids. A peregrine falcon penetrates the honied atmosphere like a bullet, also noiseless. As in walking through a di Chirico painting, all angles are odd, all shadows penetrate and discontinue.

Three birds fish far out on the water, their heads shaped like smooshed golf clubs. I walk quickly now, lost in eider thoughts, and fail to notice what is ahead. Suddenly, with muted mews, they all take off: two hundred gulls and the young eagles. I freeze, but it is too late. I have expended their energy needlessly. They rise screaming, and justifiably so: I have cost them the calorie value of several fish in their rising. Besides, it was so warm on their underwings. Curling down into a stump, I become part of the land. For twenty-five minutes my eyes strain toward the eider a quarter of a mile out. Slowly, diving, they return to shore. Big white circles around their eyes and beaks. The single male has a dark green, glowing head top and white eye plate. He rises standing on his tail, revealing a white belly, exercising his wings. Maybe, just maybe, they are spectacled eider, but for the white bellies (I have learned that color means little). Each time the angle of the sun changes, each seasonal change, a dark bird becomes light, a white bird dark. This huge and rarest of eiders usually appears on the shores of the Bering Sea and the Arctic Ocean. Yet there are the eye circles, reminiscent of spectacles, the ponderous skull, and the enlarged mandible. The range is wrong, but yet there is that magnificent shining green head.

Two hours in the curve of the stump. I watch, but again no better vantage. I must eat, so reluctantly I climb away from the beach. It is as from a romantic lover I part, barely able to tolerate a few moments away from my beloved's face. Jam down breakfast real quick, and back to the beach.

It is to a different beach that I return. The tide is out another half-mile, exposing tiny mesas on the mudflats. Three hundred shore birds pop in and out of the mud mesas and valleys: the huge dendritic drainage is a gourmet slime cafeteria. American and Eurasian widgeons flaunt their white speculums. Gadwalls suckle mud. Dowitchers poke and pluck.

What were at dawn glowing spheres floating above the horizon now reveal themselves as mere oil wells burning off natural gas. I preferred them when their mysterious form fired my imagination. As in a Ulesemann photograph of darkroom symmetry, white stones appearing to hover over and separate from the water surface have now become substantial white cliffs leading offshore in a horizontal spinal column. The opposite shore is ablaze with oil towers burning off natural gas. The sea itself appears to separate from itself at certain junctions, a choppy labyrinth of trapezoids. Oil wells glow like rocket liftoffs, silver to orange. The gas banners baste the majestic mountains with a line of dusky smog.

The omnivorous mud burps are fascinating: miniature mesas about six to ten inches high, evenly spaced, eighteen inches long. Rivers run between, forming perfectly even and efficient drainages, just as the mountains, on a larger scale, begin their rivers. Very very fine silt, the mud burps suck in foot or finger.

A crass red Dr. Pepper can draws my eye, and I drop to all fours just at the border of the mesas, reach out my left hand to grasp it, more than 4 feet out. I cannot. There is a huge sucking noise under me, and my right arm disappears suddenly up to its pit; I rock back violently on my haunches before I am trapped. Disgust. This organic mud-beast with the consistency of gelatin springs back to its exact original form before my arm disappeared. I am to learn more of its treachery later on.

To see, if I did, a spectacled eider is an honor. Back on the road I daydream, passing by labyrinths of gas pipes twisted in three dimensional mazes, like puzzles: megalithian Phillips Gas Processing Plant and Unocal Chemical companies, an ever-present reminder of this energy-rich state.

8

East/West Convergence

/ Ninilchik Russian Orthodox Church

Leaving Captain Cook State Park, I head south, the road taking me
the farthest west of any road in North America. Enticingly close to
Russia. In fact, Russian is blending itself smoothly here with Native
American and Anglo.

Our politicians are wont to divide Earth in exact lines, while
evolution is a continuum. The Kenai Peninsula is a link to those
steppingstones to Russia and to the biological hybrids in between.

The ferry leaves monthly for the Aleutians. I long to be on it.

The Aleutians are the birthplace of fierce gales, tidal waves, earthquakes, and vulcanism. They mark in a dotted line the edge of a tectonic plate, where the Pacific Plate pulled away from the Aleutian Arc
and sank. A rift with hot magma from the earth's interior rose like
steppingstones to the other half of the world. The wildlife grades
slowly into that of Asia. In fact, not only are American and Eurasian
species present, but unique species evolve where the two continents
meet and intermingle.

I would like to drop a friend of mine, a fine naturalist and writer,
blindfolded onto an Aleutian island, giving her no clue as to which

part of the world she now inhabits. I would supply her with an excellent tent, a lot of raingear, and a manual typewriter, but guide books would be out until she reached her conclusion. She would discover one clue when the song sparrow showed up larger and darker than its cousin in her backyard feeders. I would love to see her face when the first whiskered auklet winged by through the fog on its way to nest on the shores of Russia. She would observe the red-legged kitiwakes, who spend all their time at sea, nesting briefly nearby to produce more red-legged kitiwakes. The first morning, she would awaken to the tremendous bellows of a battle-scarred sea lion teaching his pup to swim.

That there is any wildlife left for her to observe is amazing, considering the plunder of long wars. Fortunately, President Taft protected these islands in 1913; pillage had increased to tragic proportions since 1869, when America purchased them. Yet the Aleutian peoples were not protected, dropping from 20,000 to 1,000 in less than a century. World War II brought 10,000 aliens to devastate the land. Ironically, the elements here killed more men than the fighting did.

On the way down to Homer there is a living, breathing Russian Orthodox church perched on the cliff above the old village of Ninilchik. There is no sign pointing to it, and I am forced to retrace my path three times before finding the right road. When I see the luminous pods of Russian Orthodoxy springing up out of Kenai soil, gold-plated and glowing against the dark gray sky, I am captivated by an ancient story of synthesis. The Russian Orthodox architecture is but a chapter in a continuous migration from Siberia and Asia begun so deep within prehistory that our collective memory has forgotten it. Diverse branches of human beings clasped here, finally, like fingers, on the Kenai. Originally home to the Denai'na Indians (Athapascan), and later to the Eskimo, the Kenai is still sparsely inhabited in roadless, scattered villages.

Ninilchik, an ancient fishing village, was here long before the Russians named it Ninilchik. Its inhabitants are tucked into the bay like ducks in the Ninilchik River. From the church, three hundred feet above the village on a cliff, one gazes down on the muddy river discharging sediments from deep within the Kenai. Up from the earth sprang peculiar forms: the bright green metal roof on three levels.

Three inverted seed pods in gold, the oldest and largest growing over the vestibule, crumbled. Each seed pod bears a cross with three bars, one with circles on the ends and the bottom rung always slanted. It makes our own seem so plain. Surely, these crosses carry more spores.

To the side of this colorful growth is a white picket fence. Within and overflowing it are many more such crosses, as if a plant had spread out an underground root system, a fairy ring in which that which has died is part of the living. Flowers grow wild, intermingled with such bones: the Oskolkoffs, the Coopers, the Steils, one Matson (perhaps related to Mr. Clark's Matson in Hope?). Many, many died in their thirties. There are many infants with no markers. Many died in their forties: a shorter life span for a harsh land. A Russian icon guards the grave of the reverend's wife. Here the Russian strain commingles with the motley biotechnics of Europe, those that migrated from the other world. The church is quite active and is still in use. Bright paint accretions ornament the walls, reflecting the chip shapes of the underlying paint: maps of the continents. Suddenly I find myself homesick for the beautiful adobe churches of New Mexico, replastered lovingly each year by the hands of an entire village.

/ September 12:   The Place Where Smoke Rises Out of Sand

On a sunny, wet day of intermittent showers and rainbows 18,347 years ago, several Siberian families were walking down the smoking beaches of a great peninsula. They knew that this was a power place because the smoke rose from seams jutting from the clay bluffs. It was a gentle peninsula, full of slumping sedimentary sea deposits and black rock one could gather in baskets and burn for warmth. The Denai'na had good reason to believe that they were the first men and women to come to this strange yet beautiful land of bays and roaring tides. No signs of people, no trails, just bears and mountain goats, moose and wolves in abundance.

Seeing great herds of caribou and moose grazing the moist land, feeling the warmth of the sun even in early winter, these first People passed by an extremely narrow arm of sea, into and out of which the tide pulsed with great velocity. Many years later, whites would call it Turnagain Arm. Blue glaciers hung overhead, and one almost reached down to the inlet. The Denai'na had to pass over treacherous mud that turned itself into jelly and swallowed a man whole in a matter of minutes. This was a supernatural land, energetic with water pouring up from the southwest, while great white snouts of ice poured down from the northeast. Greater mysteries were in store for the Denai'na.

When the Athapascans came down the last high hill above the southeastern tip of the peninsula, a deep narrow arm of sea reached far up into a land of steep ice beasts and ragged mountains, entirely different from the west side of the bay. This land was not gentle at all: humans would never live permanently in that white ice—not ever. At the tip of this land lay a long spit that curved four miles out like a dragon's tail.

If they brought livestock with them from Asia, the most appropriate would have been the dragon, long sought for its friendly assistance. (Unlike our European dragon, with its nasty appetite for virgins, the *Dragoni Asiatica* was beneficent.) Just a half-day's paddling across from the dragon tail's end lay a land carved of solid mountains, where ice spires hovered and spikes marched down to stand in the sea. The sea itself was elegant with fjords and dangerous currents.

The first Americans traveled northward to find that the long finger of sea ended in a braided stream milky with glacial flour; three hours walk above that was the snout of the ice beast. The Aleuts, the last wave of Native Americans to arrive, later were to name this place Kachemak, for the vast smoking beds of coal as far as the eye could see at the uppermost part of the bay.

Thousands of years later, along came wooden houses afloat on the seas and full of scratchy-tongued, drab-skinned, greedy men. Thus began the slaughter of sea otter to near extinction. The Athapascans were clever businessmen and became the intermediary between the Russians and the peoples of the interior, a nineteenth-century Arkansas Best Freight Company.

Yet no sooner had the Denai'na accepted the scratchy-tongue paste people than others began to come, these demanding furs to send to yet another people called "China." These new paste skins had other passions, which were inexplicable.

The English in 1890, who desired 400,000,000 tons of coal near the spit, also slaughtered whales with abandon. The Original American could not understand: they left the flesh to rot and used but one part of the great mammal. In 1907, those first Athapascans gazed upon yet another grand phenomenon: an iron beast charging down long parallel lines, devouring the black rock that smoked. John R. Bradley had discovered a commercial vein of bright yellow, malleable rock, and the quiet farming and fishing community waxed insane. This yellow metal caused great incoming waves of frantic Anglos to risk unbelievable torture at the hand of Mother Nature and the elements.

Another paste face, called by his fellows Homer Pennock, led a crazed batch of seventy-five individuals, calling themselves the Alaska Gold Mining Company, to winter on the spit in 1898. Casting aside the multisyllabic sacred names of the Athapascans, they named the shantytown Homer.

This is how I first view Homer Spit, as the Athapascans did: on foot, with deep awe. The sequin boa of lights out four-and-a-half miles accentuates its form at dusk. Across the bay, mountains so jagged and glaciers so immense that I am overwhelmed by the power of natural forces.

Today, the contemporary Athapascan still views some strange phenomena as he first enters Homer in a Datsun pickup. If he enters the Fish and Wildlife headquarters at the edge of town, he would see:

1. Boxes of dead sea birds being shipped to Madison, Wisconsin, to be examined for disease or toxins. Although they are dying in waves, he could tell them that it is only a natural fluctuation.
2. An older woman tourist is attempting to save the life of a mottled brown seabird who won't eat. She and her husband expend their energies to save a young bird who, as the Athapascan knows, is dying anyway. The abandoned-by-mother theory comes up, as urban human behavior is imposed on the bird population. The Athapascan shakes his head at such odd leaps. The young patient is a city gull; in other words, a flying garbage gob with feathers.

3. If he traveled up to Fort Richardson to visit friends on the army post near Anchorage, he would find them simmering in duck soup. He might observe pintail and mallards dropping dead by the hundreds right out of the skies. Without a gun! What eery powers these Anglos have. He would also see their bodies being shipped to Patuxent, Maryland, the heavy metal pollutant evaluation center, in order to determine why these birds are allergic to bomb sites.

4. He might also run into Poppie Benson of the Alaskan Maritime National Wildlife Refuge while she was busy shipping young kitiwakes from Kachemak back to Wisconsin. He could have told her, saving the government a lot of refrigerated postage, that there were too many born for the food supply this year: part of the natural waves of death that result from constant tinkering and subtle adjustments in Earth's delicate evolution-ary-balance machine.

5. If not entirely disgusted with civilization by now, or ready for lunch, the young Native American might be introduced to David Ward. David Ward has a lot of money to study the biology and ecology of black brants because they are game birds, useful to man. God forbid he should want to study something useless, like the fungi that tie life together. Ward wants to determine the impact of aircraft disturbances on waterfowl. The Anglo's science knows little about this smallest of goose, longest of flight; the Athapascan knows much more. He could say that it is most sensitive to the jostlings of man.

6. On a brighter note, the young man would find enlightenment in a verse by a young Homer resident on the wall of the Pratt Museum:

IF I WERE THE OCEAN
I WOULD CRASH AGAINST THE ROCKS
ON THE SAND. I WOULD WASH AWAY
THE ODD BITS AND PIECES AND WASH
UP THE NEW. I WOULD PROTECT THE
SEA CREATURES WITHIN ME. I
WOULD HELP STRANGE AND UNKNOWN

SEA LIFE LIVE AND GROW. I WOULD
FEED ALL SEA LIFE FROM THE THINGS
THAT WERE WITHIN ME.
Erika Bury, April 1980
Second Grader at East Homer
Elementary School

/ September 14: Homer Spit

Still dreaming, I come to consciousness surrounded by the slap of
water. Last night, water dreams came. In a clunky canoe, I repeatedly
sank into a kettle lake on a glacier in an enclosed room (Earth). This
lake was very, very deep, more like a bottomless tarn in a rocky cleft.
Underneath, the original sources for the Loch Ness monster kept on
conjuring themselves from a deep memory soup. Terrified, I plunged
onto a rock to empty the canoe, but it only filled again and again. I
relived a moment of 1980, when the Chama River caught me in a
whirlpool and pinned me under an overhang of rock—underwater.
Slowly, slowly, rolling with the water, I am strangling a fellow art
critic in a former life who maligned me. Rough seas.

I wake up exhausted. A crisp, cool morning spreads out silver
across the bay; I slowly feel out where I am: camped on Homer Spit.
A bald eagle sits not twenty yards from me, shoulders humped, as if
he is as yet uncertain about the day. Sore throat, achy all over: at least
I know the cause of the dreaming, although not the content. I stay in
bed and finish John Muir's *Travels in Alaska*, just where he goes sailing
up dangerous fjords in a tiny Native American craft with gigantic glaciers calving all around in earthquake-size splashes. No more Muir
before bedtime.

Fog rolls back in. I run up the west side of Kachemak Bay, twenty
miles in, to the recent settlements of Russians fleeing religious oppres-
sion in the 1980s. They remind me in dress, simplicity and shyness of
the Amish in Iowa. Two young mothers in McDonald's clothe their
cherub babies in white bonnets and pinafores. They themselves tie

their hair strictly back, wear crisp pin-striped smock-dresses, white hair covers, and opaque stockings, and could be no more than seventeen years old. Bearded, wooly fishermen cannot keep their eyes off such fragile purity.

Suddenly, the fog lifts its graceful skirts, and I see mighty glaciers across the bay. Their snouts come down overhangs, breaking up, with giant crevasses the size of skyscrapers. Thirty or more of them all begin in the Harding Ice Field, which could be more than a mile of ice built up over the last four ice ages. Science has not yet the tools to measure it, although it has tried. The glaciers come rumbling and chiseling through the Kenai Mountains. Quickly, all is hidden again; clouds slink in, wet-tongued, up to the top of the bay, all this private land, all these pure Russian beliefs. I am afraid suddenly, but I don't know why.

At the head of the bay, the flat willow marsh, a sluggish attempt of the land to rise from the sea. According to the map, the swamp should not begin so soon, but the bay is filling. The sandblasting company that cleans thousands of ships a year dumps many tons of sand and paint into the center of the bay.

Sun condenses. Liquid silver on the surface of the water. Overhead, rapid cumulus backlit, bright swirling gases. The sun again wins, reveals a water-soaked gleaming earth against the effervescent mountain scrim. Glaciers recede so rapidly that purple swatches of topographical lines mark the decade's sudden retreat on maps of the Kenai. A chaos of erratic boulders are left sitting large on the gleaming clay: the memory of the Dinglestadt Glacier, named for a Russian furrier of 1834 who first explored west Kenai.

I don't feel well. I must work in response to the weather, keeping myself warm and dry. Yet up here, that is the essence. Up here, the mind must remain flexible in response to the land. If not, in the struggle of human idiosyncratic will and nature, nature will win. Yet, in that very lack of control one is most joyous. A total freedom from those artificial restrictions of mankind allows a genuine response to the present. To what is real.

The clouds reveal deep canyons filled entirely with ice, so that the range appears flat. Only the jagged matterhorns and suggested semicircles of cirques indicate underlying stone. Glaciers break up in waves across the steep drops of vertical valleys. Between 1963 and 1985, the southern exposed glaciers, like the Yalik, have slunk backwards several miles. Where they retreat, the ice becomes hard and black, a dark rubble. A dense water crystal, hard as stone.

The oddest phenomena are the sink holes around each dark peak. Each miniature peak holds its own Hula Hoop of circular crater, and I imagine sliding down into one, all alone to explore its depths.

If I had wings like Noah's dove
I'd fly up the glacier to the one I love,
Fare thee well, oh honey, fare thee well.

Many glaciers end in water and mud, filling up their own channels with debris, much like a sick person fills his bedside night table with dishes and magazines and medicine bottles. Dixon Glacier ends in a deep dark blue fjord with its tidy band of moutonne under its lip. These slick lumps of muscular stone are scraped bare, still devoid of growth. Here I am reminded first of the preliminary stages of moss, high on the Haul Road, and the second stages in the Washington Olympics, high in the Bailey Range. Third, the lushness of Colorado's glaciated terrain, so covered now with vegetation as not to pay proper homage to its glaciated beginnings. Then I remember a high northern road in New Mexico, still with its moutonnes crowded with sheep and mushrooms, fungi one of the first to reclaim the earth.

And finally Iowa, with its four glacial stages, each older one successively softer and softer until the moraines and moutonnes, the kame terraces and kettle lakes, and long snaky eskers and eradics are translated into low rich fertile farm soil. Nothing remembered, unless one digs down to the ill-sorted material or bows low to an isolated mammoth buried deep in one's field.

A varied thrush startles me out of my gazing: one pure long melodic note, standing out like a smooth tarn of sound against the noisy grists of ice.

THE FISHERWOMAN OF KACHEMAK

On the way back I pick up a young woman in heavy work clothes, heavy and very strong, cheeks flushed in patches of red against white skin, long skeins of mahogany hair. She has been here for four years. She rolls her Rs like fish roll in the waves. Already she has become a fisherwoman. She also knows all about the new Orthodox settlers, and I can hardly wait to listen to her lyrical voice, but we stop to jump-start an ancient pickup for a young worn-out man. It turns out to be his starter motor, so we go on. "There are three new Russian communities here," she tells me. "They believed so deeply in their old Russian Orthodox religion that they left Russia and marched all the way across China, and Oregon, and finally here to freedom. Many of them are fishermen and compete with us. They are good farmers. They work very hard.

"I came here after school. I love it here, but there wasn't anything to do. No jobs. I wasn't able to do anything. Worked in a cannery. Six dollars an hour is considered good, but it is so repetitious. Doing one little bit of work over and over and over again. For three years I worked in the cannery for the six weeks there was work for 14 to 16 hours a day. But surely, there must be more to life than this.

"So I went out, up and down the docks every day, to get hired on. It is very competitive, and they don't hire women too often. It is very hard, dangerous work. But I finally found this guy who looked at me and saw I was hardy, and decided to give me a trial period. It was real hard. The halibut can weigh up to 300 pounds, and you've gotta pull him on board, wrestle him down and then gut him.

"The salmon hooks on a sinker line go flying by you and can pull you in and sink you in a moment. Then there is pulling in heavy nets full of fish, all by hand. We often cross other lines and they get cut.

"There was just a Halibut Open for twenty-four hours, so that you fish very hard and very fast in dangerous seas. We lost over half our gear this week during it, so we are going back out soon to recover it and other people's. I proved myself against an old prejudice against women. 'Even if one can handle fish, she just don't belong out there.' I did get hooked on a salmon line the first year, but didn't get dragged over. I've been a zombie for three days now after that twenty-four-hour push, and all the prep work before it. Now I'm going in to repair the nets, and then we'll go back out to the Barren Islands."

The Barren Islands, contrary to their name, are full of birds and sea mammals.

"Yeah, there are a lot of birds out there, but we don't notice 'em much. Things happen real fast up here. You got to pay attention. A friend of mine worked real hard all summer and made a bunch of money to sit well all winter. But then he went and got an idea to set up a halibut-fishing operation. Many many problems came up and he went from well off ($421,000) to broke in two weeks. You learn to roll with things up here."

/ September 15:   Skilak Lake

Predawn. Skilak Lake is a long squirrel tail of water in the middle of the Kenai Peninsula. Air temperature 27 degrees. Water 44 degrees. I was about to immerse a Canada Dry jug to cool it down, but would have warmed it by 17 degrees. For a while I do not move from my bag but prop up my head to watch light seep into the lake. A kingfisher chatters loudly, piercing the loose scrolls of clouds that lie, cool brush strokes, on the water surface up many narrow channels of this clogged glacial basin. One chilling note of a varied thrush out in the deciduous wood and down through my bone marrow. A most vascular song.

Clouds now feather during a perceptible warming, feather boas on low bluffs. The lake itself is breathing pastels. Last night the water was so clear that I could follow each island down to its base, but now it is pearly opaque. Several billion stars cast into it last night. Huge-leaved tropical bushes with 12-inch shiny green leaves turn out to be young *Populus trichocarp*, black cottonwood. Sunlight creeps, cobble by cobble, up the bank toward the end of my frost-covered bag. The thermometer is balanced at the sharp edge of dawn and damp shadow. It is still freezing there.

Suddenly dawn. The orange light hits the thermometer, which leaps from freezing to 50 degrees in seven seconds. Fog is extricating

133

itself from the water surface within minutes; the lake changes from the washes of Chinese scroll painting to the crisp realities of fish. Here, on the Kenai, Sitka alder bristle with toothed leaves. Once there were many, many mountain goats. Still in my bag, I lie reading the paper my fish dinner came wrapped in, *The Homer News*, Thursday, September 8, 1988 (name of journalist burned in campfire):

> . . . Economics is the bottom line of their argument. In late 1987, the Department of Fish and Game released an economic analysis of sport-fishing in Southcentral Alaska. The exhaustive study, done by a Sacramento, Calif., economics consultant considered to be among the best in the field, surveyed thousands of resident and visiting anglers and determined how much they spend on fishing—$127 million in 1986.
>
> The Kenai River is the major attraction in Southcentral and over $38 million was spent that year on fishing the river's salmon and trout. Included in that figure is the cost of flying to Alaska from Outside, rental cars, lodging, eating and drinking, guides, boat repairs, salmon eggs, waders and all the other goods and services.

I love the capitalization of "Outside," as if it were another country— which, of course, it is.

The article goes on and on with its economic analysis balancing act: so many pressures on the fish. It tells me that sportfishing here is big business, but that it is being squeezed heavily by other commercial concerns. As if to illustrate, there is a commotion; I thought I had been alone. Nearby a large creaking, than a splash. A single fisherman launches his boat. He looks tired, urban-weary and old, but as he floats farther out through a water-laden air he becomes a painting of himself, a singular soul passing through a beautiful time in a beautiful place.

EVENING: HIDDEN LAKE, SKILAK RESERVE

Again, odd phenomena fill my disbelieving senses: this tiny lake is packed with bright red salmon waiting to die. Red salmon, along with humpbacks, are the most common in Alaska. There are more fish than water. The brilliant red they turn is almost phosphorescent and is characteristic of brackish fresh water. It indicates the enzymes have begun turning fat, protein, ash, and water back into volatile chemicals, which already reach my nose before the fish have died. Fish flesh, or albuminous substance, standing in these warm lakes, is quickly broken down by a multitude of bacteria. Each unique bacterium has its particular job: some to the gaseous products, some to the volatile acids, some for the aromatic acids, amines, phenol, indol, skatol, ptomaines and those other products that tweak the nose. It is odd; I try to consider where the edge of life is. These fish are not yet dead, but they smell dead.

Whenever I walk near the water, 600 fish jump, flop, and splatter, a solid frantic fish flesh. Lime-green fungus grows over their hooked noses. No carrion-eaters fill the sky: they aren't even good for those death-sweepers when this far gone: no protein left. They have not eaten for weeks, since they left the ocean. The stench soon will be unbearable, but for tonight I want to sleep next to them.

Today I walked a precarious trail along a 300-foot cliff edge above the box canyon of the upper Kenai River. The bright turquoise water was covered with mergansers. Red heads flashing, they fished in swift rapids far below. At more than 200 species of fungi, I lost track counting.

I crawled over the wild riverbank, finding stinking red fish in each eddy. Deep orange with bright chartreuse fungus growing on their skin, they squirmed in azure eddies too weak to swim. Gelatinous red to burgundy, hunchbacks with malformed exaggerated humps, they glowed translucent, banging the water in the face of death.

There is a ceremony among African tribesmen to cure someone whose soul has been lost to the bush ("insane"). The first part of the ceremony is filled with people and ritual and support, blood and power and chants. The second part of the ceremony is held off for a number of months until the individual is strong enough to face himself in isolation. He is put out all alone with the spirits of nature and Earth. It is only through this power of introversion that he becomes related to the forces that assist in his making a realistic, comprehensive alignment with nature. Therapy, for us, is seen in terms of fitting one in as a productive unit in a sick society; one forgets the simple act of seeing.

/ September 16:   Palmer Lakes Basin

This morning, a dramatic howling of wind. Clouds down on the earth
cover all. I have forgotten momentarily, when I wake up, where it is I
have slept. Every once in a while clouds lift a skirt here or there to
reveal cascades pouring out of snowfields all around. From this distance, the water appears absolutely still, a piece of twisted shining
metal. Steep-angled trails climb straight up over a lip of the mountain
wall. Coming awake, I remember there may be a caribou up here.

I lie longer to absorb the cacophony of sound: chafing air, boiling
cloud, falling rock. The rain on the canopy explodes rhythmically.
Somewhere, I fall again into unconsciousness, rain confused with the
inner ear.

The wind wakes me again. Last night the heavy Coleman refrigerator ripped from my arms and flipped on the ground. In the dark,
food remains spread all over. Lost two eggs and their polystyrene
house. Picked most of it up so animals would not come, but missed
some. This morning, on top of a deep gray boulder, a red sphere of
tomato with a bright green stem looks as absurd as it does handsome.

As clouds lift, fall sneaks downward. In the one week I was south
on the Kenai, Palmer Lakes Basin has turned brilliant with color. All
morning I write with clouds pegging me in, then with a crisp tease
of sky. I eat quickly: egg, cheese, bruised tomato, smoked salmon;
then charge straight up a waterfall bed that ran with water just this
morning.

This steep graywacke ladder I climb glistens; its moss is sodden.
The climb is simple, with good hand and foot holds, steep stairs up
the waterfall, but I do not look down. Then I head north over lush
south-facing tundra, cross-country, until I meet a tenuous snowfield.
A crick tumbles under the snow arch, and I imagine sliding down
through it, coming out the bottom osterized.

An Athapascan legend tells of a man, tired of his wife, who sent
her down through a roaring river under the glacier for miles. She
popped out, bright and clean, to haunt him forever. The water is as
cold as snow, only liquid by some sheer quirk of nature. The implied
moral makes me more tenacious, and I cross the snowfield.

The glacier basin is growing more and more intense by the moment. It begins in kames and kettle lakes, the entire floor dropping away in small humps, each larger than a three-story house. My pickup is the size of a black crowberry, shiny with rain. The tops of all kame terraces are bright red with bearberry leaves. Pale greens and yellows cascade down to dark green mosses standing in water. Through translucent jades one sees the bottom of the earth. A silt smooths their light-colored bottoms with glacial flour. Water has uncanny clarity.

I am as one seeing water for the very first time: as the first woman born beside the very first lake, a million tiny hair roots ripping free as she rises, her feet a thousand tiny rabbits moving, breaking open the first seeds like miniature planets full of life. Air aerates my cerebral cortex in such a manner as to dissolve the world. As I pop over the lip of the cirque, now 1,000 feet higher, I am treated to a sight of the hidden glacial cup I could not see from below. Mountain-climbing is essential with surprises that way. Mountain-climbing is the process of constant revelation of those things higher. The perfect circumvention, the glacial cradle, the ragged peaks of matterhorns rudely sliced in half, as one slices the clay bowl still wet on the potter's wheel to examine its form. All the rest, where the glacier carved down, is muscular shoulder and buttocks, gluteus maximus at its maximum.

Water pours in silver scales across as yet unchanneled purple rock. As I continue to rise, I discover more corpuscular stone. With me is my mechanical eye for recording what I can't remember. The storm suddenly sucks light from its meter.

The talus slope is straight up now, highly unstable. I move on slim benches, placing my feet in pockets of moss. Immensely enjoying my mind at work, I watch it stumble and fold itself around new forms. Mountains unfold slowly through time, a verticality awash with fog. At foot, deep purple/black gentians unfurl their petals.

Feltwort glows black in the bog near the gentians. Leaves of the wood nymph, the dwarf hesperochirons, and mountain avens tease me with no bloom. The luetkea crouches down near the stream.

I continue straight up, losing the flowers but gaining a beautiful pale green lichen amid the moss: miniature jungles of Africa, a sketch for them begun in tundra, as if nature practiced here first her internal engineering principles before daring with great scale. Little People Bushmen. Miniature willows bright yellow and orange flap like surveyors' ribbon the dark crowberry. A mound of slimy black shit, the consistency of soft butter, shines iridescent like black pearls: somebody's crowberry feast.

Normal size gives way to microcosm/macrocosm size. Unearthly tundra glows silver against red against ghost whites, while the sky is darkly overcast. The eye of the storm pins me wriggling on a giant spindle.

I keep one eye scanning clouds. They stick their bellies down over peaks and flow with water's rapidity over arêtes, swirling back around on themselves like breakers in a slow-motion ocean. Up over the lip of the first cirque the wind is howling. I force my way into it, as well as upward. The first basin is filled with pink algae in the snow, scalloped and regular. My tongue is watching; I have finished off the water bottle, but know better than to eat this snow. It is forty degrees with a steady wind-chill factor, but I am overheated with exertion.

Then I see it!

I freeze.

Fear wells up in my esophagus like half-regurgitated food.

I freeze. An animal instinct of camouflage, as if I could be invisible. So as not to be heard, I am not breathing. On the most perfect of snowfields, an orange shroud flaps violently in the wind. It could be a tent and, judging by the shape within, a hunter's body. Lying down, he fell asleep in exhaustion and now sleeps forever. I skirt around it, half a mile away, and up the edge of the rockfall. Its bright orange nylon beats the ground like a hummingbird heart of huge proportions.

I now pretend to be a giant—not of size, but of time. Watching these surroundings by years, as years become seconds exploding forms of snowfields, exploding forms through time-lapse time, my life-span a mere fraction of a fraction of a nanosecond. I watch the forms frantically pace themselves through evolution. They are so natural in their changes. I watch the dog and the bear diverge from the same lineage and woof themselves apart. Everything makes perfect sense: no Darwin or Stephen Jay Gould to explain it to me. Then enters *deus ex machina*, no, excuse me, it is rather *homo ex machina*, the antichrist.

Everything stops. Time stops.

I head around the top of the cirque as high as I can without falling on falling talus, then come back down. Another 200 feet and I will summit out: it is so enticing, but clouds are stuck on the earth now and the wind blows. I must go down. *Now.* As I turn back, there in front of me, right in the path, is the terrible Orange Thing. I traverse the spongy tundra, which sounds like Velcro tearing off the surface of stone. I have been watching my feet and suddenly look up. There is the Orange Thing, a snowfield aflame with my terror, a bad vision. Nervous as a horse in a mountain lion's vicinity, I force-feed my eyes into the binoculars. An inordinate fear of dead bodies. I must look at it or veer far to the right and drop straight down over slick black rock without the benefit of stairs. I go toward it. A book-shaped weight holds it down. Every muscle on my skeleton is tightly wound. Fear invades me like a convulsion; it enters my brain like a chemical, re-leases adrenaline. I am sure it will spring up to feed on me. I have more fears out here than in any other wilderness, but justifiably so. This is unadulterated Earth before humans came. I am not a dispro-portionately fearful person, or I would not be here. I wonder if men experience the same sort of fear. No, yes, no, yes. They just call it by other names. It is the stuff their dragons are made of. Reading of John Muir traipsing his night glacial crevasses shames me. Some fears are appropriate, like fear of bear or fear of falling alone. Or of exposure. Or of disorientation. Such fears serve me well, to keep me safe. But this strange orange concoction! What sort of fear is this?

The Orange Thing slaps loudly in the wind. I go toward it, my head down, my heart in my throat. I go toward it inch by inch. It *has* been mauled by a bear. The lump within, though, is in boxes. Inedible equipment! I breathe again. Finally relax. Fear has blocked my aware-ness of my needs. One by one they come out. Down through the felt-wort, the arrow leaf, groundsel, trapper's tea, Rocky Mountain rock mat, vervain, explorer's gentian, Pacific silver fir, halberd willow, cinquefoil, Sitka mountain ash, cow parsnip, devil's club, orange poria slime mold, and the shrieks of pikas. A wallowy huge black marmot with two yellowish white streaks curving up its sides like Nike running shoes is no marmot at all. I am right close to a wolverine, a nasty ill-tempered wolverine. I am too tired to be scared. The gentians have teeth, for all I feel.

I sleep soundly and awake fully rested. I dream only that I was a giant with the huge voice of time. Giants speak too slowly to be heard by human ears. They are felt only as immensely low Earth moans, right before an earthquake happens, or as the prolonged chatter of crashing tectonic plates or the higher-pitched aurora's crackling in space. The sound of my own howl as it is bellowed back from moon, for no song goes unanswered.

9

In Which Winter Strikes
and I Am Entirely Surprised

/ September 22:   Healy, Alaska

This morning, a layer of white all around. Winter has arrived. Body
joints and back ache. I feel a slowing down. My self-image changes
from that of a free-spirited, infinitely energied person to that of an
older woman, a thing less valued, a thing that likes to lie still and
quiet, reading copiously. The heavy overcast sky is reflected back to
me in my face in the truck mirror. I drive to the Totem Restaurant to
be inside and arrive with the earliest hunters and truckers. They stare
at me as if a Dall sheep had walked in. Over coffee, I ritually prepare
myself to enter one of the greatest wildlife and natural areas preserved
on the planet: Denali National Park, a state of mind.

Denali embodies one of the most dramatic changes in land ownership in this country's history. Not only did massive amounts of federal land change to state ownership as a result of the Alaskan Statehood
Act, but large amounts are returning to Native American ownership
under terms of the American Native Claims Settlement Act (ANCSA).
The lands remaining federal are undergoing an important conceptual
change, from general public domain holdings (i.e., any president or

Congress can allow special interest industries to strip the public domain of resources at any time they see fit) into reserves for long-term purposes: national parks and wildlife refuges.

The exact definition of the greatest good for the greatest number of people is in sore need of clarification, not just for the United States but for the world. Even the "of people" I find vulgarly species-specific. Alaska has some of the most substantial amounts of roadless wilderness on the planet. When the first 16 million acres of National Forest (the Tongass in southeastern Alaska) were put aside in 1902, the federal government later had to reimburse the Tlingit and the Haida $7.5 million for their land. Around 1900, conservationist sentiments surfaced, based on the idea that resources are not inexhaustible. President Theodore Roosevelt's chief forester, Gifford Pinchot, demonstrated great foresight, foresight that government seems to lack now, in the time of population explosion. The resultant national public lands held in the forty-ninth state, in addition to those in the National Park system, include specific use lands, such as:

National Wildlife Refuges

	Acres
Aleutian Islands:	2,720,000
Nunivak Island:	1,109,500
Kenai National Moose Range:	1,730,000
Kodiak Island:	1,820,000
Clarence Rhodes:	8,900,000
Reindeer Stations	
St. Lawrence Island:	1,205,000
Military (Pet 4)	23,029,000
Water Power Withdrawals	
Rampart Project:	8,956,000

DENALI: THE GREAT ONE

Originally named by the Athapascans, Denali (The Great One) looms over the entire wildlife preserve and national park. The name McKinley has now changed back to the original. Late in the day and in a solid snowstorm, I enter 6,400 square miles of unspoiled land. To the northwest are the Kuskokwim Mountains, older and more colorful with sediments than the Alaskan Range. I drive (for at this slim two-week window, one is allowed to drive one's own vehicle) along the Toklat River through the Kantishna foothills. Bus travel is the normal mode here, as it is less disruptive to wildlife. These northerly mountains are gentler, sedimentary layers of the original continent.

/ September 24:   Igloo Campground

I can see nothing out. Earlier, a stunning fox in cross stage: browns, whites and reds ending in the precise black tip of tail. A young environmental analyst from Denver is traveling all over by himself for six months after quitting his job, terribly disillusioned. I befriend him because we are the only two still camped out here, and I want to tell him of the huge pile of bear shit beside my truck this morning.

Steve Merritt, for that is his name, is following the call of Farley Mowat's *A Whale for the Killing*, and will most likely end up in Newfoundland if his Toyota holds out. He shows me this scrap of Mowat's writing:

> Being a people to whom adversity was natural, they had retained a remarkable capacity for tolerance of other human beings, together with qualities of generosity toward one another and toward strangers in their midst which surpassed anything I had ever known before except, perhaps, among the Eskimos. They were the best of people, and I promised myself that one day I would come and live among them and escape from the increasing mechanistic mainland world with its March Hare preoccupation with witless production for mindless consumption; its disruptive infatuation with change for its own sake; its idiot dedication to the bitch goddess, Progress.

One could do worse than to follow Mowat; I follow Muir myself (and Thoreau and Rachel Carson), and he lets me have it. "So you want wilderness," Muir says to me, "try on this thunderstorm on top of a pine tree for size." More important, I need to try his political activism.

Park regulations, which I follow more rigorously than any set of laws, seem to me to be rose-colored lenses, predigested experience through which one must view animals. But I am being stupid and stubborn. Even the guidebook here by Kim Heacox is a fine piece of literature. It does not merely point but helps one feel. Still I resist. These regulations, which I believe in but have some resistance to, are expertly executed here in Denali. What is it in a regulation that forms a scrim between myself and the original experience? Nothing. Regulations actually serve to intensify it, because they are elegant designs for humans and wildlife to converge in wild situations.

Steve is awed by the golden eagles. In spite of extensive backpacking in Colorado, he seldom sees them. Here they fly, followed by an entourage of disgruntled ravens, charred ladies in waiting. I give him my large glasses: on the southern border of New Mexico it is still wild enough to see them, but too late in Colorado. After two days of being entirely socked in, the sky opens up astringent blue, smelling of the high dry mountains. We see marsh hawks, merlins, our first gyrfalcon. Spruce grouse with bright red combs above each eye pose for us. A dusk drive reveals a wolverine, a grizzly and her two first-year cubs grazing nonchalantly within thirty feet of our vehicle. We sit in stunned silence.

In front of us, a row of photographers out in the road with immense tripods click away with an abundance of equipment. I was at once impressed with the ease of unspoken communication between strangers, and with the oblivious stupidity of those who stayed outside their vehicles so close to the cubs. One young Japanese photographer in particular went toward the bears in a bold manner, as if she were doing fashion photography. I half-expected her to wave her hand and say, "More fur, dear! Show more fur. Now the hump . . . pivot, not like that, more like *this*." Anything could trigger the bear's maternal protection instinct. I wanted to warn her, but there was no way I was going to leave my vehicle, and shouting might upset the bears. Seeing someone ripped to shreds would ruin my day. Worse, the mother bear would be destroyed. Fortunately, just as I was getting up my courage to do battle with this blatant anthropocentrism, a female park ranger drove up and gave the Japanese woman holy hell. Instantly, I felt deep gratitude for rules and regulations.

On all fours, the mother grizzly would measure up to my chest; the cubs, thirty inches at the shoulders. They eat constantly, nibbling sparse remains of willow buds and invisible food within the grasses. It seems it would take forever to build up that much fat with such a proportionately tiny food unit. Park personnel have done a superb job in keeping the bears wild here. Their hardest animal to educate: people.

We are supplied with house-sized metal locking sheds for our food at the campsite. Even toothpaste and soap go in. Still, my truck is full of lovely smells of cooking and I sleep lightly down by the river. The next morning there is an enormous pile of berry-textured shit on the narrow path past the driver's door: a calling card, a reminder of whose house this is. A ranger arrives, casually kicking the slimy pile open, and says, "Oh, that's just *dog*. Nothing to worry about," and then launches into her standard bear lecture. If that's dog, it weighs 200 pounds.

I remember keenly the doglike muzzles of the bears and the enormous claws. The hump on her back is all muscle from digging. They wave their heads from side to side constantly: it is a blurry visual soup they live in, but one of distinct olfactory edges. I wish I could know how she perceives our substantial row of seventeen human bodies; we stand so still and make no sound but the crisp clicking of cameras. To her it must smell like a wall of electrified olfactory chainlink, passive unless poked, blackened urban-soiled spikes, a putrefaction of flesh decorated with the tinsel of deodorants and perfumes, the sequins of makeup and cream rinse, an occasional flower of cordon bleu or a black orchid fart. Her cubs have no fear of this wall and head right toward it: their world consists of such walls, either in groups along the highway or in single rangers of smell. She herds them sideways with deft movement. How is she to train them, these youngsters for whom there is no adverse sting from human?

/ September 25:   Teklaneeta River, Denali

8:09 a.m.: Entirely enclosed in white. Twenty degrees out. Snowing at a goodly rate in doily-size flakes. Climbing stiffly out of the back of the truck, I open the refrigerator to let in the cold, then walk down to the edge of the earth.

There, along the rocky river channel of the Teklaneeta, predawn smells of tracks and mysteries. I can't quite grasp what I smell. I smell the river, a wild animal, and winter coming. Clouds, like a papyrus basket, contain and float at once. They begin to singe with pink diffuse light.

There!

Wolf tracks along the opposite edge of the river where I thought I had seen him the night before. Beyond the gentle gurgle of a river confused by its own channel, silence.

Sun pierces through on a parabolic curve from another dimension. Later, Steve is up. We decide to go on a long hike up the Toklat River on the west side of Pendleton Mountain. There, we see and hear for the first time one of those power-phenomena one's senses do not believe:

We walked along, deeply engrossed, arguing environmental ethics, unaware of our surroundings. Suddenly, the sound of locomotive engines roared toward us. Bearing down. Bearing down. I looked for earth moving, an earthquake, but the land did not move. The two of us watched in awe as a 9-foot wall of steel gray water came toward us down the dry river channel. So bizarre: the beginning snout of a river, a freight train coming out of a fireplace, roaring down. Instantly I understood a braided river: the water stumbles to find its channel, searching here and there, and then turns suddenly, unsure of itself despite great momentum. Surges thrust against bulldozed wreckage of the last stream and the piles of hard wind-driven snow.

Never as in the far north have I seen the forces of wind, water, and ice so turbulently visible, changing instantly from one force to another and back. The chocolate water devouring the snowcrust in odd ways, carving it back in scallops, leaving Henry Moores or the muscular fragments of Michelangelo hovering unlikely above the churning. We stood as two toddlers, eyes wide in awe, watching an event we had never seen before, with no adult to explain it to us, cradled in a trust that this too shall be explained, pinned down, dissected with the dull blade of language.

That was yesterday. Today at dawn on the Teklaneeta River: bright sparks of snow burn holes in the air. I love this cold!

River rocks here are beautiful, varied nuggets of Earth history; I am awed. The jeweler: the seven to eight geological eras each contains. Plate tectonics. The flysch and melange of mountain ranges.

The northern slope of the Alaskan Range is one of the most abrupt slopes *in the world*, rising from the plain at 2,300 feet to more than 20,000 feet in a matter of miles. The perennial snowline on the north flank is at 7,000 feet. Many glaciers go below 4,000 feet. Rocks from this range include undifferentiated Paleozoic fossils several thousand feet thick and composed of alternating layers of black slate and argillate, graywacke and quartzite in varying degrees of schistosity (squished together under great heat and pressure). Intermingled with these rocks are some hard siliceous conglomerates, thin-bedded black limestones, and, in places, black or gray limestone beds that reach a thickness of thirty feet. All these rocks are abundantly seamed with quartz veins or reticulated veinlets of calcite.

The sandstone is cross-bedded, indicating dunes. Near the upper Toklat there are stocks and sills of greenstone, which are now distributed at my feet as polished green "jades," often cross-cut and ovaled by white and blue chert. Birch Creek schist forms beautiful river rocks. In jet black stone, sudden flecks of red could be jasper. Capturing these polished stones, have I landed on another planet?

7:46 p.m. 28 degrees. Another cold one.

Again down to the river at dusk to watch the wildlife. Just hunker down and watch. 8:15; 25 degrees. Steve keeps thinking of things to yell at me from the back of his pickup, where he is warmly bedded down. I wonder if I should go sit on his tailgate and talk, but it is way too cold for ass-on-metal. I have learned so much from his company, and our words pour out to each other like water quenching long thirst. He has the ability to make one feel wonderful and capable. Ah! The enlightened male.

/ September 28: Beauty and the Beast

A thought occurred to me this morning. Bearing the burden of too
much beauty demands attunement and atonement. I was driving out
east of Anchorage along the most gorgeous stretch of road I had ever
seen. That started me thinking about men who perceive beauty versus
those who perceive the environment in terms of its usefulness to
them. Those operating on beauty have a broader instinct for the survival of the whole planet. I'm throwing out all my aesthetic philosophy courses: out goes Kant; out goes Santayana; bye-bye Suzanne K.
Langer; smoosh to Susan Sontag (we'll hold on to Aristotle for a
while). I'm deciding that beauty springs from a sense of continuity, an
all's-right-with-the-world, a deep sense of ecology, the elegant symbiosis of whole. Beauty is not a luxury but a necessity.

The quintessential road would be one that hangs on the fringe of
mountains as they plunge to the sea, while the sea itself wound in a
narrow channel into the interior of a deep mountain range. Each of its
curves would soften the mountains behind it. This is it, this drive
from Anchorage to the Kenai Peninsula. On one side is Turnagain
Arm, that arm of sea that promises to be the Inside Passage, stinking
of exotic spices and foods and animals, clattering with exotic tongues,
heavy with blunt-edged Otherness, the infinite possibilities of being,
that mysterious tunnel from East to West. On the other side is the
Chugach Range, diving from talus cliffs to muddy bore tides in slightly
less than a mile, from high drafting eagles to singing belugas in a
matter of breaths. Such juxtapositions are found "beautiful," and this
beauty made greater by the proximity of danger. Such a road reminds
me of other inward passages, tunnels in and out of the collective
dream we call history. "The Far Away Nearby," as Georgia O'Keefe
has seen.

The gray water of Turnagain Arm takes on no form as I first see it,
although I know it is full of life. My eyes are dull. Just some greasy
waves. No whales. No seals.

It is only when I am not looking that they appear, not leaping with
Walt Disney idiot grins, but as dirty-off-white swells. A toothed whale
with an imposing hump, a sophisticated sounding chamber, thirty to

fifty—no, eighty!—belugas playing blind in the heavy glacial silt of
Turnagain Arm. No doubt they are delighted in their large brain
chambers that this is an abundant year for salmon. They gorge in the
bore tides.

White hulls inverted in the murk. A hundred white backs slipping
through silty meringue. Bald eagles circle. Locals are out in force:
mothers in rusted VWs with toddlers watching. The tide pulls on our
strings. In a churning of chocolate backwater from Portage Glacier the
bore tide is fifty yards out. On one side the tide roars in, and on this,
the north side, it rushes back out, creating standing walls of water up
to three feet high. The river runs backward, like Deception Pass in
Puget Sound through its narrow neck of rock at the northern tip of
Whidbey Island. Being a desert rat, not a water rat, I remember hanging over Deception Pass Bridge clinging tightly to my bicycle, watching
the vertiginous blue waters froth backward while oblivious western
grebes fished in the powerful eddies.

At times of extremes, the water of Turnagain Arm varies forty feet
between low and high tides in its narrow channel. A substantial volume of water is pumped from Cook Inlet. Like pouring too much
water into a funnel too fast, it swirls and slops. Finding its power seductive, I sit as far out into it as possible. Its movement captivates me
no less than the sudden blasts of storms. A maelstrom inside water.

Watching metallic eddies over unseen rocks, I see as a river kay-
aker, not as an oceangoer. Parallel lines squirm and drum in a noisy
corridor. In an hour this will be all mudflat. Not barren, but broken
in Paul Klee cubism, each section gleaming a different earth pastel.
Steve Merritt, my environmentalist analyzer friend from Denali, called
such mud in suspension "the disturbance of uniformity." I sit and
read an old newspaper (*The Anchorage Daily News*) July 16, 1988:

TIDE'S BEAUTY HIDES ITS DANGERS
Accidents heighten rescue teams' awareness of tide's deadly force
By Marilee Enge

One week after a young woman drowned on the Turnagain Arm
mudflats, Wasilla paramedics were awakened by an emergency call. A
woman had been dipnetting at the mouth of Fish Creek and she was
stuck in the mud.

As the Matamusks-Sustina Borough divers hit the road in the
rescue van, they were remembering the tragedy of 18-year-old Adeana
Dickison, who died the way nobody should have to die. She stood
helplessly with one leg buried to the knee in glacial silt as the tide
immersed her in 38-degree water.

"We were saying, 'Oh boy, not here, not now,'" recalled Bob
Hancock, leader of the Mat-Su dive rescue team. "That was definitely
the main thing that was on our minds."

This time, though, companions had pulled the woman out of her
hip boots which were held fast by the mud before the rescuers arrived.
When Hancock and his team got to Fish Creek, she was warming herself
by a fire.

Such predicaments occur so infrequently that no one knows exactly
why they happen or how to rescue someone hopelessly stuck.

In the past three decades, at least three people have drowned after
sinking into the ooze of Knik or Turnagain Arms. An unknown number
of duck hunters, clammers and others who ventured out on the mudflats
have been pulled out, some in dramatic rescues that illustrate just how
treacherous and unforgiving the glacial silt can be.

Nothing illustrates that better than the death of Adeana Dickison.
Early on the morning of July 15, she and her husband drove a four-
wheel all-terrain-vehicle down a trail near Ingram Creek, just south of
Portage. They planned to mine for placer gold in a nearby creek. The
tide was low and they began to cross the broad, gray, rippled mudflats.

The four-wheeler got stuck in a deep tidal slough. It's not clear what
happened next, but Dickison and her husband, Jay, apparently tried to
push it and in the process she became mired in the mud herself.

The couple had a dredge for placer mining and Jay Dickison used it
to pump the mud away and free one of his wife's legs, according to
Harold Rohling, assistant chief of the Girdwood Volunteer Fire Department. Before he could get the other leg out, a belt on the dredge slipped.

"I don't know if that's when he went for help or tried to dig her out
some more," Rohling said. "They just didn't know that, 'Hey, this is
going to be full of water in a few minutes.'"

By then, the tide was coming in, filling the slough with icy, glacier
run-off. Jay Dickison found some tourists and one drove up to the
Tidewater Cafe at Portage to call for help. The call was received at 7:53
a.m. and Jay Dickison later told rescuers he had been trying to free his
wife for two or three hours.

Alaska State Trooper Mike Opalka arrived at the scene first. He ran across the flats to where Adeana Dickison was trapped and assured her that the rescuers would get her out. The tide was at her chest and she was panic-stricken.

Opalka and paramedics fought against the mud, the rushing water, and the cold to free her. She begged for them to save her. Opalka gave her a tube to breathe through as the water covered her head, but she was suffering from hypothermia and unable to hold it for long.

The rescuers finally had to give up. They couldn't pull her loose and they were numb with cold. Six hours later they retrieved the body, one leg still firmly trapped.

What is it that makes the mudflats of Cook Inlet so unpredictable and so dangerous? Geologist Susan Winkler of the United States Geological Survey said it is the unique character of the grains of silt that are washed down from surrounding glaciers.

Winkler, who recently transferred to the USGS Denver branch, spent several years studying Cook Inlet sediments.

"The grains are highly angular. They're in contact with each other in a delicate balance," she explained. "When you step on it, you cause it to become more mobile. Then when it resettles after you've disturbed it, it tends to be more compacted around your foot. The grains are so angular that they're just locked together.

"You have these grains that are just balanced and they have lots of water between the grains. When you disturb it, the grains rearrange themselves and the water flows out and when they rearrange, they're more compact."

Tidal channels, like the one where Adeana Dickison died, are the most dangerous places because the mud is more highly saturated with water, she said.

"Of course, when the tide comes in, it comes in the channels faster." Cook Inlet sees the second largest tides in North America, with a range of nearly 40 feet.

Winkler had a frightening brush with the quicksand effect of the mudflats during her research. A helicopter had dropped her in the middle of Turnagain Arm where she was taking measurements.

"All of a sudden it liquified," she said. "The surface was just like a water bed. It just waved. An area of 20 feet all around me had liquified. I had been walking for a minute or two. All of a sudden, whatever I did, it just went." She was lifted off the quagmire by the helicopter.

Some tales of successful and unsuccessful mudflat rescues have worked their way into the local mythology.

Many have heard the story of the duck hunter who was stuck in the mud on either Knik or Turnagain Arm in the 1960s or 1970s, depending on who tells it, and was pulled in half by a helicopter, leaving the lower half of his body in the mud. Some locals remember the incident vividly.

There is no evidence it ever happened, but the story has become an Alaskan legend.

Hancock, the diver, said the story may be based on a rescue attempt on Turnagain Arm in the late '60s. As a young fire fighter with the Girdwood fire department, he remembers hearing about a hunter who drowned when rescuers were unable to free him. A helicopter may have been involved, he said.

On September 17, 1961, a 33-year-old Fort Richardson soldier named Roger Cashin drowned when the tide washed over him after he had been trapped in the mud of a tidal slough near the Knik River. According to an interview with one of the rescuers, published in *The Anchorage Times* in 1981, the barrel of his shotgun was removed and held for him to breathe through, but he was panicked and eventually drowned.

The next day, the story reported, a recovery crew tied a rope around him and a helicopter tried to pull him out. The rope broke from the strain, possibly giving rise to the legend.

Tony Chain of Anchorage was rescued from a Knik River slough by an Army helicopter crew on September 1, 1981. Like Cashin, he was out for a day of duck hunting. And he'd hunted in the area most of his life.

"In the process of unloading the boat, I just stepped in a hole," he said in a recent interview. "I tried to get out. I've been stuck before. I knew exactly what to expect.

"I just kept sinking. One leg went down and, trying to push myself up, both went down. I ended up chest deep. It seemed like it didn't take any time at all."

The story of how Chain was finally pulled from the mud by the helicopter was told in a 1986 *Reader's Digest* article. It took 45 minutes of Chain digging himself out as the chopper pulled on him.

"You would think if you got overhead leverage like that it would just suck you right out. Let me tell you, it didn't happen. It was a slow process," he said.

"In this country that kind of area is extremely dangerous. I knew that and I was always careful. Hell, you step into a hole and it's just unforeseeable."

Adeana Dickison's death has prompted Anchorage area rescue

agencies to think hard about techniques for rescuing such victims. The Girdwood and Mat-Su fire departments both have portable pumps which have successfully washed people out of the mud in the past. But in Dickison's case the water was too high, by the time paramedics arrived, for the pump to do any good.

The question asked most often by second-guessers is "why didn't they cut her leg off?"

"That's easier said than done," Rohling answered. "Sure, that's better than death. But she might not have survived anyway . . . that would take somebody with some real skill. We don't carry the right instruments."

"It's not going to be quick and easy," said Trooper Sgt. Paul Harris. "I've taken a lot of moose legs off and I'm telling you, it's not going to be quick and easy."

And both Rohling and Harris said the liability factor from such a procedure would be great.

"If the water comes in and drowns her, that's nature that drowned her. If you cut her leg off and she dies, you killed her," Harris said. . . .

/ October 1: Glennallen Highway from Anchorage to the Richardson Highway, then South to Valdez

Last night the ground rocked back and forth where I slept on Eklutna Lake fifty miles north of Anchorage. I grabbed the keys, thinking that tsunamis could be set in motion in this long glacial trough, but driving back to town under talus balanced at the critical angle would not be smart either. Once I made the decision not to move, there was nothing to do but enjoy the ride.

This night I am awakened in a whiteout by what sounds like seventeen howling wolves: actually, eight on the ridge and nine "howling back from the moon." Wolves howl in dissonance, on adjacent or harmonic notes, never the same, giving an impression of great numbers.

So it is with weariness that I get up in a pouring rain at 4 AM and head south to Valdez to study the terminus of that long singing snake I have followed almost 700 miles from the North Slope.

6:50 AM: COPPER CENTER ROADHOUSE

The Copper Center Roadhouse sits like a ptarmigan on the Klutina
River, waiting. It is September and snowing. There are no more sane
people visiting. To enter the all-wood and memento-laden lobby is to
step back to 1902: the hand-carved banister, the wooden hotel desk,
the cheerful knotty-pine wall paneling covered with animal heads or
pictures of animals. There is not a soul in the lobby, as if inhabitants
cease to be on October First.

The television set is on with nobody watching. I turn it way down.
Always the television. My bones say it is warm and dry. Knotty pine
murmurs years of miner tales, catastrophe, loss of life, people leaving
for the Lower Forty-eight, gunfights, gold, and bears. Tales hang in the
air like burnt gunpowder. The restaurant is stuffed with pine tables,
each with plastic flowers and attractive settings, as in a place named
Chez Something. Still no persons. I sit and write for a while, and examine my placemat, which is an abbreviated map of Alaska. Abbrevi-
ation is welcome.

The cook materializes. She is speaking to someone unseen. In the
midst of conversation, without a pause, she takes my order. No ac-
knowledgement of my presence. This is all right; she is an efficient
cook. I am not sure I exist, except that she does serve me eggs and
someone eats them. Going to the door of the kitchen to help myself
to more coffee allows a glance about the inner sanctum. Eventually I
coax the cook's invisible conversation partner, Jean Huddleston, out
of the kitchen. This roadhouse is living history, her ancestry made
audible.

Jean taps out her thirteenth cigarette butt and arranges them all
artistically in the ashtray near my food. She settles in for her story in
mock protest of my demands that she talk. She is eager to tell, and I
to eat, so this is equitable.

"This is the oldest roadhouse in the area, built in 1898 for the
gold runners off Valdez Glacier. If they survived hauling a thousand
pounds of supplies over the Valdez Glacier, then they floated down
the Klutina River in rough-sawed boats. Many drowned in the rapids.
A Swede, Mr. Holmes, built the original two rooms, and later Mrs.
Barnes, an Australian, built on the second story, the lobby and the

kitchen, and turned it toward the new road. She owned it until 1948, when my parents, Mr. and Mrs. George and Katherine Ashley, bought it from the Barnes estate. They since then have remodeled it to the feel of an old English inn.

"The old English roadhouse feeling is for real: Arthur Laverty was hired to remodel the original log buildings. Although he was exceptionally fond of whiskey, he was a fine craftsman. He carved that banister, and planted enormous tomatoes. When he was old, he lived on in the family roadhouse and delighted the children with tales of England. At Eaton, England, he went to school with Winston Churchill."

"What was it like growing up in an Alaskan gold outpost?"

"There were touches of cultures, like Arthur Laverty from Victorian England or the Swedes or others who came through. And there were real derelicts. I always granted them their dignity and their rights, and sometimes they would blossom right before my eyes. All these people had value and knowledge. They were full of old legends, like Chuck Nelson, a fellow admired for his great mining ability. My mother hated him because of his impropriety, but my father still respected him. He used to tell me stories, like the night an abominable snowman, Chitma, lurched against his cabin. They came from the Wrangell Mountains walking upright.

"It was a great place growing up for kids. We had correspondence lessons from Calvert School in Baltimore, Maryland. School was really quite different for us, and we actually scored higher on tests than our counterparts who sat in boring classrooms. When we learned, it was under the careful supervision of our parents and quite intense. This was counterbalanced with chores, so that schooling was a welcome relief to physical labor. It was like Christmas when the school supplies arrived in the fall.

"And now we serve old-time Alaskans who have been coming here for years. Politicians, hunters, fishermen, statesmen . . . there are lots of huge salmon up the Klutina."

A young Athapascan woman and her son arrive, grinning from ear to ear. It seems that she was once a part of the extended family that makes up Copper Center, on intimate terms with everyone. For five

155

dollars she cuts my scraggly hair, which has been abused by sun, wind, and lack of cleaning. A well-traveled Athapascan, she has lived all over the states and in Hawaii. "I love Seattle," she croons, "the Pike Market Place and all those beautiful fresh fish. Rows and rows of colored vegetables. But I knew I could not raise my son there when he protested, as I dumped a live crab in the pot, 'Mommie! You'll hurt it!'

"I want him to learn to hunt. I want him to learn that you must kill to live, and that animals are here for us. I just dressed out a moose last week. Here I can live for free because I have free housing, and the federal government sends me a check for my son. It has been hard, the isolation, but I want to live in the right way. I want him to be raised in the old way."

We touch each other's hair, comparing the texture. It is not that different: hers is silkier, longer.

BOOK THREE

Dream, Ritual, and Conversation for Return

10

Easy Dream, Easy Money, Deep Water

Prince William Sound has long been one of the most coveted pieces of submerged real estate in North America. Explored then claimed by three nations in one year (England, Spain, and Russia), it is the most northerly deep-water port in America. Twenty-one glaciers come down to the water, and another thirty hover a short distance away. Goats, salmon, ducks, geese, ptarmigan, grouse, moose, bear, and goeyducs abound. These latter, members of the clam family and resembling certain humanoid parts, are grasped by the light of the moon or lantern in the winter and during early morning in the summer. The grabber then slings his or her body weight backward with force, and the shoveler takes over, sometimes having to dig three feet down. The Chenga natives of Zaikoff Bay on Montague Island attribute their ancestors' slanted eyes to always looking sidey-ways for goeyduc geysers.

Valdez, the small city butted up against the steep glacier, was the beginning of the original trail over the Chugach Range to the Klon-

---

This description of Valdez is basically unaltered from the way I scribbled it in my

dike: synthesis of dream, easy money, and deep water.

On south I drive, while the weather grows colder and sloppier. It is darker each day. The nick in the high coastal range called Thompson Pass, the last gasp of the Chugach Range before it plunges down to Prince William Sound, forms a funnel for the moisture rushing up from the ocean and the cold pouring down from the Arctic. Oil and weather pumping down to the Alyeska nipple, where the tankers slip up the narrow chute. Although the educational signage is handsomely designed for public consumption, the Sound and the shipping terminal appear to be a disaster waiting to happen. We, the public, are given a sense of security because the designs of man are so superbly "adequate": nets, scoops, and oil-gathering devices lay over the waters ready to react to any natural disaster, or so the signs tell us. (I don't see but one coil of boom in the center there adequate for, say, 200 gallons of diesel fuel.) A superfine processing system for the ballast water tankers hold on the way up north and then flush out purifies the water before it reaches the bay, the signs tell you. An Alyeska manager holds up a vial of the stuff at a state environmental hearing. "Why, even cleaner than drinking water!" he says of the stuff from the bowels of the tanker. "So, bottoms up, Mr. Alyeska!" calls out a local town official.

Local lore says otherwise: the water is oily and pollutes the Sound. Nearby many birds croak and breed; an array of wildlife coexists blissfully with the mountain size tankers, the signs say. The signs say

---

black notebook six months before the March 24, 1989, Exxon oil spill of more than one million gallons of crude oil into Prince William Sound.

In 1989, Alaska lost her wilderness virginity—twice. First, the *Exxon Valdez* oil spill spread oily fingers around the Kenai Peninsula, through the Aleutians and, eventually, on the bottom, back to Prudhoe Bay. It left a wake of death in the prime rookeries of the planet and affected fishing all along the coast of Alaska.

The second, quieter disaster was unfolding on land. Major flaws in the welds in the Alyeska Pipeline were discovered, which meant that they would have to be redone at astronomical cost.

On August 2, 1990, Iraq's Saddam Hussein took over Kuwait. Oil is perceived to be in short supply. Prices at the gas pumps have skyrocketed. With no mention of the first pipeline's flaws, pressure is on to drill in and pipe oil out of the Arctic National Wildlife Refuge. Oil companies are delighted. As I write, we expect war at any minute.

the tankers curl up with the mountain goat and the bear and are perches for great blue heron and tiny water shrew. In the middle of this stands an Alyeska worker, clothed but naked, gently holding the nose of the bear and the tanker's grounding wires, wearing a god-smile.

The truth lies within the larger scope of Prince William Sound. Supertankers loading at Valdez encounter huge icebergs within the narrow shipping lanes. The icebergs come from the Columbia Glacier, which has begun breaking up after years of stability. Intense calving began in the summer of 1979, when a large rift appeared in the front of the glacier. Only nine miles away, the forty-one-mile-long ice river winds down through the Chugach Mountains to Columbia Bay. It had remained basically stable since Vancouver's cartographer, Whidbey, first mapped it in 1794. Cruise ships and ferries pass as close as is safe under the front ice cliff, which springs 262 feet straight above sea level. Now, water extending a mile from the base is clogged with glacial calves and teems with water plankton, sea animals, fish, kittiwakes, eagles, orcas, minke whales, harbor and Dall porpoise, and the endangered humpback whale.

Supertankers up to 400,000 tons must slip through a narrow channel deep enough for them. Even though night traffic was outlawed in the late '70s, owing to the glacier's recent activity, visibility can still be near zero. At that time, radar could not read ice, since it reads no different than water. Night traffic obviously was reinstated sometimes, when nobody was looking. In 1979, various schemes were proposed for controlling the recalcitrant icebergs: a 2.5-mile-long rope, 10 feet thick, to hold back tons and tons of ice for only $32 million? Or lasso them with tugs and pull them out of the lanes? Or perhaps develop a highly sensitive radar that could differentiate ice from water? One typical quarter-mile-long cube can weigh more than a billion tons, 5,000 times heavier than the tanker.

The original arguments against ending the pipeline here and transferring the oil to ships: the narrow Valdez Arm, the frequency of storms, winds and high waves, the thick fog always along the route, the highly active seismic zone that lies under Valdez and the Columbia Glacier (Manella 1979).

Against a warlike backdrop of tight security, bright red trucks move through wild sealife: American and European widgeons, the ubiquitous mallard, my first Gadwell, lots of geese (Brants and Canadian), goldeneyes, bald eagles, seal faces poking above the water, curious otters. Several herons creak off with rusty complaint from just behind the tourist propaganda post. A corny but inspiring statue by Malcolm Alexander sports the brave slogan of the pipeline: "We Didn't Know It Couldn't Be Done." Oddly enough, it looks like a leftover from World War II, until one sees the men and women are holding welding devices, building tools. Aesthetic similarity to the gung-ho nationalistic and technocratic naiveté of our most popular war is no accident, despite the fact that this is a national view that has outlived its time.

The woman with the long braid, of well-built, sturdy beauty, working alongside men is designed particularly to twang feminist heart strings. Underneath the list of owners that form this octopusian Company:

Amerada Hess Pipeline Corporation
Arco Pipeline Company
Exxon Pipeline Company
Mobil Alaska Pipeline Company
Phillips Alaska Pipeline Corporation
Sohio Pipeline Company
British Petroleum Pipeline, Inc.
Union Alaska Pipeline Company

It is an impressive and extensive piece of human cooperation. The Company built the largest privately constructed project in Earth's history, 800 miles in record time, 1969 to 1977. I cannot keep myself from admiring its technology, its complex response to conservation concerns, its environmental checks and balances. What worries me most lies settling in the graveyard near where Valdez used to be before the Good Friday earthquake of 1968. There, soggy grave stones sink akilter, one up to its cross-armpits in muck. People of Russia, Denmark, New Zealand, Holland, California, Colorado, England, Ireland, and even New Yorkers lie thumbs up to catch the washout from the next ice-dam flash flood. This road, this new city, and, alas, the Al-yeska Pipeline, exist here only by graces of the gods beneath conti-nental plates.

I retrace my tracks back up through Thompson Pass after watching a sea otter resting calmly on its back in Prince William Sound. The way up the Lowe River is loaded with wet eagles sitting, uncharacteris-tically, on their haunches. They look like erratic boulders on river gravel; their mottled color matches stripes on stone. Dead trees con-vulse with gestures of empty limbs: a boreal holocaust drowned trees from the earthquake's flash flood. The quake dropped the entire re-gion a hundred feet, so everything is out of whack. Punkers have no concept of heavy metal until they have seen the Jurassic fault line just above this range of mountains: the mineral there is so heavy that it actually is magnetic. The oldest layer of dark rock shoots 400 to 700 feet straight up from the valley floor, and over it pour sheer veils of white falls. Siltstones, conglomerates, and Sitka graywacke lie in a rippled torte. Gold-bearing quartz squirts through it.

I tilt my head back, eating a passion fruit from the market in Val-dez. To watch a waterfall from underneath is mesmerizing. It comes down in pulses over ragged black slate, in scallops over no channel still connected to its mother glacier. The newly sunken Prince William basin welcomes it with open sea arms. This breath-halting topography is not inhospitable here, but it is very tenuous in purchase: quakes, slides, Earth in chaos.

/ October 2, 7:18 P.M.:   Worthington Glacier

Northbound again on the Richardson Highway, I am disappointed to find myself entirely socked in. The shores of two pristine alpine lakes where I had planned to camp are so windy and wet that I can't stay. Instead, I sleep at the Worthington Glacier in order to catch a glacier waking up early in the morning. At 2,677 feet, Thompson Pass is made of airborne sea from Prince William Sound. When it finally ceases to rain, an omniscient light spreads from the snout of the glacier. At the ice snout, metamorphosis squeezes the air from compacted ice; the light rays it bounces are blue. The firn, an intermediary stage between deep ice and surface ice, contains small air pores that barely communicate. The ice grains have begun to fuse.

I am tempted up to the ablation zone, the line above which snow always accumulates and below which it breaks and wastes away during summer. And accumulate the snow does, the most massive snow records for all of Alaska. It is an odd sensation to be on ice so near the sea in a relatively warm environment: here it is snow accumulation that counts, not temperature.

This sphere of hallowed pillars and spires, sink holes, tunnels and caves, ice falls and queer ice bore holes is otherworldly. The tall pillars between two crevasses, at their intersection, melt into thin walls and spires called seracs. Mill holes sink unexpectedly and beautifully, sculptured punctures in blue ice where water spirals down in the negative inversion of a narwhal's tusk. The relatively warm rain water bores down into the bowels of the glacier. These holes would be the envy of the most florid of Gothic architects: scalloped, fluted, undercut, they channel the water into ice caves and disgorge it in a labyrinth of vaulted sewers at the glacier's base.

I scramble up the rocky side of this glacier, gazing down the randkluft between the rock and the glacier, where the blue ice is repulsed by the warm dark stone. Not far away, over the névé, lies the zone of accumulation. Familiar, yet mysterious, the Bergshrund crevasse forms where flowing ice separates from its stationary mother. It is the Bergshrund into which a leaping glacier-skier would disappear were he to attempt such a stunt. And if the Bergshrund did not devour him, the long crevasses parallel to the movement of the glacier would.

Varying layers of speed and malleability, the lower connected to the shape of land and the upper with the tensile strength of the ice mantle, are marked by deep cracks. Where the ice-over-rock below is gnarled and tumultuous, it is reflected in the ice above. Water containing carbon dioxide, dissolved out of limestones, dolomite, or gypsum, melts out as karsts: caves and sink holes.

I lie on my belly in drizzling fog, observing the rippling silk of alternating dark and light bands of ice. These seasonal depositional patterns torque across the surface of the glacier. Ogives, baroque pillars of ice, are formed by seasonal flows down icefalls. At the bottom, Worthington disgorges and shoves ice into a glacial output lake, opaque with silt, which hastens its demise: ice melts twice as fast in water as in air. All is blue and gray, layered, twisted, whorled, and rundled.

Inside the warm wet truck, I read more about the ice beast called Worthington. It seems that this is not one of the larger glaciers in the Chugach Mountains. It was only 1,000 feet long at the turn of the century, and it tops out at 6,200 feet above sea level; 800 feet below my former homes in Santa Fe, New Mexico, and Manitou Springs, Colorado.

It then tumbles down four miles of bedrock to an elevation of 2,600 feet, where I sit cross-legged in a tin cracker box. Gazing up at its chaotic power, I can't imagine how miners loaded with equipment made it up the Valdez Glacier, then down the Klutina Glacier, down the rapids to Klutina Lake, then on to Copper Center Lodge. Canadian Mounties would greet them at the top of the pass to require that they bring at least a thousand pounds of equipment with them on their backs to see them through the first long winter. A strong quake shook the area in 1908, and many miners lost their lives in the avalanche that followed.

Several years later, a trail was completed up the Lowe River through the narrow shaft of Keystone Canyon. Twenty-one point seven miles from Valdez, a sign says City Limits, recalling the old city before 1968. One hand-hewn tunnel is a vestige of the great railroad war, which decided whether the railroad would originate in Valdez, which would have brought prosperity to the town, or near Seward and up over the Portage Glacier passage. Seward won. This much safer trail over the Chugach Mountains must have pleased the newest miners. They gazed from under heavy loads at the dark siltstone crenelated and criss-crossed with quartz, which held gold with their names on it. This rock was also the leg-resting point for many Alyeska engineers as they labored to solve extreme earthquake problems.

/ October 3:   Lazarus Returns from Near-Dead on Mantasta Lake

Morning. Apollo is off duty. Just a dank protoplasmic black, then an imperceptible warming, like cranking up a wood stove in the Colorado mountains at minus 20 degrees. I drift down a tunnel of incandescent light at 50 mph, a sort of Alice in Frozenland.

The Tosina River, full of silt, appears as a tube of cellophane enclosing liquid silver. Its convolutions match precisely those of the volcanic ash bluffs it has carved into white pointed erosion cones reminiscent of New Mexico's Tent Rocks near Bandelier.

At Mantasta Lake I stop to consider the two roads out of Tok Junction: one down to Whitehorse and home—the sensible route, considering the winter—and one up, north to Eagle. Suddenly I see white-winged ghosts, Yeats's symbols of beings going from the Here to the There, Lazarus, many of him, coming back from the brink.

The black lake is serene with great white birds, inspirations for ballet, for love poetry, for grace, for soup tureens. I had thought that they were near extinction, poisoned by lead in Yellowstone and hunted for meat up here. In the mid-'30s, there were only sixty-nine of them left on the planet. Sitting as still as stone down by the shore, I fade into the bush. The great white birds are aware of my presence, but slowly they gain trust and begin a horrendous honking. This must be one of the most primeval sounds on the planet. It creaks across the water and into the surrounding taiga. The trumpeter swans, *Cygnus buccinator*, bugling down the next century.

Trumpeters are the largest of all waterfowl. The cob weighs up to 60 pounds or more and has a three-foot wing span. Buccinator— "horn" in French—refers to the twisted sounds coming from elongated necks. It is not the gentle creaking of the smaller tundra swan, but a great horn-blowing. Their population is estimated at 10,000 now; conservation efforts have successfully reined in the trumpeter's main predator—man. Native people and pioneers found their meat delectable, similar to young beef when properly roasted. In fact, the word cygnet comes from French cuisine, indicating a young bird tender enough for gourmet tastes. Many more trumpeters vacationed in Europe in the form of feather boas, powder puffs, and various feminine apparel, as well as quills and flute parts. Protected since 1916, the swans have made a dramatic comeback in many areas of Canada and the United States. Across British Columbia, Ontario, and Washington, agriculture encroaches on swan habitat, so I was amazed last winter to hear their bugles up and down the west side of the Cascades. I thought I saw six on the Columbia River in late February while driving with my sister along the border between Washington and Oregon. Sara was horrified when I slammed on the brakes and demanded that she extricate my WW II binoculars from the jumper cables and tire chains in back of the seat, then rejoined the 60-mph stream of traffic with a squealing of truck tires. Who says bird watching is for the faint-hearted?

Recognition is problematic: the tundra swan, North America's other indigenous species, has yellow in front of the eye and is smaller. According to species distribution maps, trumpeters dip south in a thin curving line along the Cascade Mountains, following the abundant river sloughs in the foothills. The bottom tip has apparently extended down past the Columbia River deep into Oregon.

On Mantasta Lake, there is a nursery tended by four adults, a particularly intelligent arrangement. One pair of tundra and one pair of trumpeter adults watch over a clutch of six mottled brown young, who are slowly swimming toward the bank I sit on. Soon they will be close enough for detailed examination. I am patient.

While I wait, I read in my bird book that the young hatch from clutches of five to nine eggs in June to July in nests that both parents weave. One 325-gram egg is said to be enough to feed a large man an entire meal. In the first two weeks, three to six of the clutch will be trampled by a parent's large feet, become entangled in the nest and drown, or fall to cold or predators. Only two to three join their parents in the fall migration, already almost as large as the pure-white adults. The young's bright pink beaks and dirty brown feathers accentuate the awkward state of adolescence: from ugly duckling to elegant swan in a matter of weeks (Armitage 1986).

Seventy voices begin creaking in unison, a contemporary orchestra made up of creaky doors, French horns, trumpets, trombones, and bucket-pulley devices. John Cage at his finest. When comfortable, they begin to trumpet, fully and melodiously, waving their necks out in front like snakes in a cobra act. They cry out to one another, perhaps signaling that it is too dangerous to stay on this small lake much longer. They need long runways to take off with their heavy weight, and soon the lake will freeze. It has been unseasonably warm this summer, and they have stayed way past their normal departure date.

In a curious, if not humorous, symbiosis, smaller waterfowl trail the immense swans like a courtly entourage. European widgeons and buffleheads stick at the skirts of the flotilla of birds like dirty pom-poms. Bobbing up and down, they eat plankton brought up by swan-foot-paddles. A marsh hawk circles above. The ravens keep close watch on their magnificent antitheses.

There is a familiar pinging sound, and an Alaskan family in a bus with unmuffled engine stops right behind me. For some reason, they do not turn off their engine. As it idles it revs up. They come out scrambling and howling: "How wonderful they are!" The swans, meanwhile, are retreating hastily. "What a menagerie!" shouts the mother over the bus engine. I am not sure whether the label applies to her nursery or the swans'.

The family leaves but its disquietude stays. The swans are restless, moving about. Their song has turned from abandoned bugling to throttled cries of distress. Eight decide it is time to go. Four pairs lift off like flapping PBK's, forty-pound eggbeaters at their sides, amidst the grand orchestral finale of loud bugles.

This lumpy oatmeal of sound is accentuated by the insane-sounding quacks of mallards, widgeons, buffleheads, and gadgets. Yelping like puppies, those left miss those who have taken off. For a long time I lie still and listen: the vivacious brass orchestra begins again. It is clearly a developed language, in three senses: first, in the incredible variety of sound, the compassionate tenderness, the entire lake creaking and cooing; second, the rise and fall in both volume and mutual excitation seems to have an intelligent form to it; third, the communication goes distinctly from bird to bird. The swans' specific message is not easy to determine: it could be a food call, a fear call, a warning call, an aggressive challenge, a mating song, etc. The meaning of each call, although emotionally "apparent" (misinterpreted) to human beings, is almost impossible to decipher, since that would mean determining intentions that are not necessarily synonymous with behavior.

Yet another danger of anthropomorphism lies in the fact that bird calls are produced by mechanisms very different from the larynx that vibrates to produce the human voice. The voices of birds come from the syrinx at the bottom of the trachea (windpipe) and from the two bronchi, (branches into the lungs). Actual sound is created by air rushing over the membranes or vortices caused by such a mechanism. Thus do birds produce their enchanting variety of trills, whistles, songs, and orchestration, as well as an ordinary speaking voice. The oscines, or forty families of "song birds," have great muscular control of the syrinx muscles and air flow. The reed warbler and thrasher are able to sing two separate tunes simultaneously. The brown thrasher can actually utter four different notes in one instant, through a mechanism not understood (Burton 1985).

I am reminded of the Eskimo women who play one another's throats as musical pipes, one blowing hard into the other's open mouth, thus vibrating the other's windpipes for them. This is combined with a chanting sort of song on top of the larynx, which is vibrating like a bagpipe drone. The song meant to evoke serious gods usually ends in hysterical giggles.

The musical sounds from the avian syrinx can be made by changes in the trachea airsacs, causing low resonation, as in the trumpeter swan and the whooping crane. In certain species, extra loops in the long coil of trachea can create a lower drone-whistle mating call. Other birds puff up airsacs under their throats, often brightly colored to seduce the mate, while other birds enhance their songs with drumming instrumentations: feet, wings, hollow logs, or clattering mandibles (Burton 1985). The cobra dance of elongated swan necks is not unrelated to the trumpeting trachea inside, suggesting that neck length evolved both for food gathering and for trumpeting.

Where song becomes pure vocalization, or "call," is uncertain for me, as both are very seductive. The noisy creaking of migrating cranes, the underwater gurgle of cooing mourning doves on my grandmother's window ledge, the loud honking of geese in the sky, the uncanny hooting of nocturnal owls—are among the most evocative sounds on Earth. From lugubrious to exuberant, birdsong's liquidity or mechanical simulations capture us humans as does no other sound, as if in some cross-species fertilization of the heart and mind.

I leap as a rifle shot punctures the silent taiga. My eyes comb the black-spiked spruce for man, and I am strangely reminded of the snaggly spears of ocotillos in the Big Bend of Texas. This country feels even more primordial than does that southern sorcerer's land: the eerie cries of the loons, the bone-hollowing howl of wolves engenders the same feeling as do the dry rattle of legume pod, the infant-dying cry of coyote, the persistent vultures in cottonwood trees down on the Rio Grande. Here one hears the creaking trumpets of swans, mumble of earth underneath, and the gurgles of active volcanoes close by.

11

Darth Vader's Hometown

/ October 4:   Chicken, Alaska

Here blows a fine wind of radio murder mysteries.

On the Taylor Highway north to Eagle, the tundra is no longer the elegant hues of fall—burnt reds, saturated yellows, earthen greens—but somber, as someone thinking she had color film in her camera would shoot black-and-white. There is still time to turn back south, only forty miles to join the sensible Alcan Highway home, but I continue north, flirting with the possibility of a massive snowstorm. In Eagle, people choose to spend the winter roadless and isolated.

Wind whips up as I sleep on the tundra. My mind has begun dealing with the return to civilization with deep dreaming, worrisome dreaming. This stormy night, some *nouveau riche* folk have a huge, catered party up in mountains full of natural phenomena: blue pools and waterfalls in the rock ledges, tall aspen growing right up through the open-air rooms. People are handsome and young, standing in small clusters talking quietly. A talented hostess has prepared gourmet tidbits for the affair, such as anchovy eyeballs rolled in truffle filaments and lightly dusted with lavender gastropod sperm. I wish I was not there.

My relatives are embarrassed by me. There is only one way to leave: by bus to Anchorage. This is a bus that floats through air, since this is a roadless area suspended high in glacial seracs and mist. The people who have floated here in airborne sports cars with flotation devices exude golden penumbras and tinsel auras. I float out to wait for public transport.

On the bus I take a harmonica out of my hair bun and give it to a young black man behind me, honoring his creativity and talent. Others have been ridiculing him. I turn to the bus driver, a bloated ugly man, and say, "If you don't mind, this young man is going to play Bach." The young man begins to play intricate baroque improvisational riffs never heard before, melodious progressions like waterfalls. We hold our breaths to catch every note; we are in the presence of genius.

"Yes, I do mind!" snaps the jowly bus driver. "That is against bus rules." On that note he climbs heavily from the bus and moors it, still floating, to an old-fashioned lamppost. I could see then that he was terribly deformed.

As I record this dream, it becomes lucid. It is the subconscious's preparation for the journey back to civilization. The harmonica, my own creativity, is taken from the hairstyle of a well-dressed, acceptable young professional and handed to my creative part, the young black man. It always causes me to fall off the Acceptable Career Path: to produce and consume as much of Earth's resources as fast as and in as conspicuous a manner as possible. The old deformed man is an angry Lower Forty-eight drone who has lost touch with his body, the wilderness. The house made of ledges and spectacular phenomena represents Nature in the Lower Forty-eight. Even though many of the phenomena are inherently dangerous, they are used as status symbols or to entertain people. Everything appears under control, *but nature under control is fictitious and dangerous.*

Eating in Alaska is falling into a mattress of white bread: soft, deep, and empty. To talk politics up here is to return to the isolationism of the 1930s. I pass a mine abandoned in the 1940s. Ravens line the gravel heaps of stream devastation, a child's version of Darth

Vader's hometown. Eventually will be a time when natural beauty is more valuable than gold.

A road crew directs me through a mile of treacherous highway repair. No turning back now. Once through the bad part, I have to keep going or get stuck. What I see ahead is ghastly: deep mud up a steep quarter-mile hill in undulations about three feet high at each apex. I gun the engine, put it in second, both hands grasping the wheel, and accelerate. The truck slams bottom; my head slams top, skull banging loudly against struts. At the top I begin to fishtail and barely make it. The crew chief walking back down barely steps out of my way, looks me in the face and laughs.

In Chicken, I learn that many of the tourist trailers don't make it, that they often are more torn up by the road crews hauling them out than by the mud. The crews are obligated to pull out mired cars, but they do so with blasé nonchalance. "It will be finished soon!" is sardonic Chicken humor. It is called Chicken because the original miners wanted to name it Ptarmigan, but none of them could spell ptarmigan. Actually, chicken does mean ptarmigan, and stupid chicken means spruce grouse in bush lingo. In Chicken I meet several delightful women in the one-room-shed Post Office, and we exchange necessities of the road: I get Clorox for drinking creek water, since I am running low of stove fuel, and I give them cans of pop, brake fluid, windshield fluid, a camper light, a box of condoms, and other paraphernalia that has fallen off an ill-fated RV.

/ October 5: Eagle, Alaska

On the third house in Eagle is a huge sign:

> PARK SERVICE EMPLOYEES AND ALL
> WHO SUPPORT THEIR VIEWS NOT WELCOME HERE—
> PARTICULARLY THE ANTIQUITIES ACT!!!

Yet another sign reads:

> ANTIQUITIES ACT UNLAWFUL.

I sleep near the graveyard, which I peruse early the next morning as a way to glean firsthand the town's history. This was a military post, and many anonymous men with only first names are buried here. Next, I learn that many of the old markers have been replaced by cheap white kickboards—in the name of orderliness, I suppose. Third, I learn that people die young here, often in violent deaths:

CHARLIE WILMA	DAVID W. WALLER
OSTRANDER	BORN
WENT HOME TO BED	MAY 7, 1961
AUGUST 9, 78	SHOT AND KILLED
AGE 37.34	JUNE 1, 1981
JAMES PATRICK SCOTT	CHARLES OTT
1942–1973	1944–1968

Eagle was never a normal town, not a town in which families of settlers built slow steady concretions of what we call culture. In fact, except for abundant Biedermans, there seem to be no family histories. At least not buried here.

I make an obligatory journey over to the Yukon River: slow, huge, fat with silt. I dream of kayaking 154 miles to Circle by myself, taking ten days to do so. The mighty Yukon, fourth longest river in the United States, is outclassed only by the Mississippi–Missouri, the Mackenzie, and the St. Lawrence. Perhaps I could begin at 1,060 feet elevation at Dawson City, Canada, and float the border, drop down to 820 feet at Eagle and to 200 feet at its confluence with the Tanana River, then on into the Bering Sea. This float trip would have to be done during the 155 days when ice does not cover the river. During mid-May breakup, my small craft could be crushed between the huge blocks of pack ice. I might find myself swept down by one of the ice-dam floods, the river swiftly rising over the banks, lost in the pine forest in a kayak. I doubtless would grow quite confused where the Yukon flattens out to 20 miles wide in Yukon Flats.

Better yet, I could begin at the river's headwaters in Marsh Lake, only a stone's throw from the Pacific Ocean, to which the Yukon used to flow before the Alaska Range docked against the continent's quiet continence. Floating silently through Athapascan territory, I would

hear a beautiful name for the river falling off the tongue like salmon
leaping, meaning Big River. I would float through roadless Eskimo
villages unmangled by civilization's "superior" maw. There I would
hear it called Kuikpak, also meaning Big River, and learn to love it
as sacred and as survival. Finally, after snapping through a minus 81
degrees temperature record at Snag, Yukon Territory, I would be disgorged at Emmonak at the Bering Sea, 1,993 miles later.

Looking down from a high crumbling cliff, I am mesmerized by the
swirls and eddies that cover the surface of the green artery. All sorts
of culture, ships and dreams float past. Kayaking changes the heart,
and with it the way of reading the river.

Before leaving town, I ask a Christian storekeeper to explain the
anger toward the National Antiquities Act. I figure if I ask a Christian
in a Christian bookstore with 300 Jesus faces staring at us from the
tops of lamps and the bottoms of ashtrays, I won't be driven out of
town. This is how I understand the act:

Passed in 1906 under Theodore Roosevelt, it is designed to protect
America's national heritage and grants a president the right to create a
National Monument: Roosevelt created quite a few himself. National
Parks are created by Congress; National Monuments by the president.
All over the Southwest, the land is prickled with warning signs invok-
ing the National Antiquities Act. Still, ranchers, politicians, and
thieves (categorically not mutually exclusive) vicariously or directly
dig up prehistoric pottery of great beauty with backhoes, breaking
quite a few in the process. But who gives a damn what other artifacts
you trash when one pot can bring $5,000? Through lack of proper law
enforcement, politicians once turned a blind eye toward their hungry
constituency. (I've never actually seen a Southwestern politician
holding a shovel, although some need to.)

"The National Park Service used it illegally to get all our lands up
here. It was a sneaky way, backhanded. The government blatantly
used it to steal what is rightfully ours from people up here. It was
some [and here, the air is pregnant with foul language the Christian
could not speak] Udall back in Ohio. They don't have any land left
back there in the East, so they used the Antiquities Act to grab all of
Alaska for themselves. The National Antiquities Act has absolutely

nothing to do with us up here," she says, heating up now. "It just applies to some stupid ruins down in Arizona.

"I sure wish you could talk to my husband." She sputters to an angry halt, noting the color in my cheeks. "He could tell it to you real straight"—i.e., with less God-inhibited language.

The people of Eagle are strong, individualistic, prideful and exuberant, considering that they live in the dark most of the time. I ask a handsome young woman how she copes with the dark: "It feels quite mysterious and special. I walk out early, early in the mornings, and it is so quiet and so beautiful. I love it here. I love it when all the tourists leave [with a pointed glance in my direction], and we are bundled in for the winter. Because it is so odd, the dark is beautiful."

A remarkable tenacity.

To drive down from Eagle is to sink through layers of time and sea. Down through ultramafic rock heavy with iron, dark with magnesium, a littoral Gregorian chant. Narrow chutes of rockfall alternate with trees tipped at 45-degree angles, also sliding down with roots in the solifluction, "drunken forests," as they are called. Dark red-brown blood means Tertiary rock, while fresh roadcuts vibrate light green/ pink/lavender/purple, similar in hue to the Chinle formation in the Southwest of the Lower Forty-eight.

Deep army-green serpentine is so fibrous it crumbles in my hand. White fragments of sea are belched up through the green where fossils still wiggle. The gobbledy-goo of sea has not yet metamorphosed, so that green stems of a primeval compost heap keep crumbling, and the black shale is still a leafy mess, disintegrating like charcoal, becoming fossil fuel right in the palm of my hand. Highly magnetized mafic is cracked and veined with white: six million years ago smack up against five million years ago! Such disconformities are disconcerting to those of us with a brevity of lifespan.

A roadcut reveals an ice lens suspended in black mud above the permafrost. In plain sight, the 14-foot-long and 5-foot-high perfect lenticular shape drips icicle fangs. Fragile tundra swells upward above its bulge. Shining dully, this black ice with concave ripples could contain a mastodon or a woolly mammoth, it seems. The day is warm.

Elephas primigenius jump-starts his circulation and stumbles up from his knees to his feet, ambles off bewildered, stretches hind legs out and smells odd smells. Then, with no pause for existential contemplation, he begins lunch on exotic new vegetation. Some he remembers from the Pleistocene Epoch: the rich mosses and lichens. Some, like wintergreen, he does not. But it is all quite delicious anyway. Climbing on up tundra, he devours cassiope, arctic bell heathers, small evergreens he does not recognize. He finds the pungency of Ledum, or Labrador tea, the small boreal evergreen with thick alternating leaves, delightfully strong when bruised between his immense teeth. The wild geranium, whose name means crane in ancient Greek, is also strange to his palate. He does not stop to ponder how the Greeks saw a crane in such a plant. And Epilobium he adores, its flaming red and fleecy seed pods. He little cares that its name translates as "upon capsule," for the way the perianth surmounts the fruit. He's just real, real happy.

As sun strikes his thick coat, a color is revealed that has not been seen since the twelfth century: the color of woolly mammoth fur, deep pearlaceous black.

Related to the modern Indian elephant, *Elephas primigenius*'s relatives dispersed from Asia. Although he is less progressive than his Siberian brother, *Elephas primigenius* is beautifully adapted to this arctic climate. In the tropics he had longer legs, while in harsher northern climates he was stunted, hardier, more active. Man also developed and dispersed from Asia, parallel to, and perhaps in symbiotic relationship with, the mammoth. In fact, it is theorized that it was humankind that eventually led to his demise (Digby 1926).

He is not pretty by *Vogue* standards, with tiny eyes, smaller ears than the Indian elephant, and a sharply sloping stern. His tusks are nine to ten feet long and two and a half feet around at the base, weighing more than two hundred pounds apiece. Early Europeans and Eskimo alike were hard-pressed to explain the immense tusks they found buried. One legend had it that these great beasts lived and moved under the earth, and died immediately when exposed to air.

E. primigenius may long for his parentage, 400,000 years ago in the Pleistocene Epoch, when his kind wandered from Washington, D.C.,

to Alaska and across the Bering Land Bridge. Yes, those were the days.
They had clout then. Even the Greeks had their legends: Pliny mentions a giant beast that shed its tusks only once every ten years and
buried them immediately. The largest of *E. primigenius*'s brothers was
found in Nebraska, the imperial mastodon.

As I am gawking at the mammoth, a young Athapascan driving a
red Toyota pickup comes barreling around the corner. He sees something incredible. He knows his four-leggeds warm-bloods extremely
well, being an expert hunter and a student of zoology at U. of A. in
Fairbanks. He returned to his homeland, above Eagle on the Yukon,
equipped with a knowledge of evolution and archaeology. He studies
Darwinism and paleontology and reads *Natural History* magazine
religiously.

As I was saying, he comes whipping around this corner in his
pickup of Asian descent and there, standing in the road, is something
he knows exists only in books: a living, breathing, grazing woolly
mammoth. Losing control of his truck, he plunges into the thick mud
ditch with enough force to knock loose the lenticular ice slab, which
covers him and deep-freezes him instantly.

Two ice ages pass. A superior race descends to Earth and, to its
horror, discovers a planet in crisis, losing a thousand species of flora
and fauna a day. This superior race convicts and imprisons for two
epochs an East Coast power establishment dependent upon raping
Earth's last resources for immediate wealth and control, thus saving us
from ecological demise. One day, hovering around this very corner in
a gyrocopter, one *deus ex machina* watches incredulously as something
ancient emerges from the black earth. He quickly scans his computer
data bank under "Archaeology; Siberian migration; Athapascan."
He reads:

> arrived in three separate migrations from different points in Asia . . . the
> American Indian, Athapascan Indian and Eskimo-Aleuts each crossed
> the Bering Land Bridge at distinctly different times, beginning up to
> 35,000 years ago . . . the Athapascan is different biologically from all
> other American Indians . . . yet linguistically he cannot be traced to any
> Asiatic language. . . . "

Then this superior being records his find in the computer archaeological bank: "Found in the year 32.5*][4c, one male Athapascan Indian contained in a red metal coffin with the following items intended for ritualistic use in his Afterlife:

1. Siberian Canine, blue-eyed, male
2. 1 instrument of destruction filled with metal cylinders
3. 2 ptarmigans with wounds to their heads
4. 20 paper tubes containing shredded leaves
5. 1 internal combustion engine
6. 23 aluminum cylinders marked "Rainier"
7. 1 cassette tape marked "Dvorak: New World Symphony, Rafael Kubelik conducting the Chicago Symphony Orchestra"

Tired from my encounter with prehistoric fauna and future Supreme Beings, I drive on down the Taylor Highway and to the Canadian border, where a young boy charges $3 a gallon for gasoline on the U.S. side, and the Top of the World Highway, which continually squiggles away from underneath my tires. On down from Dawson City, I encounter the Klondike River.

/ October 6: Hammer Water

Mental-kayaking on a mighty river through 100-foot rock fingers in the middle of the Klondike, I imagine the sleepy-looking water lives up to its Athapascan name, Hammer Water. Yet this does not refer to whitewater, but rather to the salmon traps that were pounded into the riverbed. Drowned in the thick sludge of buried names, *Tthi-cho Nadezhe* means rocks standing up. In the late nineteenth century, gold was discovered on its tributary, Bonanza Creek. By 1899, all the important streams had been staked and claimed, and the word Klondike no longer meant river water, instead becoming synonymous with the greatest gold rush in the world.

A roadsign informs one that the Tutchone People lived here, entirely "unknown" until explorer Robert Campbell "discovered" them
and claimed their home waters for the Hudson's Bay Company. Imagine their surprise and delight upon being discovered, finding that they
existed. Governor Sir John Henry Pelly's name fell to the tributary on
which they had fished and lived since before time. Imagine their surprise and delight in discovering the name of the unknown river.

I drive on down to Whitehorse and out the Alcan Highway,
sleeping just below its junction with the Cassiar dirt road. The next
day I proceed with my exploring and eventually end up at a most
beautiful lake, which had captured my heart on the journey north.

/ October 9:   Kinaskan Lake, Cassiar Highway

Evening glazes the lake's surface red: it stretches out for miles around
Mount Edziza, a National Park of rugged lava rock terrain. A ring-
necked duck feeds nearby. I prepare a Rock Cornish game hen in
tinfoil with onions, thyme, and the innards of one orange. Game hens
are very good for traveling because one buys them frozen and they
keep the cooler cold as they defrost. They do, however, make the
local ptarmigan nervous.

Materially, I am in heaven. There is abundant cedar firewood
neatly cut and stacked for odiferous crackling fires. I have not had
fires because there is not much wood on the tundra, which is too
fragile to recover from fires. Here, the luxury of fireplace and the
elegance of tailgate and table prove that desires can be scaled down,
happiness becoming simple and cheap, yet as satisfying as ever; that
home is any place where the ruffed grouse, spruce grouse, common
goldeneye, and a bright rose-red flock of pine grosbeaks hang their
hats. The drab brown of a goldeneye's head turns bright rust in the
setting sun. Tomorrow is Canada's Thanksgiving, and if I am feeling
slightly alone, the red-necked grebe dissolves such feeling.

For the second time, I stretch out my bag under a clear sky, completely vulnerable but completely satiated and entirely happy. Clear, still air. Somewhere an owl hoots. Under Mount Edziza, the volcano whose birthday was a mere four million years ago, I lie a flyspeck on a huge dome of andesite, dacite and rhyolite, and basalt. Successive layers flowed higher and wider, finally reaching more than ninety miles in length. A mere 10,000 years ago, Edziza plugged itself, but smaller volcanoes constantly erupt here and there. Earthquakes are commonplace: like a giant pot of boiling kidney beans, the lid being the coastal range. A huge inferno spurts out one side and down the pot, layer after viscous layer, until one has a high lava plateau. I lie in the chaste night air waiting for plate tectonic gods to create ground oscillations, or at least a good fiery eruption or something, waiting as I always do for the show to begin.

And it always does, but never to my specifications.

Yesterday I visited Telegraph Creek, the closest community to the volcano. For the seventy-plus miles up through grand lava canyons of the Stikine River, the road sits tenuously, like quicksilver, on the very side of the canyon. It is so narrow and steep it disappears beneath the nose of a truck. This is another one of the Great Drives on the planet. There are now rumbles within the Canadian Parliament to create the Stikine National Park. Owners of the abundant mining operations, needless to say, are not amused.

Surely, though, there is a way for mines to coexist with nature-lovers: the purists, of course, would be rid of all mining operations, yet these western mines bring in substantial income to Canada. I find them colorful punctuations of the land, but hope for a technology that renders their slag heaps harmless.

To the west, through Raspberry Park, the Collins Overland Telegraph strung its fragmented link between Asia, North America, and Europe. After two hundred and fifty men spent $3 million on it, it was instantly abandoned on June 26, 1866, after the successful laying of the transatlantic cable. At its end, Port Fleming is named after a possible Scots ancestor of mine, Sanford Fleming, a civil engineer. He was the first to survey for the Canadian Pacific Railway from 1871 to

1880. The port, which also was the point of arrival for miners in the Klondike, is too shallow to have become a major northern port. Else my ancestral name might have been famous (Orth 1967).

There are many inexplicable sounds now, as constellations begin to delineate themselves. A sad two-note mew repeats over and over. Fish flop. Froglike chants. A plastic mug ticks in contraction. A grouse calls as if through a plastic nozzle. In spite of the dark into which all sinks, the lake is gold. The sound of protest from a goldeneye is heard. Each voice a language repeated to perfection through the eons.

Thrushes call. A muskrat breaks the water's surface in long gold V's. Then, about ten o'clock, I am annoyed: the eastern half of sky has a dull glow in it, which ruins the stars. I was so looking forward to naming the constellations with a star chart. It must be the moon. But no, it is not time for any moon. Layered waves of what must be clouds lit up from the sunset are drowning the stars. Vapor trails criss-cross the Milky Way, which looks just like the many-armed galaxy it is. Loons cast about night with lugubrious quavers. I close my eyes and fall away through the veils of consciousness. Suddenly, my eyes open: the sky is all curtains of heavy white silk, lines down from pure sources shimmering, moving in undulation, their bottom edges quick as sidewinders, twitchy, then fluid. I gaze up between the curtains, between the energy lines, into dark patches of deep space shaped like crabs met head-on, or like desert animals as I would see them on my belly.

Instantly, rays come down on all sides, east and west, across the entire southern sky, to the perimeters of Earth and beyond, feeding the dragons over the edge. They reach down to me as well, but I cannot see them within a mile above me, and thus dark shadows take their place. These shadows are constantly undulating wherever the rays end. They are lifelike; the Angel of Death tall and wavering in his fearful mimicry. Other relic medievalry, snakes and winged Evil, wave in a visual ululation: I am ecstatic.

It was Pierre GeSindi, scientist-philosopher, who named the aurora in the sixteenth century. Since then, scientists with rockets probe, measure, and delineate it, but never touch its magic. I know that nitrogen emits red and oxygen emits whitish green, and I understand that the illuminated gases are shaped in elongated ovals out from each pole of the planet, outlining the magnetic field cavity. Thoughtwise, I know of its origin in the solar winds of up to a million degrees, which cause surges of subatomical activity. I've seen video from *Challenger*, which viewed the full aurora from space, 1,000 miles long, sixty miles high at the corona-convergence point; and that exact mirror image extends from the South Pole, as well. From reading the rivers, I comprehend the vortices and eddies that form in the highly charged field of gases.

I recently read about heated gases that oscillate not in gradual color gradations (rainbows) but in discrete colors. I should not be as much in awe as I am. But I am. I barely breathe. The eddies and swirls get larger and larger, the magnetotail pulls out farther and farther until, like an oxbow in a river, the loops reconnect and close, separate and float off into space: the passage of vast plasmocides.

All the rays then come to Earth from a place exactly overhead; the entire sky fills with a burning as bright as an overcast day. I see each branch and pebble clearly. A Zarathustra theme of red nitrogen atoms is released, then a Samuel Barber shimmer of green oxygen molecules on the horizon, deep into space; I am allowed to see directly into those reptilian gods where no other human is allowed. I fly through the plasma of space without my body. I am between lives in the *Tibetan Book of the Dead*. Cast at impossible speed for a soul without a ship, changing color from the Doppler effect, I fly inward and outward simultaneously. I remain flat on my back for several hours, not breathing, flying through space. . . .

And then I don't remember.

/ October 10:   West Coast, British Columbia

Stewart, British Columbia, and Hyder, Alaska, are two little communities from two different countries linked together like a man and a cat on a wet liferaft. Hyder's sixty-odd people cooperate with Stewart's in using Canadian currency and in local politics, as well as in celebrating each other's holidays. Until 1971, when the new blacktop was blasted down through the Bear River Valley of the coastal cordillera, there was no way to Stewart or Hyder except by sea, up the narrow saltwater fjord called Portland Arm, which marks the southern boundary of Alaska. Before 1965, there had not even been a wagon trail through coastal rainforest thick with salmonberry, Devil's club, stinging nettles, slide alder, hemlock, and spruce.

Everywhere on this road, work crews always wear hard hats and plant signs warning one not to leave one's vehicle. Treeless chutes attest to the seriousness of these signs. Nowhere am I able even to hop out for a moment to collect alluring ribbons of *Aleuria aurantia*, a Day-Glo orange edible fungus. Bear Glacier, glowing azure, constantly calves Henry Moore sculptures into a small turquoise lake screwed tightly down into the deep canyon. The Bear River leaves from here, lathing its way through glacial-fluvial deposits. On the north it is confined by the faultline wall called Bear Ridge. There is no way up to its 3,000-foot top in that wild country, except by miner helicopter, so that naturally is exactly where I want to go.

In Hyder, a small pleasant restaurant is holding Canadian Thanksgiving. Telegraph Creek, some fifty miles north by raven, and Anyox, to the south, rely entirely on Stewart for transportation, supplies, communication, hospital, and recreation. The Granduc Mine dominates everything local; in fact, the area's entire history before the 1971 highway is mineral history. The road forebodes ill: a dreadful new industry is arriving, which may stymie the mines; it attracts people who want to preserve the topsoil and vegetation just to *look* at it. Imagine that. Just to frigging *look* at it.

In said Hyder cafe, a kind local man changes my hundred-dollar Canadian bill at a very favorable rate while he growls, "I hate tourists. I'll be glad when they're all gone."

Hyder is at the mouth of the Salmon River, 55° 55′ 00″ N and 130° 01′ 30″ W, the easternmost village in the forty-ninth state. In 1907 it was known as Portland City; in 1915 it was named after Frederick Hyder, a mining engineer. In 1945 there were only 254 Native Americans living here, and by 1967 it was almost deserted

(Orth 1967). Now, with the resurgence of the gold-mining industry, it promises to become again a boomtown.

I have ordered a massive green salad in a large container, even though one is not offered on the menu. All eight customers watch the cook through the counter window as she prepares it. It seems to be one of the more intriguing events this evening in Hyder. I would kill for romaine and die for fresh spinach. She has white cellulose lettuce. I am in crucifer withdrawal. A local says, "Don't put it in *that* bucket, the one with the mop in it."

As always, the conversation moves freely from table to table with none of those invisible barriers city folk maintain at intimate tables, where, shoulder-to-shoulder, they divorce and merge, claim bankruptcy and start love affairs, and feign ignorance of the next table. I rather like both styles. Here, I ask what they like and what they find difficult about Hyder in the wintertime. In a Greek chorus, they say: "Isolation, quiet, remoteness, independence from either country. Don't like people. Especially tourists."

"Especially nosy funny ones who write in notebooks," adds the toughened blonde who commented on my salad before.

It seems that such tenacity originated with a man named Bruges, who came with sixty-eight men on the ship *Discovery* in 1898. He promised them productive placers, which were never found. Abandoning them, he traveled farther north to Alaska. Among the men who could not continue north were Brightwell and Cook, skilled miners who found a mineralized float and vein material just north of Stewart. A float is a term for a pocket or plane of mineral-bearing intrusions that hold great promise and actually appear to "float" inside the matrix rock. "Dad" Rainey then founded the townsite of Stewart at the foot of Mount Dolly. John and Bob Stewart came in 1902, attracted to the stench of gold. It was John who left his name stuck on the wildcat town. The town was emptied by 1910, when a series of wild speculative rumors brought the area ill repute in mining circles to the north.

Then Premier happened.

Premier, Alaska, began 150 million years ago when Mesozoic rock (the era spanning 70 to 240 million years ago, from the birth of the

Alaskan continent to the age of dinosaurs) came smacking up into the plutonics of the coastal belt. These plutons consisted of augite, diorite, and quartz monzonite in tiny dykes to extensive batholiths. Augite is a precious black silicate stone of high luster, while diorite is a gray to green igneous rock occurring in connection with other precious minerals. It is in the quartz that there is gold.

This mineral-laden ore is overlain and mixed in with marine sediments of the Bowser Strata from the Jurassic Age (150–200 million years ago). Bowser Strata appear as handsome gray matrix stones with vivid red, green, and purples: green limestone is cut through by rhyolite flows and bright red littoral debris. It is during the Jurassic that terrain is added that will be called Alaska.

All this geologic mumble gumbo allowed fifty properties to produce in excess of 5.6 million tons of gold, silver, lead, and zinc ore between 1910 and 1968. The Silbar Premier Mine alone produced more than 4.7 million tons, while others stockpiled tons of tungsten copper. Western British Columbia is vital to the Canadian economy, owing to this particular combine of sea and vulcanism. Environmentalists wishing to preserve any part of coastal B.C. will have to deal with mining operations.

Up the steep Salmon River grade, the water is so full of its dead namesake that breathing is intolerable. All the way up, the gold-mining operation has tossed utility poles akilter over the ground like pickup sticks, road included. Old beater cars drive up on my tail fast and pass impatiently on blind curves, their drivers late for their shifts at the mine. At the Y for the mine, I proceed up past the gatehouse, which miraculously tells me that they are not mining here for two days: this will be the last time a civilian will ever get to see this splendid glacier and valley. The road turns ugly with mud, requiring constant acceleration. Crew chiefs in bright yellow slickers stand in gray rain, glowering through the debris of yellow machinery.

Once past this, the road hairpins and joins on again to Salmon Creek, which has mysteriously become the Salmon Glacier without so much as announcing what it was doing.

/ October 11: Salmon Glacier

I awake this morning to a dawn that illuminates the tops of spires and peaks with salmon color, as if filling these pinnacles with an apricot mercury. It then slides down the glacial thermometer and divides evenly with the ice to the northwest and southeast, casting the parallel moraine cadmium orange. The rock ledge on which breakfast is getting itself cooked hovers 400 feet above the glacier. The air is surprisingly warm: 58 degrees, at 56 degrees latitude in the middle of October (Greenhouse Effect already?). Two huge pink pine grosbeaks alight on top of one another in a solitary stunted pine. A bald eagle thermals high over the canyon. Below, it can see abundant mountain goat, black bear, an odd grizzly or two, moose, lynx, deer, wolverine, fox, porcupine, and it may dive to feast on shrew, vole, mouse, baby bird, martin, mink, marmot, squirrel, pack rat, abundant salmon and Dolly Varden trout. If I were gifted with eagle eyes, I could watch the intimate lifestyle of *Mesenchytraeus solifugus*, the ice worm. These clever adaptations live near the surfaces of glaciers in meltwater pools, which fill the ablation hollows at 2,500 to 3,200 feet of elevation. They are barely visible to the human eye. Their body temperature stays just above freezing while they feast on the debris that floats in the wind or the algae growing in the snow.

After breakfast, a short "just-down-the-road-a-piece" turns out to take five hours to travel. Cut high over the glacier in a rock wall, the road drops off suddenly to a road running parallel and way below. I meet a mining equipment operator and his wife attached like a limpet to his side. He says he works here seven days a week all summer long, doing exploratory work for the Mining Company. "I'm the one who destroys nature and tears up trees to build roads and rip open mountains," he says with a spate of conscience. But he makes extremely good money, enough that they can buy a house in expensive Victoria on Vancouver Island.

His wife, who seldom sees him, looks desperate by his side. She never makes eye contact with me, even when my eyes fall directly on hers to acknowledge her presence. She resents me as another female perhaps? No. This is talk of mines, mountains, money, and earth-movers. She wants no part of it.

He tells me that it is owing to his exploratory digging over the last six summers that they are opening up a mine: he found enough gold to make it profitable. He states this apologetically, as if he were personally responsible (if not he, then someone else). I tell him about all the Colorado mining roads I followed to their ends and beyond as a kid. I do not say that the mule wagon trails of the nineteenth century are a far cry from the bulldozed strips of the twentieth. A hand-dug pit straight down into the ground is a lot more colorful and tolerable than are the huge all-inclusive scrapes of DC9s. I tell him what joy miners' roads have brought my exploratory urges. Why am I so damn diplomatic this morning?

Miners often are the first to slice into Earth's torte layers, their diggings fascinating at first, and sore, drab rubble later, leaching out dangerous minerals artificially released from inside the planet.

Now it is raining softly, and the old miner's road is dropping down radically to the glacier. The cold air surges up from bottomless crevasses, which gape hungrily. Rockfalls now cover the road, requiring quick scrambles over large scree, and I constantly watch above me. The intense reds, greens, and lavenders create a littoral aurora with a crystal structure. Throughout is pyrite—or possibly gold?—galena, sphalirite, and rusty minerals.

The road becomes a narrow trail, a whiff over tumbled ore with bright colored string to delineate it, as if there was anyplace else to go but straight up or straight down. I decide to return.

It is raining hard when I get back to the truck. During a quickly cooked supper, black storm clouds swirl over the ridge behind me. I am apprehensive of the glacier-edged road and its slop bucket of horrors. The first is Tenajon Silver's hand-slapped sign, "Pass at your own risk," a vertical chute of silver ore that could sweep down 800 feet at any time. I drive on, examining the surface of the filthy glacier and the fog pouring over the ridge in a tangible wall. The "road" shoots down the precipitous valley wall and around a sharp curve, which turns back in the opposite direction.

Recent rockfall and debris from a Cat has left the road full of sharp edges that play Russian roulette with my tires, quick and sassy little turns, me hoping one of them doesn't continue over the edge. The road then jogs sharply back to the west over excruciatingly slippery ruts, down through big yellow trucks with broken axles and Cats with tread width equal to the length of my long-bed pickup. Through Ancient Growth rainforest goes a whistling white river of glacial silt opaque as a high-tech kitchen cutting board, muscular as a Rodin sculpture. This road is dropping 1,999 feet to sea level in 28 miles. The river rushes over and snaps at the road.

That evening I come back out of the small notch of civilization at Portland Arm and continue on the Cassiar Highway until I reach the Yellowhead blacktop down to Terrace and Prince Rupert. There I will board a ferry for Vancouver Island.

/ October 12:   Prince Rupert, British Columbia

I am sitting in an oriental cafe listening to some fish guts being spilled in the plastic booth behind me. On the wall hang plastic items of China made in Taiwan. Red and black plastic decor items on each table are counterbalanced with a bottle of cheap double-spigot soy sauce. Mine sits in a pool of brown goo.

"If there's no more herring, then there's no more herring! I want those multi-permit guys off the board! Gill-net herring and halibut. Who the fuck cares if them Indian's are making a living!"

A soft spoken voice: "But them Indians need it. That's the way they always done. That's the way they done it long before we came." I twist around just long enough to see a Vietnam tee-shirt on the soft-spoken one.

"Yeah, but there's these Indians I know who sends an entire case of fish home to his family every week. Fuck him, the bastard! Fuck him! I don't even get a case a week no more. Fuck him!"

"That's cool. It's legal. They use it to live. Let him live."

"Fuck him!" Silence while the waitress brings them their oriental fish dishes. Quiet sucking noises ensue. "I don't want to be penalized

189

just because some new guy comes in who don't know how to fish yet either," says the first.

"Yeah, but they got as much right to come here to fish as you did to come up from New Zealand, or wherever it was you just was."

"Fuck 'em all. There ain't enough fish left for all of us. New Zealand had it right. You don't mess around down there because they fine you thousands and thousands and jerk your license away for life. But the problem here is that it's not evenly enforced. So everybody cheats. It's totally unpredictable here, their enforcement. So I have to cheat, too." His tone reminds me of a three-year-old.

"When did you lose your license down there in New Zealand?" asks the perceptive friend.

Later, I squat on a glacially scoured rock with pitted humps and slick grooves. In front of me a black river rushes upward and inland. Hovering over another series of glacial drumlins in the backwards rapids are large sculptured sponge forms the size of llamas and mucky tan. These seem to be animated by a nervous system from another planet, for they all quiver in unison. In combination with the black thunder of bore tide, this sunken glacial valley has an eerie effect.

The kaien, or foam, of Kaien Island stands high in the rapids created from whipped up tannin, cedar tree juice in the water. It is uncanny and abundant on these powerful rapids down the glacial chute of the Skeena River. When the tide water rushes back in over the drumlin islands, noisy bore tides stand fourteen inches high.

Drumlins make queer seal-back-shaped islands with long flutes and grooves out of bedrock, horizontal columns of a submerged civilization. An ancient sideways Parthenon.

The Skeena River, the same river that led me into this journey three months ago, is an odd river, cutting rapidly through layered sea sediment that is lightly metamorphosed. Shallow lakes lie in thin basins scoured out of the bedrock, and all the fjords and steep canyon walls are near bedrock. To gaze into the primordial mud of these canyons is to gaze into the Black Box of the biosphere: the road cuts into mud boils of sea goop that shines like afterbirth.

There is tremendous climatic variation here: in terms of precipitation, 200 inches of snowfall just above Prince Rupert, 400 inches at

Premier, and 1,000 inches at Tide Lake. Just on the other side of the Coastal Range it looks like the dry sagebrush hills of New Mexico. A topographical map indicates much bare scraped rock and scattered moraines, and still ice caps over much of the area.

Glacial memory is everywhere: scoured, polished, stepped, sharp-ridged, serrated, round humps of moutonnées, the funny humps of kame terraces, ice-stagnation heaps, undulating mounds of unsorted glacial drift. Diamictons are one of the few natural features that rate uglier than the tracks left after a bulldozer convention. Slides of rock leave debris, avalanches triggered by the failure of a thin surface layer of water-saturated colluvium and glacial deposit. Random heaps of rock and directional ridges of swales up and down the valley are downright ugly. The planet looks much newer, much rawer up here.

Exfoliating bedrock falls off in sheaths, leaving linear devastation. All along the base of avalanche-streaked cliffs are colluvial aprons of stone: talus balanced at its most precarious angle and subjected to frequent rockfalls; vegetation begins only at 30- to 35-degree angles. Irregular surfaces left by the melt of dead ice in contact with the re-working of drift lie at the base of stagnant glaciers or where long ago a glacier came to a halt. Eskers, ridges of poorly sorted under-ice river deposits, left in long tunnels of ice at the base of decaying glaciers, are also visible in these glacial paths to the sea. Kame terraces march up valley sides, like mountains with agricultural intentions.

Prince Rupert's deep-water port exists because of the glaciers grinding down to the sea. Former fjords, such as the Kitsumskalum-Kitmat trough and the lower Skeena Valley (Prince Rupert), contain deltaic, marine, and glaciomarine deposits exposed since the close of the last glacial period. Raised fjords are full of deltaic platforms left by the snout of a retreating glacier. River valleys are radically different from any I've seen in the Lower Forty-eight.

The sea has been bouncing up and down since the first of the four glacial periods in the beginning of the Quaternary Period. The entire period alternated intervals of glaciation with climates similar to our own. During the Fraser Glaciation, 25,000 to 30,000 years ago, there was vast precipitation (even more than falls on cyclists in Seattle now), which built up the great ice sheets of the Piedmont Complex that were

to cover most of British Columbia. Inside uncovered pockets were
the keys and bridges essential to life forms: the musk ox, bison, and
smaller organisms new to the New World. The Queen Charlotte
Islands were important such pockets. The Canadian Cordillerian
Glacier Complex expanded well-nourished by abundant precipitation
to cover the entire western part of British Columbia with flow patterns of its own. It became so huge that it was no longer controlled by
surface topography. Instead, the powerful dynamics of ice sheet mor-
phology took over and controlled its own megalithian movements.
Some conjecture that a huge ice dome formed during this ice age, with
all the flow away from its center. It slowly shifted its axis eastward as
the one over the Rockies drifted west.

Earth's crust was isostatically depressed by the great weight of ice,
so that the oceans here reached 200 feet above current sea level. Old
deltas from the sides of the once-shrunken fjords visibly lap their way
down the exposed cliffs: at Terrace, B.C., for example.

In between ice ages, the Olympia nonglacial period laid down extensive deposits in the Straits of Georgia. Determining climatic conditions is a paleoecological task; the collectors of prehistoric muck
and bugs tell us that this period was remarkably similar to our own.
Beetles, pollens, and oxygen-isotope data say this region was just a bit
cooler and wetter than it is now. For this data, scientists dipped into
the Queen Charlotte Island peat bogs, finding they truly were the In
Spot for large vertebrates and other yuppies of the mammalian age.
Even the small horse *Equus conversidens*, a bison larger than today's,
and *Mammuthus columbi* chortled and cavorted in their ice sandwich of
time. The Tanganyika people had already been here for two thousand
years, dropping stone tools.

There were not filthy glaciers, such as the Salmon; they retreated
too quickly, finishing up around 10,000 years ago. By 80,000 years
ago the sea had fallen to its present level, leaving irregular complex
patterns of fertile sedimentations soon stabilized by vegetation. Still
under water, the land bridge to Siberia now stopped the slouch of the
Rough Beast away from Bethlehem, or toward it.

12

Rough Beast's Progress Report

/ October 14:   The Queen of the North

Ship rides are rites of passage for me; a sense of completion covers one in fog soup as the land one has known so intimately, in such detail, melts into sea. I remember the opening passage of *Zorba the Greek* by Nikos Kazantzakis, the long passages of Joseph Conrad at sea, Herman Melville, Coleridge's infamous journey with albatross, and my favorite sea passage of all time, from Rachel Carson's *The Sea Around Us*: the fog room at the beginning of Chapter Ten. It is at sea that we become vulnerable, have to listen to our inner workings and confront the monsters beneath.

I sit across the big ferry benches from Françoise, a French lady who moved from California to remote Alaska, now traveling down to San Miguel D'Allende to build an adobe house for winter living. She gives me a piece of moose meat from the animal she has killed, dressed out, and hauled all by herself. In her fifties, she appears to be in excellent condition, but she is not a large person. The meat is so well cooked that it is hard to taste the mooseness of it, but it is firm and tangy, as if spiced. I shared with her Dijon mustard and blue cheese.

Together, we speak of life, of independence, of marriage, of men, of truth, of self-worth, and then proceed to solve the problems of nuclear energy based on the French government's system of uniform high standards, and make it so that all countries are one, and that we have no boundaries. We go on to conquer the problem of Washington, D.C.'s, and Ottawa's apparent disdain for the natural world of the West. We attempt to decipher why these governments are motivated only by population base and short-term economic greed when the health and wealth of the planet is at stake. This one we fail to solve.

We are now in a long narrow channel with a white man's name; Grenville, between Kitiman mainland and Pitt Island. Farther west another narrow slit, the Principle Channel, then Banks Island. Deep fjords run rhythmically out to the sea about every twenty miles. Their rivers and glaciers eroded the evenly spaced northeast-southwest faultlines.

I stand out on the deck of the *Queen of the North*; she is huge and the engines throb. Françoise and several other passengers have seen fit to point out that it is very cold-wet-windy-rainy-blah-blah-blah to me, but I have dreamed of this intimate flirt with deep fjords from the perspective of the sea, longed for geology's ability to unlock the stars, to toss me one of the keys to the planet, to hogtie me to the vastness of time. The dreariest roadcut becomes an open book, and the stones, engaging mind games ever since Mr. Ratliff in high school bounced around the room gesturing passionately, as if each epoch were of explosive significance to our pimpled adolescent lives. Which, of course, they are.

Out here, slicing smoothly between parallel islands, an air of mystery, where the sea glows light green when the sun comes cracking through the mottled clouds, then bright chartreuse, then a slippery rubescent green. These greens are picked up and reverberate through the purple bruised greens of the islands, to the deep blues-dusky greens of the mainland mountains.

One hour out, and the *Queen of the North* has barely passed the first inlet of mainland, the Ecstall River. It cuts deep into the Douglas Channel before it whimsically curls around in a curious spiral, almost cutting off an island. Log roads are knives in the steep sides of these mountains; sudden verticality, bare and nauseating. Back farther on yet-steeper slopes, ear-lobe-shaped mountains plunge to the sea. There are multitudes of cascades straight down to the sea from thousands of feet above and avalanche chutes. I've never seen a coast with no pause at the shoreline, no low land: just mountains crotch-deep in sea. I am reminded of Lake Powell, its red sandstone spires now flooded, covered forever, popping up unexpectedly out of the depths like the Loch Ness Monster. While driving a cruise yacht with a computerized depth finder, I would read: 301' 302' 305' 301' 303' 12', and suddenly a pinnacle would have risen out of nowhere to the bottom of the boat.

The northwest-southeast troughs, perpendicular to the main slant of fjord drainages, slice off islands from the mainland. Low connector islands of scraped bedrock slither in between. I theorize to pass the time: a set of faultlines caused by subduction of the Pacific Plate came later than the original faults caused by the doming of the cordillera. But then that may be just too small a perspective from our tiny ships' passing. Western British Columbia is on the edge of the American lithospheric plate, which, in turn, interacts with the Juan de Fuca, the Explorer, and the Pacific plates in the northeast Pacific Ocean.

Diastrophism is the process that changes the internal and external structure of Earth, forming new continents, reshaping oceans, and building mountains. It consists of tectonic plates pushing around while changing land and sea relationships. Under the present plate tectonic regime, the west coast of Vancouver Island and the Queen Charlotte Islands are being uplifted, while the mainland is slowly subsiding. As an ice age transfers water onto the continents, the landmass underneath redistributes itself in what is called isostatic distribution. These redistributions shift most intensely at the edges of the ice masses. Here, the mountains stand right in the sea.

Eustatic changes in sea level vary in direct relationship to the glacial ice. Because these changes occur all over the planet, there is nowhere one can stand on the planet to avoid isostatic adjustment.

Right here it is visible: earthquakes measuring up to 6 on the Richter
Scale occur frequently; floods, erosion, landslide, snow avalanche
sculpt the Northwest's history with a crazy man's chisel.

Islands float past us now as if in a dream, a white lace line where
the sea reaches eroded rock. Chafing waves tighten their rhythms in
the constricted channel, squeezing down on the *Queen of the North*.
Cross waves catch her skirts and rock us. Clouds obscure the tops of
the high forested cliffs; cascades originate mysteriously in the heavens.
Islands have infinite concavities here, a jigsaw-puzzle piece gone
cancerous.

Struck deep in a pensive mood by the rhythmic slap of waves and
the darkening atmosphere, I imagine these strange islands being colo-
nized by the Greeks, attracted to their deep green wetness. Greek
philosophy would have been altered, our system of government different. I would be curious to know what long dark winters would
have done to the Socratic dialogue or Plato's *Republic*. Personal free-
doms might have taken a second seat to the way of the tribe. Huddling
together throughout the long wet winter might, in the long run, have
lain a firmer basis for environmental connectedness instead of all-
celebrated individual gain.

The smell of cypress would have been the odiferous Western red
cedar; olive oil replaced by salmon fish oil. A finely honed aesthetic
would have come out darker than in the blaze of gold hills under olive
trees stripped of their Ancient Forests by ancient warring navies. Humanity's very thought structures, which emanate so much from the
land, would have been more interdependent, perhaps more tradition-
cast, and instead of fighting so hard to escape and conquer the forces
of nature we would have fought to be one with them. We would have
taken on animals for ancestors and named ourselves eight to ten times
throughout a lifetime based on the deeds we had done for our fellows.

In fact, the people who did live here believed that the Animal
People from whom they were descended had souls, spirits, certain
abilities and emotions, just as Human People do. They felt themselves
part of a dreamlike whole, once more closely related to the animal
ancestors than now. Transitions between animal and human, even
between dying and then living again, were fluid. But alas, now we have

lost the power to see animals turn themselves into their human forms, except under extreme conditions: sickness, fasting, or far out at sea.

How different the Tlingit were from the Europeans in their relationship to the natural world. Even before the Classical Age in Greece, these sea-going people were creating an elaborate language, totem poles, ocean-going canoes, and manifesting the abundant wealth they claimed from the sea in reciprocal giving feasts called potlatches. These were excuses for passing down inheritance to generations, honoring a specific event or person, or observing a rite of passage from one stage of life to the next. It was a way for the host chief to prove his wealth and proclaim his rights to use certain songs, dances, names, crests, and privileges given to him by the ancestors and by the people he led and protected.

Potlatch originally came from a Nuu-chah-nulth word meaning gift or Indian business. Potlatches also gave the Native Peoples here on these rainy coasts a way to cope with new diseases, missionaries, schools and governments, which forbade their languages and ceremonies. The potlatch gave them strength, community. The potlatch wove the tribes together, making reciprocal trading a matter of honor and unifying isolated tribes. The Haida, Tlingit, and many others have a history of moving and intermingling all the way down to the Washington coast, all the way up to Alaska, and inland along the roaring white water to mix with the interior people. Their culture was rich, their craftsmanship beautiful, their ceremonies elaborate. They lived graciously in this land of rugged islands and fjords: the Bella Coola, the Tsimshian, the Kwakiult, the Nootka, and the Coast Salish. All nations relied on the abundant salmon runs, at least until the salmon were depleted by nineteenth-century canneries. They gathered each resource in its own time: sea-bird eggs, clams, mussels, sea urchins, crabs, seaweed, berries.

Although there were slaves and lower classes, everybody had access to food and shelter. Their system of law was tribal, not individual; chiefs settled disputes, if possible, through consultation with others.

Language grew from the land: a system of sounds in which modifiers contained the subtle varieties of shapes and textures of the infinite natural world. The multiple syllables created an onomatopoetic language that seemed to murmur like the rivers as they came out from under the glacier.

I pause in my thoughts about the Peoples here and notice all is mitigated, softened by vegetation and mist. Fifteen gulls sit on one log, all facing the same direction, the log a bleacher for some infinitely slow game of ball. It is cold.

Inside, Francoise and I choose to sleep under the benches against the walls for the protection and darkness they offer. All over, people still are moving and mumbling among themselves, past the generous seats where we sleep. I drift in and out, and hear a girl in passing: "But bears don't have an open season on man." I fall to sleep under the ferry bench, remembering parking in Whitehorse to go to sleep in the pickup. All night long the man sleeping in the van next to me garbled his snores, gasped in bad dreams, and choked and growled, sounding like a dog. All night long there were periodic scratchings on metal and his stomach snarled with a bad meal. The next morning I discovered that he sounded like a dog because he was a dog.

I am dreaming now, in full sleep, of scraping caribou gut and seal stomachs, or filling seal carcasses with unplucked auklets and letting them ferment and freeze, then digging into feathers and all in mid-winter in my subterranean house. But that is the Eskimo people. Dreams aren't so choosy, except on a level one can't know. I dream of steelless tools so clever as to capture the largest mammal on Earth in six-foot seas from a dugout canoe. I dream I am standing high in the canoe, my fellows paddling silently with spear-shaped paddles designed for silence, following the sealskin floats at incredible speed over the black back the size of drumlins, and hurling an ironwood shaft as hard as I can, then back-paddling out of reach of the mighty tail. Under the waves I hear a chorus of us who have been lost at whaling, chanting under the black swells.

I sink down through the sea of all memory, the superstition, the beliefs that grow like fungi around the original impulse, seeking to explicate the most powerful natural phenomena, or, at least, to domesticate them. Wild animals and plants put arms and roots about the People and their beliefs so that they are overgrown and transformed

198

through years by the fine net of mycelia: choked by it, changed by it, words popping like fruits overnight through the soils of experience.

I turn on my back to feel the deep throb of the ship's engines, fall to sleep hearing the cogs turning a high frequency on my spine. I raise knees to press my spine directly to the metal floor through the rough Moroccan spread that serves as bed. Its thick, uneven cotton weave has the softness of peasant clothes. Above me float 500 puffy faces of all nations, expressions slack, dreaming with the rock of the ship in its narrow channel.

13

An Oceanic Ending/Beginning

The ocean should be our rule of thumb,
green as blood, numb as vision,
abnormal, singular and all motion.

Fossils are monsters shrunk through time,
prehistoric miscarriages,
drunk with dream of feet and lung.

Compulsively I pick them up.
Each is digited in years, drowned
souvenir of leagues, then reappears.

Out of their league these thoughts
won't let go, known combines with unknown
in seductive undertow.

/ October 15:   The Lost Continent of Cascadia

As our ferry docks on Cascadia, dawn ratchets into gear, and it stays dark. It is usually raining on Cascadia.

I am out in the rain at the snout of our ship, leaning into the airborne sea, squinting toward a succession of land mounds, a line of submerged dragons, dorsal-finned, grazing headless, each dimmer than the last.

Our ferry docks on Cascadia. Or a vestigial fragment of it. Vancouver Island. Cascadia rose and fell into the sea four times, each time collecting a shroud of sediment, a thick limestone mumbling with fishes, shells, trilobites, amphibians, and reptiles. After its last submersion, Cascadia left behind only this comma-shaped afterthought perched on board the continental shelf. If only I could have scheduled an earlier ferry—say, 25,000 years earlier—I could have docked among primitive forms of rhinoceros, pygmy camels, musk ox, tigers, mammoths, and monkeys, before they left over the last land bridge south, back to Asia.

Stepping off the boat, I would have encountered an isolated enclave of animals; some are still here. Drowsy from lack of sleep, I expect them to appear as crosses between mangoes and mammoths treading air in trees.

There is a legend on Texada Island, a crescent shape north of here, of the grandest beaver that ever lived. The phenomena of size fascinates our species. Much in evolution seems against hugeness: the giants of Earth ebb and flow with the solar flux and the ice flux. In those queer pockets that had lengthier times between ice coatings, such as the interior of Alaska, Vancouver Island, and the Queen Charlotte Islands, giant raccoons, mink, elk, deer, and martin left their supernatural skeletons in the slime.

I hit the land running. Up toward the northernmost point of Vancouver Island, roads are few and scenic—if you like clearcuts. Drive With Caution means: "We don't want interference with our duty of stripping the rainforest as fast as we possibly can." Although the grizzly isn't here, one of my least favorite predators is: the fast-rolling log truck. It's not that the men behind the wheels are bad drivers, or even particularly unkind; it's just that they drive as if they own the roads. They often do.

I stagger through the clearcuts for a long, long time: roads are not marked, so I am lost in the maze. Keep on trying for the far west coast of the island. Thus, one enters the Old Growth Cathedral with a good deal of psychological readiness. Ugliness really does produce a stress, which is the emotional equivalent to me of walking downtown L.A. at midnight in a short skirt in bare feet over broken glass with a lot of small bills.

/ October 16: St. Josef's Camp

Living Spot Extraordinaire, St. Josef's Camp is a small oasis of Old
Growth left by the timber industry for the public. It is a magnificent
site, with columnar Douglas fir and western red cedar. The floor is
striking: absolutely flat with an even cover of red pine needles. At the
base of a red cedar 5 feet in diameter grow gargantuan amanitas the
color of traffic warning signs and twelve inches across. Their caps are
flaked with veil remnants and blush at the center. It is so wet here that
the human eye can almost see them expand. Infant amanita buttons
protrude through the needles, looking like innocent and tasty puffballs
before breaking their veils and expanding into umbrella-shaped poison.

Above, the fluted columns of red cedar are the envy of Greek
antiquity, while down in each tannin-hued pool a bureaucratic nymph
or water spirit distributes oracles. The camp is surrounded by lagoons,
which are covered with the ultimate biomass of the planet: 300-foot
giants stroking the heavens, appearing topless in the mist.

Northwestern forests produce the grandest biomass accumulation
per acre *in the world*. California's coastal redwood, *Sequoia semper-*
virens, produces the greatest biomass, estimated at 4,000 tons per
hectare (one hectare = 2.47 acres). Here the Douglas fir/western
hemlock forest can average 868 tons per hectare; the Sitka spruce/
western hemlock 1,163 tons per hectare, making it grander even than
the tropical rainforests of South America, which produce an average
of 461 tons per hectare. Leaves and surface area in these Pacific forests
grow very slowly, so that the concept of quickly raising trees as crops
is null and void. Downed wood takes another 200 years to add to the
immense biomass, as it decays and is literally turned back into new
trees. Rows of young cedar sit with arched roots over their decaying
elders. Although our Northwestern forests take longer to reach
growth climax, their biomass, and thus their breathing potential and
assistance to a healthy atmosphere, is one of the greatest anywhere on
Earth.

So we clearcut them.

Respiration rates have been estimated at 150 tons/hectare/year for
a 450-year-old Doug-fir, compared to 15.2 to 15.9 for a tulip/poplar

forest in Tennessee (Franklin and Waring, 1979:62-3). Therefore, the health of the atmospheric skin of the planet and its effect on biosphere depends greatly on such massive forests. While condemning Third World nations, we are cutting down our own forest at a rate proportionately faster than they are. In Washington State, another square mile falls each week. It is faster in B.C.

I am startled by the angry chatter of a tiny black-gray squirrel coming toward my truck in an approach-avoidance dance: a chickaree squirrel 6 inches long and with a 5-inch tail. According to the Peterson field guide, it is not supposed to be on this island. It competes with its counterpart, the red squirrel, in the mainland forests for the title of "most-obnoxious-noisemaker." At the base of the huge Doug-fir he has piled pine cone fragments, but he much prefers my morning's dishwater remnants. It is the simmered flavor of soap and tidbits that sends him into rapturous vulgarity. He is a beautiful subspecies of the plebeians that raid our birdfeeders on the mainland: distinct black fringes along the edges of his body make him more intricate and streamlined.

A fragile voice trills from the underbrush with the tremolo of silky flute. I am stilled by the song. Frozen. My skin cast with goose pimples. The song comes closer, its liquidity so seductive I soon find myself on hands and knees creeping and squiggling through dense marsh vegetation, wetting my knees, scratching my unfurred skin, falling elbow-deep into tannin water. All for a brief glimpse of *Cistothorus palustris*. She reveals her identity by a tail flick, although the Audubon guide does not extend distribution this far north. She is a long-billed marsh wren with bright yellow and white breast and wren-shaped round body. Once every eleven minutes or so she grants me a brief audience, rising high on a berry branch to investigate this cumbersome intruder; then she plunges back into nothingness to sing in a rapid woodwind pulsation. For a quick pull on the heart-string, I am back on the slick rock of Arizona and Utah listening to the canyon wren.

Leaves drip constantly, collective drops of three-inch-wide dough balls rolled in the flat sticky needles above until they are loosed and land with such force that even the pine carpet explodes on impact.

With sodden sound, they gather together to become rain. I plan to hike down the coast today, a brief hike to gather the prolific mushrooms and to study the Old Growth Forest. This forest is Hans Christian Anderson illustration animated and three-dimensional: miniature paradises hidden within Earth's giants.

/ October 17: Cascadia: The Northernmost Tip

Cape Scott protrudes, a finger beckoning north toward Queen Charlotte Islands. By the time the cape snagged the first Europeans, the original humans had been here thousands of years. These secretive people called themselves the Saa-Kaalituck, the Nimpkish, the Kwakiutl, the Upatse Satuch, and the legendary "lost" tribes of the Masolemuch and the Kakalatza in the interior (Lillard 1988). In the interior there were legends of a fearful savage place, of tribes who were not actually human at all, but spirits of the dead; places where it was so dank that even salmon feared to go.

Nootka legends warn of the supernatural center of the island. They also advise one of the infinity of creation that thrives within the rainforest. Once again, an ancient, pre-technological people's folk wisdom foreshadows and contains contemporary truths greedily ignored by the industrial revolution, now rediscovered by biologists and foresters. Now these mysterious pantheons are called by such names as "diversity and abundance of speciation," "ephiphytes," "fungi," "seedladen squirrel and bird scat," "nitrogen-fixer," and "ecological system." It is the same folktale, but founded on a different empiricism.

The Quatsinos, the Native Americans who now live between here and Alert Bay, must have found the early white man strange: he killed so many fellow creatures and left the meat. Then there were the Kwisskaynohs, so named because heads of infant aristocrats were bound to show status. In 1904, near here, a skeleton of a child with a long tapered skull was found preserved in a cedar box. The Quatsinos, called Kah-cheen-ah by themselves, are the sole survivors of a massacre a long time ago, before memory.

How beautiful these white beaches and jigsaw coves must have appeared to the first Anglos: immense red trees hovering over the shore, fresh running rust-colored streams that tasted sweet, and abundant sealife for the taking. And take they did, in great and voracious harvests. Captain Hanna came in 1786 for countless pelts. August 1, 1786, trader James Strange stuck another white man's name to the point, that of his friend, Mr. David Scott, and named the Queen Charlotte Islands after the Queen Consort of his monarch, George III. St. Josef Bay was known to the first settlers only as the Little South Bay, where the ship *Consort* was wrecked in 1860. First settlement was Dutch, and since then the Brits, Americans, Russians, and Spanish have all claimed what was never theirs. (Peterson 1974:4–17).

Perhaps in fear of the great dark rainforests, white man's towns hovered cautiously along the coasts for some time, his lumber and trade villages shipping out from the east coast. The interior seemed wild, and the west coast fragmented and inaccessible. It was not until July of 1852 that Hamilton Moffatt of the Hudson's Bay Co. first crossed the island via the Nimpkish River (Lillard 1988). The dirt roads of the northern part of the island still twitch nervously over the confusing terrain and lead to only a few of the many small, isolated fishing villages on the west side. This shore remains one of the most chopped-up and dangerous coastlines in the world, so, of course, I try to go there. Until my ship comes in, most likely a '60s kayak covered with silver duct tape, I must make do with hiking out to St. Josef's Inlet, where the timber industry has graciously left three miles at the end of Cascadia unstripped.

To walk down through it is to plunge into a deep tunnel of rainforest canopy through powerful Modigliani roots, past abundant mushrooms and jungle bird calls. It is dark, yet so light. Sun filters through the 200-foot-high canopy with the intensity of laser beams. The atmosphere is thick with red cedar odor. One can bite it. The ferns are greener than green, each lit by a miniature tensor lamp under each leaf. Their ancient symmetries are soothing.

ODE TO OLD GROWTH

There is nothing else on this planet, perhaps in the universe, so ordered for deep resonance as is the Old Growth Forest. My Forest Service friend Jay Wells, over in Idaho, said of trees: "Of all living things, they seem the most comfortable with their existence. It is hard to imagine a tree looking out of place or at odds with its surroundings. The suppressed and misshapen have wonderful character and diversity to them."

Perhaps it is the immense biomass, or the tremendous complexity, or the filtered beams of sunlight and the columnar antiquity, or the smells of cedar and decomposition: whatever it is, I have never felt such awe and serenity. The death of this ecosystem will be our own demise.

Swamp water stands throughout the trees, back to rust, filled with bright yellow skunk cabbage. The yellow is not actually the flower but a bract hiding a spike of minute flowers. At this late date they are almost gone, but their color remains stark on the retina. *Lysichitum americanum*, an outrageous plant!

I cross over St. Josef Creek, where the canopy above is slightly unzipped and lets in more light. Muscular water gleams as the returning tide climbs through its ladder of fallen trees, each in itself the theater of new life out of old. Constantly, there is squeaking, creaking or chortling. Yet, just as constant, there is a silence that pounds in one's skull.

The trail spits me out at the ocean, which has roared and thudded with a pitch lower than hearing for the last mile. Such pounding always sets our organism's excitation level at open throttle. The beach is long and smooth, studded with sculptured tree bones, remains of great forces. The Pacific Ocean at its thundering best: green, moving. Stones like Inges portraits ripple and curve in precise chiaroscuro.

When the sun comes out across the Pacific's pounding bay it is from no one source, but rather scattered through a viscosity of ocean suspended in air. Slowly it unwraps Earth like a Christmas ball, layer upon layer of white silk ribbon, here and there, a bright treasure.

On reaching the ocean, the sun backlights the gray waves until they become green jade with white veining. Forces constantly recarve them as horizontal, potent totem poles, as ornate and symbolic as they are momentary.

Far out, a loon fishing in the breakers watches me carefully. Few people come here now. Drawn inevitably by tall rocks pounded into concavities, I am at first frightened by the power at their bases, the roar of wave, and then enticed. As the tide goes down, hidden crannies like skull holes expose niches of vegetative pantheons unique to Cascadia. Rough rock stands as a series of sea stacks and spires straight up out of the flat cobble to a 100-foot-high pinnacle. On top of each, the very same western red cedar that stands in columns back at camp here is distorted, braided by the wind, the trunk shooting out parallel to earth or making plunges down toward it.

Just before reaching ground, the limbs shoot back upward. A loon catches a silver flash in its mouth, flips and jerks its club-shaped head to get it parallel to its long beak, then swallows it whole. Cedar trunks torque down over undereaten basaltic rock. Michelangelo was here without the constraints of human form, free to sculpt muscular bulges in stone, constricting and pulsing them at will, carving veins whose bases emerge from the gentle spray of barnacles. A black organic slime colors the lower rock, until the rock rises high enough above the waterline to be stippled with army green rosettes of lichen. A mosaic of khaki and ruined leather clings to mountainscape of red and tan lichen. Fine-grained sheaths of rock exfoliate, cauliflower lava pounded by the sea. Glacial striation streaks the rock. In bas relief, a pale lime-white of embryonic lifeform is underlain with a gray flesh consisting of multitudinous balls of round-mouthed spore bodies on stems: club moss.

As the grand finale of this crowded organic tapestry, a delicate pink lichen grows outward in perfect ovals, like oil paint dropped in water. A last trickle of sea highlights stone, white jewels on black rock. Grasses curl down. Fuzzy strawberry plants drip with mist. Berries black as moon-warts crawl over a bonsai pine.

I have been so caught up in observation that the sudden sound of a raven's wings immediately overhead startles me. The raven here, like coyote in the Southwest, is Trickster. He is here to startle my bland assumptions, perhaps to change me.

Three miles back out through the Old Growth, three miles of archetypal passage, three miles of branches draped thick with epiphytes. Fluted trunks twelve feet around, wide and graceful limbs to pass under, limbs low and horizontal to the ground, new roots grabbing the earth.

"Living" here is not a stop-and-go proposition, as we humans perceive it, but huge trees constantly reconnecting themselves to Earth. Trees upon trees upon trees. Water upon water upon water, moving sluggishly in tannin stain, cedar soup from trees steeping in ox-bow pools, 200-foot reptiles stretching in dark water. Even stumps isolated in mid-lagoon sprout paper birch 14 inches in diameter, oblivious to their watery graves. Twelve deciduous trees atop one old log whose end is submerged in black pond: a dozen bright white columns of birch glow against Ansel Adams–dark liquid. Every surface area is crammed with growth, growth on top of growth growing on old growth. Mushrooms and alders grow profusely from every knob above the water. Giants steep in rich coffee. Pan could be playing his pipes, but then I couldn't hear the fungi calling.

I jump. Something breathing breaks the surface; large rings.

To come to such unabashed growth and diversity is to come as a small beetle among giants, to feel one's actual place in the biosphere. Our niche is quite small, considering our hubris. Being and Nothingness *á la* Old Growth.

Underfoot, tan sticky bubbles pile up on protrusions.

The tide is surging back into the bay in broad scallops. Four mallard females take off only three feet away. I cross slippery planks, a tangle of logs, filled with new seawater, volume increasing. Undermined, the chaos of roots carves dams and dirigibles. The sun streams through grand fir, *Abies grandis*, which has been caught growing three feet a day, 140 feet in fifty years. A Douglas fir can grow 170 feet in seventy-two years, and trees 300 feet high live along coastal British Columbia (Arno, 1977:67). This site is too soggy for the western hemlock, which grows best inland at elevations up to 3,500 feet and is part of a luxurious undergrowth of original forests. I am particularly fond of hemlock, which has a wonderful manner of catching light rays just before they hit ground and casting lacy exaltations upward.

Sitka spruce, Alaska's signature tree, flourishes within thirty miles of salt water (although we found one seventy miles inland on the White River in Old Growth slated for cutting next to Rainier National Park). It likes tide waters just fine and revels in cold, wet fog. Two hundred inches of rain a year and it can march right up onto the tundra in Alaska. The Sitka exerts a particular grace on sea stacks and sheer cliffs. One can love its ability to contort, to form mysterious huge burls, and to serve as a proper throne for our national human-endangered emblem. From here down to Oregon it grows to the world's grandest proportions: records of 16.5 feet thick and 216 feet high (Arno, 1977:53–59).

Here Jack the Ripper is MacMillan Bloedel Ltd. I read in a B.C. newspaper that the company enjoyed both record sales and earnings in 1987, passing for the first time the three billion dollar mark. Profits were better, though, the company moaned, when there was no required stumpage system. Damned heart-rending! Like the Third World, Canada is cutting and exporting its national heritage so fast that it will soon be gone. Yet we are all one country, one territory: we breathe one another's air, float one another's water, dream common dreams.

We have had the Germanic approach to order and clean forest floors in American forest management for too long. Single-species forests are dying. We are faced with the disasters of narrow genetics. Tim Schowalter, an entomologist at Oregon State University, among other scientists, has definite proof that the single species forest is vulnerable to disastrous insect infestations. Predators that control such pests are eliminated in single species forests. In my own state, the clearcuts are in checkerboards of about twenty-five to fifty acres each; here in B.C., clearcuts are enormous and blatant. According to recent visiting members of the European Congress, the heads of companies doing such cutting would be imprisoned in Europe. Liability should be high enough to cover damage to the planet on which we all depend, capital punishment for the murder of entire ecosystems not out of the question. But here's the rub: with liability so high, owners of mega-lithian fuel, timber, and shipping industries would not take the risk. They would go elsewhere. The price of oil would soar; the price of raw building materials would become prohibitive. What we now consider our normal lifestyle would go only to the wealthy. Once again that ugly ball is back in our court, John Q. Consumer.

Scientists have found that a minimum of 600 acres of forest must be left standing to protect against wind and storm. Instead, our forest policy (1988) dealt out smaller northern spotted owl habitats scattered and isolated across three states. The result: genetic isolation, death by disease.

My country's National Forest "Management" Act calls for 123,400 acres of Old Growth to be cut within the next fifty years. It is disappearing at the rate of a square mile per week, and at least as fast here on Vancouver Island. The argument for jobs is a spurious, cruel invention of the Timber Industry: between 1979 and 1986, 30,000 jobs were lost in Washington and Oregon while production increased by a billion board-feet. Twenty-five percent fewer workers produced ten percent more lumber; sawmills are going under. A fast buck for the industry does not a rosier job market make. In Washington State alone, we *buy* half a billion dollars more wood products than we export!

The timber industry is not all good for the local economies, as they would have us believe. Profit goes back to boardrooms and stockholders. The timber industry giants are basically nomadic, moving from place to place until the trees mature enough to cut are gone and then pulling out, leaving economic and psychological devastation in the very communities to which they once brought wealth and prosperity.

Oops, sorry. I am raving again. On to more cheery and subtle pleasures, delights of tongue and eye, engaging the mind in naming spongy pieces of the Divine Biosphere. Mushrooms again.

MUSHROOM LIST:

Amanita muscaria

Coprinus comatus, shaggy manes (ate, but was too watery to have much taste, as opposed to New Mexico, where they are tough, wizened old birds, bullets of minerals to be softened in delicate cream sauces)

Huge puff balls of all sorts, too squishy to consume

Pleurocybella porrigens (delicious! all over the downed logs like
  dove winds, related to ostreatis, the oyster mushroom)

Pleurotus ostreatus (found only one characteristic black beetle
  and was not sure; they look so different here than in the
  Southwest)

Amanita flavoconica (slugs have eaten away at cap; slug lies dead at
  its foot, but, I believe, not owing to mushroom ingestion)

Lactarius deliciosus

Naematoloma fasciculare (sulphur tuft with pale green tinge; flesh
  bitter on tongue; many on rotten wood; quite beautiful!)

Aleuria aurantia (funnel cupped, translucent orange; exotic!)

Cantharellus xanthopus (lovely orange, chantrellish)

Fluted white helvella

Laetiporus sulphureus

Green tacky russula

Mycena inclinata

Collybia something

Strobilurus trullisatus (on fir cone, yellow stalked, thin and
  cinnamon, bell-like)

Tricholoma pessudatum

Suillus luteus

Coprinus disseminatus

Ah, fungi! Their mycelium webbery crochets together the entire forest, an ecosystem of complex circuitry, exquisite in the necessity of each part to the whole. The lungs of the planet. Mushrooms, the fruiting bodies, are all that appear of the fungal world. Their roots, the mycelia, spread for miles and miles throughout rotting logs, through and over every inch of the lofty trees, and down through every smudge of soil, carried within the bowels of animals, chemically changing death into life!

The fungi make the rotting logs fundamental to the forest economy, powering and stabilizing the roots of new trees, passing on and creating energy by releasing organic material gathered by once-living trees into nutrients for the next plants. They store and carry water, and are wonders of conservation. Nothing is wasted or extra in fungal activity. A system of loops of energy, everything dead and dying is once again transformed to alive and living, mostly through the fungi . . . down in the darkness of the soil's black box, rising like Christ through microbiology, a self-renewing, life-giving fountain.

We know only a minute fraction of the full complexity of this system. The timber industry is like the primitive warrior who rips the protective siding off a sophisticated space station from another star's planet, a spaceship that could unlock knowledge of other solar systems for us. Then, claiming to have "scientifically farmed" this knowledge, he blows up the ship.

/ October 18:   Coming Out of the Rainforest into the Light of the Clearcut

Cosmothetic, I emerge as a dead man in the jokes of the living.

Some of them are pretty funny jokes, though. Like the sign warning one to be careful of the log trucks: ELEPHANT CROSSING, with pictures of red elephants crossing the road. Or the huge cedar log on top of a crushed 1968 Chevy; on top is a standard yellow highway sign, which reads: EXPECT THE UNEXPECTED.

Everything wet gleams on the way out. I can barely steer, having touched nothing mechanical for days. I hate to leave the thirty-foot limbs dipping down as if protective. I hate to leave air that is palpable with 10 million possibilities of life per square meter, all oddly humming. I hate to leave the sky tube spiraling always overhead wherever I look, its elegant symmetries converging toward a vanishing point. I hate to leave the hollow logs, each filled with its unique miniature cosmos, and the cobwebs backlit: the logic of eight-legged jewelers.

/ October 21:   Cowichan Bay

As I walk back to switch laundry from washer to dryer, a very old
fisherman catches up to my stride and continues a conversation we've
been having for the last eighty-seven years. . . .

" . . . and so they've got a sidewalk in here now, eh? I told them a
long time ago that they oughta 'ave a sidewalk in 'ere forty years ago,
I says to them . . . I told them back then . . . I took a look at these
women 'ere in long skirts pushin' them big baby carriages ahboot 'ere,
jus' right up next to this dock 'ousing . . . quite dangerous it was.
These women 'ere pushing these carriages. One of them could 'ave
fallen off 'ere then! Or even now. . . . "

I glance down about twenty feet to the boat dock level; it used to
be quite a drop-off before they put in a new railing. We walk out in
the street, off the half-done boardwalk, on level with the second
stories of dock buildings. I decide to hold up my end of this timeless
conversation:

"Yep," I say.

"Yhup, I came 'ere in '36, I did. I came from the big prairies—
too cold to freeze your derriere. Forty below, it was, and that wind!
I didn't need that! No, certainly not!"

"Nope!" I say, in an inexplicable bad mood, but grateful for his
company.

"You fish?" I ask.

"Yhup," he says quite sadly, "but not no more. Now I got another
business. I watch the loons. They come, you see, they all come into
this one area near this bay and then distribute all around to feed. I
keep this log book. I kept this log book all these years, you know. You
know a captain has to keep a log book. A log's a fine tradition, it is,
and it goes way back far—sea captains, you know. Captain Cook,
Vancouver and all."

"When your memory fails you, and memory fails me a lot now,"
he continues, "when your memory fails you, the log gives you good
information. I go back over my log notes and find out exactly where
my birds were and what date. Find out ahboot my birds, you know. It

is having a life over again. And the log book is good for your business too, you know. Should anybody bring a case 'gainst you, you say exactly where you were at exactly what time. Or in case someone else wants to know where my birds are later on, when I'm not 'ere to tell 'em."

He has seen the large black notebook under my arm. It goes with me everywhere. I am very sad, and this man knows it. This man, this old, old man, knows more about me than I do.

"Yup," he continues, as if I had said something intelligent in between, "that journal's your life there, all I got left of mine, good women, good boat, good fish. You go back over that to get the information. You go back over the log book. . . ."

With that, the old fisherman leaves as he came, in mid-thought and mid-stride.

I think, "I am afraid." Afraid of what? Afraid of being swallowed back. Of forgetting. Forgetting what? I've forgotten. Of urbanity, of routine, of forgetting. All the way down to Victoria, driving in pouring rain, tears pour down my face.

/ October 21, 4 P.M.:   Coho Ferry, Juan de Fuca

It is exceptionally hot and packed in Victoria, and I have decided not to stay. Always so terribly British and elegant and with a superb museum system, I usually love Victoria. But not today.

I book passage on the Coho Ferry immediately. Sailing from Victoria to Port Angeles, she is an American ferry full of American-sounding twangs. We are crushed in together on the dock waiting for the customs official to come by our cars. Wretched smells of exhaust. The two people beside me chain-smoke in an air-conditioned luxury car with the windows up and the engine idling for an hour and a half.

I can hardly wait to drive onto the ferry and get out of this god-damn vehicle. What once was my home, my castle-studio-cocoon, is now my prison.

As soon as the ferry is launched, I brace myself against the bone-chilling wind on the top deck, as far into the wind as I can get. The deck empties of people as soon as they feel the sea wind whipping past. I am alone again with my birds. To ease pain, I watch birds. A Buller's shearwater slices the air very very fast. Kingfishers, geese, and cormorants float right in town. Two grebes fight over a fish. The phlegm of city floods out, while sun, an hour before being swallowed by the steely Strait of Juan de Fuca, leaves a strip of liquid gold between eye and horizon.

The sun, four fingers above the water, an hour before setting, leaves water pewter on either side of the sun strip. There is no horizon line. Just a low moan of airborne sea. The white hum of a continuous curve. Ships appear as black stones floating above where the horizon line should be.

British civilization has disappeared in a gray sludge. I am traveling from the known to the unknown, thinking of nineteenth-century explorers. I think of discovering new, unseen lifeforms, like in the rainforests of the Amazon or somewhere in the Aleutians. I dream of the drawings I will send back to explain life there. I am dreaming of suddenly coming upon an isolated zoologist, lost for years without any of his own kind in proximity. After his initial fear, I peel back layers of synthetics, down, silk, wool, polyesters, to examine the tiny pink hapless man protected by only a clever but vacuous brain.

I snap out of my reverie as a cormorant speeds by faster than the ferry on double wingbeat, twice as fast as gulls. In a stupor, I seem to be grogged from city driving, numbed by practicalities. I watch the archaic bird and imagine him as a last vestige of dinosaur.

The Olympic Peninsula, once a dark shapeless mass, is distinguishing itself with trees, and branches on those trees, and needles on those branches—sort of as a long thought takes form from a nebulous feeling, branches into structure, and finally is filled out with the particulars of words. To the west, all floats in a thick fog backlit by sun, which itself is a red contusion on a white sphere. All that passes between the sun and my eyes, the swath of translucent gold molecules, itself becomes electrified and transparent; the east is dark gray, each ship furry at the edges, blurred. To the west, a small sailboat too near us in the fog.

The man in his small craft works rapidly to bring his ship around in a fickle wind, passing into the gold strip of sun: instantly, what has been a dark silhouette turns into a blazing pink membrane, all metal of rigging and engines, all polished wood of deck and wheel, set ablaze in a firework of refraction. I suck in my breath. The man simply continues his frantic work routine, unconscious of the beauty his ship is casting.

Select Bibliography

"Arctic Coast Wildlife." *Wilderness* 50, no. 173 (1986): 4–5.

"Arctic Refuge Battle." *Congressional Quarterly Almanac* (100th Congress, 1st Session). Washington: Congressional Quarterly, Inc., 1987.

Armitage, Doreen. "World's Largest Waterfowl Staging Resounding Recovery." *Canadian Geographic* 106 (June–July 1986): 46–48.

Arno, Stephen F. *Northwest Trees*. Seattle: The Mountaineers, 1977.

Bland, John. *Forests of Lilliput: The Realm of Mosses and Lichens*. Englewood Cliffs, N.J.: Prentice-Hall, 1971.

Boslough, John. "The Latest Word in Oil Rigs Hits the North Slope." *Smithsonian* 12, no. 2 (May 1981): 82–87.

Bradley, Hassel. "Courts Slowing Alaska Rush; Nevada Gold Mining Gets Easier." *American Metal Market* 96 (October 4, 1988): 5.

Bulkis, Lawrence, and Louis H. Barton. "Yukon River Fall Chum Salmon Biology." *Chum Salmon and Stock Status*. Anchorage: Alaska Department of Fish and Game, 1984.

Burton, Robert. *Bird Behavior*. New York: Alfred A. Knopf, 1985.

Cirkle, Fritz. *Chrysotile-Asbestos: Its Occurrences, Exploitation, Milling, and Uses*. Ottawa: Canadian Department of Mines, 1910.

Daumal, Rene. "Mount Analogue." *Parabola* (November 1988): 10–87.

Digby, Bassett. *The Mammoth and Mammoth Hunting in Northeast Siberia.* New York: D. Appleton and Co., 1926.

Franklin, Jerry F. and Richard H. Waring. "Distinctive Features of the Northwest Coniferous Forest: Development, Structure and Function." *Forests: Fresh Perspectives.* Corvallis: Corvallis Press (State University of Oregon), 1979.

Hanson, Dennis. "Alaska Energy: Oilmen's Woes, Coal Contract." *Audubon* 78 (September 1976): 127.

Harbottle, Jean Connoly, and Fern Grice Credeur. *Woman in the Bush.* Anchorage: Pelican Publishing Co., 1966.

Hawking, Stephen W. *A Brief History of Time: From the Big Bang to Black Holes.* New York: Bantam Books, 1988.

Kizzia, Tom. "Can Caribou and Oil Coexist?" *Sierra* 71 (September–October 1986): 20–23.

———. "Feuding Groups Make an Oil Deal." *Sierra* 71 (September–October 1986): 76–77.

Kopvillem, Peeter, Flora Evans and Heather Stockstill. "Mining for Regulations." *Maclean's* 98 (Nov. 11, 1985): 77–78.

Krieger, Louis C. *The Mushroom Handbook.* New York: Dover Publications, 1967.

Kurten, Bjorn. *The Ice Age.* New York: G.P. Putnam's Sons, 1969.

Larsen, James Arthur. *The Role of Physiology and Environment in the Distribution of Arctic Plants.* Madison: University of Wisconsin, 1964.

Levine, Robert D. *The Spoken Word.* Victoria: British Columbia Provincial Museum, 1983.

Lillard, Charles. "The Ghost People of Vancouver Island." *The Beaver* 68 (April–May 1988): 46–50.

Lincoff, Gary H. *The Audubon Society Field Guide to North American Mushrooms.* New York: Alfred A. Knopf, 1981.

Manella, Lorin. "The Columbia Glacier: A Glacier in Alaska May Begin to Retreat." *Sierra* 64 (May–June 1979): 64–65.

McIlvaine, Charles, and Robert K. Macadam. *1,000 American Fungi.* New York: Dover Publications, 1983.

Mowat, Farley. *A Whale for the Killing.* New York: Bantam Books, 1972.

Nance, R. Damian, Thomas R. Worsley and Judith B. Moody. "The Supercontinent Cycle." *Scientific American* (July 1988): 72–80.

Orth, Donald. *Dictionary of Alaska Place Names.* Washington: U.S. Government Printing Office, 1967.

Osgood, Cornelius. *Distribution of the Northern Athapaskan Indians.* New Haven: Yale University Press, 1936.

Peterson, Lester R. *The Cape Scott Story*. Vancouver, B.C.: Mitchell Press, 1974.

Porsild, A.E. "Plant Life in the Arctic." Ottawa: National Museum of Canada (papers), 1951.

———. "Vascular Plants of the Western Canadian Arctic Archipelago." Ottawa: National Museum of Canada (papers), 1955.

———. "Illustrated Flora of the Canadian Arctic Archipelago." Ottawa: National Museum of Canada (papers), 1957.

Richardson, David. *The Vanishing Lichens: Their History, Biology and Importance*. New York: Hafner Press, 1974.

Schaefer, J., and John A. Day. *A Field Guide to the Atmosphere*. New York: Houghton Mifflin, 1981.

Spellenberg, Richard. *The Audubon Society Field Guide to North American Wildflowers*. New York: Alfred A. Knopf, 1979.

Thompson, D'Arcy Wentworth. *On Growth and Form*. Cambridge: Cambridge University Press, 1971.

Thompson, Ida. *The Audubon Society Field Guide to North American Fossils*. New York: Alfred A. Knopf. 1982.

Thompson, William Irwin (editor). *GAIA, A Way of Knowing: Political Implications of the New Biology*. Great Barrington, Mass.: Lindisfarne Press, 1987.

Van Ballenberghe, Victor. "Giants of the Wilderness: Alaskan Moose." *National Geographic* 172, no. 2 (August 1987): 260–80.

Viereck, Leslie A., and Elbert L. Little. *Alaska Trees and Shrubs*. Fairbanks: University of Alaska, 1986.

Young, Steven B. *To the Arctic: An Introduction to the Far Northern World*. New York: John Wiley & Sons, 1988.

Zukov, Gary. *The Dancing Wu Li Masters: An Overview of the New Physics*. New York: William Morrow and Co., 1979.

/ About the Author

Susan Zwinger has been fine artist, art critic, and museum curator of contemporary art in Santa Fe, New Mexico. She has worked for the National Park Service in Alaska and has been an environmental educator in Maine, New Hampshire, Wyoming, and New Mexico. She received a B.A. from Cornell College in Iowa, an M.F.A. from the Writers' Workshop, University of Iowa, and a Ph.D. from Pennsylvania State University. She now lives in Seattle, Washington, where she is a nature writer and environmental activist.